SHOW CASE

DEVELOPING, MAINTAINING,

AND PRESENTING   RAFAEL JAEN

SHOW CASE

A DESIGN-TECH PORTFOLIO FOR   SECOND EDITION

THEATRE AND ALLIED FIELDS

Focal Press
Taylor & Francis Group

NEW YORK AND LONDON

First published 2012

This edition published 2015 by Focal Press
70 Blanchard Road, Suite 402, Burlington, MA 01803

and by Focal Press
2 Park Square, Milton Park, Abingdon, Oxon OX14 4RN

*Focal Press is an imprint of the Taylor & Francis Group,
an informa business*

© 2012, Taylor & Francis.

Notices
Practitioners and researchers must always rely on their own experience
and knowledge in evaluating and using any information, methods,
compounds, or experiments described herein. In using such information
or methods they should be mindful of their own safety and the safety of
others, including parties for whom they have a professional
responsibility.

Product or corporate names may be trademarks or registered
trademarks, and are used only for identification and explanation without
intent to infringe.

Library of Congress Cataloging-in-Publication Data
Jaen, Rafael.
 [Developing and maintaining a design-tech portfolio]
 Show case : developing, maintaining, and presenting a design-tech
portfolio for theatre and allied fields / Rafael Jaen. -- 2nd ed.
   p. cm.
 Originally published in 2006 under title: Developing and maintaining a
design-tech portfolio.
 ISBN 978-0-240-81926-6
 1. Theaters--Stage-setting and scenery. 2. Motion pictures--Setting and
scenery. 3. Television--Stage-setting and scenery. 4. Art
portfolios--Design. I. Title.
 PN2091.S8J33 2011
 791.4302'5--dc23
                                    2011018486

British Library Cataloguing-in-Publication Data
A catalogue record for this book is available from the British Library.

ISBN 13: 978-0-240-81926-6 (pbk)

Preface   ix C O N T E N T S

Introduction   xi

PART I   WHAT IS A DESIGN-TECH PORTFOLIO?

Chapter 1:   What is a Design-Tech Portfolio?   3

             The Winning Design Portfolio   4
             The Winning Technical Portfolio   15

Chapter 2:   Traditional Portfolio Development Techniques   23

             Planning and Creation   24
                 Models, Styles, Dimensions, and Handling   24
             New Trends   30
             Inside the Case: Supplies and Materials   31
                 Multiring Refill Pages   31
                 Three-Ring Binder Sheet Protectors   31
             Specialty Layout Materials and Supplies   32
                 Where to Find Specialty Materials and Supplies 34
             Basic Strategy to Get the Right Materials   34
             Brother MFC-6490CW With Wireless   35
             Product Review: Brother MFC-6490CW   35

Chapter 3:   The Effective Showcase   39

             General Considerations   40
             Organizing the Body of Work: Beginning, Middle, and End   40
                 The Beginning   40
                 The Middle   41
                 The End   41
             Presenting Visual Content: Page Layout Options   43
             Opening Page   45
             Horizontal Layout   46
                 Vertical Layout   49
             Inserts: Adding Conversation Pieces   49
             Featuring Best Artwork, News/Media Reviews, and Photographs   52
                 Back Pocket: Research and Organizational Paperwork   55
             The Designer and Technician's Archives   56
             Marketing and Networking: Identifying Portfolio Requirements by Venue   56
                 College Applications   60
                 Organizations That Offer Portfolio Reviews   60

Chapter 4: Types of Portfolios   **65**

Know-How   66
The Right Stuff   67
Buy the Book, CD, or Website   67
Everybody Says Don't!   69
No Techie Left Behind ...   69
The Basics   70
Scenic Design   70
Costumes   71
Makeup and Hair   73
Lighting   73
Sound   77
Specialized Technicians, Crafts, and Allied Fields   80
Technical Director   83
By the Book, CD, or Website: The 21st Century Multimedia Portfolio   83
Production Design   88
Portfolio Photos   91

Chapter 5: Portfolio Development Techniques Do's and Don'ts   **101**

Portfolio Development Do's   102
Portfolio Development Don'ts   105

PART II   WHAT IS AN ELECTRONIC PORTFOLIO?

Chapter 6: The Effective Digital Portfolio   **111**

Working with Collaborators   112
Relearning and Learning for the First Time   113
New Capabilities and New Uses   115
Conclusion   115
What Is a Digital Portfolio; What is it For?   116

Chapter 7: Digital Portfolio Developing Techniques   **121**

Graphic Design Principles and Branding   122
Software Applications and CD Showcases   125
PowerPoint and Adobe Portable Document Format (PDF)   127
Photo Editing Software   130
Websites and Web Archives   130

Multimedia Sharing and Social Media   139
About Interactive Portfolios   152
Final Words: Things to Know When Designing Websites   154
    What is a Domain Name?   154
    What are Domain Name Registrars?   154
    How Do I Know I Am Buying from a Real Registrar?   154
    What Are Some Recommended Resources for People Starting Out?   155

Chapter 8:   Digital Portfolio Do's and Don'ts   157

PART III   PRESENTING AND MARKETING THE PORTFOLIO

Chapter 9:   Portfolio Presentation Techniques   163

The Professional and Appropriate Appearance for Portfolio Presentation 164
Foundations of Presenting   165
    Being Present, Presenting, and Leaving a Present   165
Post-Interview Maintenance   170
Self-Evaluation   170
Networking: What's Next?   171

Chapter 10: Portfolio Presentation Techniques Do's and Don'ts   173

Do's   174
Don'ts   174

Chapter 11: Design-Tech Résumés, CVs, Business Cards, and Stationery   177

Intent and Purpose of a Résumé   178
How to Present Your Work History and Education   178
The Design-Tech Résumé: Specific Expectations   179
    Résumé Formatting   180
    A Blueprint for an Effective Résumé Presentation   181
The Bio and the Curriculum Vitae   184
Other Marketing Tools: Business Cards and Brochures   185
    Tips on Successful Use of Business Cards and Brochures as a
    Marketing Tool (or as a "Present")   185

Chapter 12: Design-Tech Résumés, CVs, Business Cards, and Stationery Do's and Don'ts   191

Questions a Résumé Must Answer   192
Design-Tech Résumés, CV, Business Cards, and Stationery Do's   193
Design-Tech Résumés, CV, Business Cards, and Stationery Don'ts   193

PART 4   PORTFOLIO MAINTENANCE AND NEXT STEPS

Chapter 13: Establishing Goals and Reviewing, Choosing, and Updating Work   **195**

Rafael Jaen Teaching Points 1: The Carrying Case   197
Rafael Jaen's Teaching Points 2: Featured Works   197
Rafael Jaen's Teaching Points 3: Portfolio Size   198
Rafael Jaen's Teaching Points 4: Communicating Process   199
Rafael Jaen's Teaching Points 5: Organization   200

Chapter 14: Self-Assessment   **203**

The Basics of a Self-Evaluation   204
The Comprehensive Self-Evaluation   204

Chapter 15: Planning for the Next Job   **209**

Why Planning? What Planning?   210
Putting it Together   210
The Big Picture: The Design-Tech Career Concept   210
Your Concept: Identifying Practical Considerations   210
The Small Steps: Your Blueprint for Short-Term Goals   212

Chapter 16: Words of Wisdom: Do's and Don'ts Highlight Summary   **215**

Portfolio Development Do's: Good Practices   216
Portfolio Development Don'ts   216
Digital Portfolio Do's and Don'ts   217
Theatre, TV, and Film Portfolio Presentation Techniques Do's and Don'ts   217
Résumé, CV, and Business Cards Do's and Don'ts   218

PART 5   CONTRIBUTORS

Chapter 17: Contributor Bios, First Edition (2006)   **221**

Chapter 17A: Contributor Bios, Second Edition (2012)   **231**

I first got interested in portfolio development in the 1980s. While in college, I created an art book sampler that helped me transfer from a renowned architectural school in South America to the BFA Theatre Design Program at New York University—not a small accomplishment for someone who didn't speak English! Later, I used various formats to get internships in my field, get into graduate school, get jobs, and get a teaching position in higher education. Through the years one thing has remained constant: Every goal I set up for career development has been dependant on a portfolio. These combined experiences inspired the first edition of this book. After the book's publication, I had the opportunity to present many workshops across the country and observe numerous trends. I have also had the privilege of chairing portfolio reviews for various regional chapters of the Kennedy Center American College Theater Festival (KCACTF), the U.S. Institute for Theater Technology (USITT), and United Scenic Artists (USA) 829. These opportunities, combined with the growing interest in digital portfolios, branding, and marketing, have refueled my interest.

Why a Second Edition?

I wrote the first edition to assist others after I realized that there was a need for a comprehensive reference book. With the second edition I want to expand the chapters and explore 21st-century approaches, including branding, social networking, and interactive e-portfolios. As a comprehensive guide, this book's main objective is to bring excitement to the process of building a portfolio, helping plan and develop details such as personal presentation, pages layout, content variety, aesthetic sequencing, marketing, and next steps. It also covers a wide range of aspects, from the beginner's portfolio to the advanced portfolio and from the traditional portfolio to the e-portfolio. Each chapter features interviews, essays, and updated visual samples plus lists of "do's and don'ts" provided by experienced professionals in a variety of design-tech fields. In addition, I have been able to gather a superb cast of contributors at different stages of their careers, including recent graduate students, officers of renowned organizations, and international theater artists. The book also features art directors to represent narrative artists in the allied fields of film, TV, and other media. To this end the book is designed as a reference guide, workbook, and inspirational tool. The final objective is to assist the reader in the process of developing an excellent showcase that can be used to apply for graduate school, to pursue new jobs in the field, and for career marketing purposes.

The Parts

The book consists of five main parts with various expanded and updated chapters. Each chapter has beautiful graphics. Part 1 is dedicated to the realization of effective portfolio showcases and identifies materials and techniques used to produce them. The chapters in this part also identify specific requirements by discipline, including scenery, costumes, lighting, and sound, and cover the various portfolio requirements to apply for graduate school, jobs in the field, and professional organizations and to be used for promotional purposes. Part II is dedicated to the development and use of e-portfolios and looks at digital approaches, software options, and Web servers in this area. Part III is about presentation and marketing; it covers first impressions, how to develop personal presentation techniques, and how to build effective résumés, business cards, and brochures. Part IV offers key information in regard to the maintenance and updating of traditional and digital portfolios. Each chapter features real samples from a wide range of professionals in the field and a page of "do's and don'ts" with comments from experts in each design-tech discipline. Finally, Part V contains the biographies of the many contributors.

This book also includes detailed information on helpful subjects such as:

- Steps to develop and maintain an effective traditional portfolio
- Steps to create an effective e-portfolio, digital slide show, and/or a website
- Considerations in choosing software and Web servers for e-portfolios
- Personal presentation and rapport-building tips
- Steps to develop versatile and/or purpose-specific résumés, business cards, brochures, and stationery
- Planning next steps in developing existing portfolios and marketing plans

In Conclusion

A design-tech portfolio is a showcase of a designer or technician's process, resourcefulness, and artistry. This showcase is key in opening new doors and getting into choice colleges, obtaining scholarships, and getting new jobs in the field. With new expectations in the 21st century, putting together a (traditional or digital) portfolio for presentation can seem like an impossible undertaking. The process can become time consuming and challenging. The objective of this book is to offer useful information that can motivate and aid in the process of developing and maintaining a design-tech portfolio.

I hope you find each chapter useful, inspiring, and helpful!

Best wishes,

Rafael

Introduction to *Developing and Maintaining a Design-Tech Portfolio: A Guide for Theatre, Film, and TV, First Edition*

At the time that I finished graduate design school as a costume designer, a portfolio was a fairly uncomplicated affair. It consisted of a case: leather if you could afford it, plastic or fabric covered if you could not. We had all been encouraged to draw large sketches in school, so our portfolios were, out of necessity, also large, usually measuring 24 × 36 inches. Inside they were equipped with flimsy plastic pages, which we eventually replaced with the infinitely preferable, but also significantly heavier, polypropylene (vinyl) pages.

The rules were simple: produced work in the front, class projects in the back, strongest work first, update it regularly, and be prepared to show it *anywhere*.

Although the guidelines for assembling and maintaining a portfolio were straightforward, my classmates and I spent countless hours working and reworking our sketches, poring over and selecting photographs, reorganizing layouts, and critiquing each other's work. Before long, opportunities arose to present our portfolios to obtain work as costume designers and assistants.

I showed my portfolio *everywhere*. I showed it to producers in their offices, to designers in their studios and costume shops, and to directors wherever I could. I showed it sitting on the floors of rehearsal rooms. I even showed it in restaurants. "Oh! Do you do weddings?" the waitress exclaimed, looking at my production of *Faust*. I found that directors always asked about the other directors, and producers always asked about budgets. Costume designers always looked the most carefully and asked the widest range of questions.

Every time I showed my portfolio I came across something to remove and thought of something new to include, so I managed to keep it regularly updated. The advent of color copying and resizing capabilities added to the flexibility I needed to refurbish my portfolio. Suddenly, I could show many more sketches in much less space. I could include work from more shows, even my research. The possibilities were endless.

I had been out of school for many years when I found that the need to show my portfolio to get work was lessening. Because I was looking at it less frequently, I was not maintaining it as regularly. And, gradually, I found I had less and less time to devote to its upkeep, although the amount of material I wanted to include was increasing.

As a guest lecturer, however, I was frequently asked to display my portfolio to students. Although somewhat outdated, it was the perfect layout with the perfect amount of content to display in the space of an hour, the average amount of time for such a presentation.

Although in a display setting I seemed to achieve the ideal length and layout, there still remained a considerable amount of material that I had yet to add, and my portfolio was already extremely heavy (I practically needed the services of a sherpa to help me carry it around). It seemed impossible to include everything, and I discovered an even greater dilemma in the question of what exactly I wanted to show. I found I no longer knew how I wanted to represent myself through my portfolio.

For many years I had been reviewing portfolios for the United Scenic Artists (USA) 829 costume exam. Initially, the exam consisted not only of this review but also, more important, an extensive home project that was legendary for its ability to terrorize applicants. At that time, the portfolio was only half the equation.

A few years ago the home project for costume designers in the eastern region of the United States was eliminated. It was determined that the costume business had changed. Designers no longer had to demonstrate that they could design a wide range of events chosen by the exam committee. If they were being hired for jobs with companies that had a collective bargaining agreement with International Alliance of Theatrical Stage Employees (IATSE) USA 829 and had both a portfolio that fulfilled the union requirements and three letters of recommendation, they were qualified to join. The exam committee laid out the new portfolio requirements very carefully. In their eyes at least, the portfolio gained a new level of importance.

The portfolio requirements are specific; applicants are not encouraged to put too much energy into making a concise book for presentation to our panel of reviewers. Instead we ask to see two complete projects for which the applicant has been the principal costume designer or first assistant within the past two years. These projects must include a full set of swatched, full-color sketches, production photos, bibles, and research. We also want to see other projects, spread out around a table or stacked up in groups, as well as supporting production photos, research, and bibles if the project has been produced.

Even as I was helping students and young designers prepare their portfolios for work and union interviews as well as graduate school applications, my own portfolio quandary loomed large. I wondered about the possibilities. Maybe I should consider a smaller portfolio? Did I need an archival portfolio? What about digital? A friend sent me a copy of a portfolio she was sending out for review for a tenure position. It had pages and pages of scanned sketches, photos, and design statements. It was beautiful. On the other hand, another friend had dispensed with portfolios altogether and just took a large sheaf of sketches with him to his interviews.

What does one do, I wondered, when one is changing direction and there are no longer teachers and classmates to turn to for feedback? How does one think objectively about one's portfolio?

When I heard about Rafael's book I was delighted. My own dilemma aside, I am aware that not all schools can devote an entire year or even a semester to portfolio concerns. Discussions of portfolio creation and presentation often occur at the end of a student's academic career, when they are busy trying to finish their final projects. When they finally have time to work on their portfolio, their teachers may not be available for comment and critique.

Rafael's book is exhaustive in its treatment of the whole topic of portfolio composition. He very carefully covers all the various types of portfolios and the strengths and weaknesses of each. He presents different types of layout, details the materials necessary to create each one, and lists sources for those materials.

He examines the differences between traditional hard portfolios and digital portfolios. He also covers résumé writing, business cards, and promotional materials, and last but not least, offers presentation guidelines and techniques.

The remarks and advice from expert designers and educators included in the book are extremely helpful in answering questions one might have about the merits of digital versus traditional portfolios and what designers, producers, and educators are looking for in portfolios presented to them by prospective employees and students.

The specifications for constructing a portfolio have not changed all that much: produced work in the front, classwork in the back, strongest work first, update it regularly, and be prepared to show it *anywhere*—these rules still apply. However, the range of choices for presentation has expanded dramatically, offering designers and technicians myriad ways to present themselves and their work. Rafael's book takes us through all the options and makes it possible to choose among them. He also includes guidelines for self-evaluation that enable one to objectively assess one's own work, portfolio choices, and presentation style.

This book is useful to a wide range of people: students applying to college or graduate school, graduate students looking for jobs, designers aspiring to join a professional organization, teachers seeking university positions, professors applying for tenure, and anyone who has found that that the direction of their life has shifted or who wants to make a change.

Rafael's book offers all these people direction and the tools necessary to make portfolio decisions for themselves. He addresses the issue of change, making it clear that portfolios need to be modified depending on the purpose for which they are intended. I was especially impressed by the final chapter, in which Rafael urges the reader to make plans and set short-term goals, thus leading to the drafting of long-range ambitions and to planning the creation of a portfolio that will aid in the achievement of these objectives.

Rafael's belief in the power of a portfolio is absolute and inspiring.

And I, for one, have been inspired. So now, if you'll excuse me, I am finally going to go and update my portfolio.

Kitty Leech
Chair of the Costume Design Exam Committee for the
United Scenic Artists Local 829
TDF/Costume Collection's Advisory Committee Chair
Design Faculty, NYU Tisch School of the Arts

Introduction to the Second Edition

When I finished my undergraduate degree at the University of Iowa in 1969 I had several watercolor renderings on 16 × 20 inch cold-press illustration board, a handful of very rough draftings, perhaps a dozen 5 × 7 inch photos of the three designs that I had done in the old Armory at Iowa, and a handful of art projects of varying sizes and shapes. My plan was to apply for grad school or a job somewhere in theater. My wife took a job teaching eighth- and ninth-grade English in a small town in Wisconsin, and I started sending letters of inquiry to a number of schools, theaters, and individuals. Most of the responses that came back to me requested a portfolio. I knew what a portfolio was, but I had no idea how to put one together or what it should look like.

A trip to the library at the University of Wisconsin was less than helpful. I found books on artists' portfolios, photographers' portfolios, and one book on architects' portfolios, but nothing about theater portfolios. Armed with an assortment of the portfolio books I began the process of making mine. Because most of my materials were on 16 × 20 inch illustration board it seemed obvious that I should start with those materials. I matted the renderings with different colors of mat board and created a book by gluing two matted plates back to back with a fabric hinge. I then made a front and back cover from illustration board covered with black felt. I cut letters out of white felt to spell out "Donald J. Childs' Portfolio" and glued them to the cover. I then started sending it off to schools, theaters, and individuals. Each time it came back I sighed a big sigh of relief that it had actually been returned undamaged. I guess it worked because I got a number of offers from schools and an offer of an apprenticeship from Jo Mielziner, which I was unable to accept because I thought I was about to be drafted into the Vietnam War.

Since then I have created at least 15 other portfolios, discovered art stores with materials and supplies that made the process of portfolio creation easier, and learned to be especially concerned about protecting my work. One school where I applied for a teaching position kept my portfolio for over a month, and I was nearly apoplectic by the time it was returned.

When I got the announcement that a book was being published entitled *Developing and Maintaining a Design-Tech Portfolio,* my response was "Finally!" I purchased the book at the next USITT conference and, even though I wasn't working on a portfolio at the time, I read it immediately. As I was reading it I frequently found myself thinking, "Wow, I wish I had thought about that!" or "Good idea" or "Where was Rafael when I was creating the first portfolio?" Or, for that matter, "Where was he (and his book) when I was making any of the fifteen-plus portfolios I have made over the years?" The inclusion of comments, portfolios examples, and ideas from working professionals, coupled with Rafael's high level of expertise, made the book a must-read on my bibliography for any class I have taught since.

When Rafael asked me if I would write an introduction to the second edition of the book, I accepted without hesitation. The second edition has taken on the challenge of a sequel and moves solidly into the 21st century.

As in the first edition, Rafael turns to working professionals in all areas of theater design and technology for expert advice and praiseworthy examples of portfolios from a number of perspectives. In addition, he includes guidance from professionals beyond the theatrical arena to provide the reader with multiple resources designed to assist in the process of preparing, presenting, and marketing oneself as a professional. The book is a true bible for creating a complete marketing package, from the selection and arrangement of materials through the proper way to present oneself at an interview. Rafael successfully taps experts, from marketing agents to psychologists, for this process.

Rafael also turns to students and recent grads for examples of working portfolios and marketing packages. He draws on the full spectrum of practitioners to give the reader a well-rounded perspective of what is happening and what is working for theater artisans at all levels of experience and development.

The expanded section on digital portfolios and networking alone would keep the book on top of my bibliography of must-read books for students and professionals, but it goes way beyond those areas. Rafael addresses the issues of today's marketing tools as well as those of more traditional marketing. Again, as I read through the manuscript for the second edition, I frequently found myself thinking, "Wow, I wish I had thought about that!" or "Good idea" or "Where was Rafael when I was creating the first portfolio?" but now I can say I'm honored to have the opportunity to formally introduce this book to all the readers who will benefit from its contents. This book will make my next portfolio, presentation, or exhibition so much easier to create and to display.

Thank you, Rafael.

Don Childs
Director, Stagecraft Institute of Las Vegas

A PORTFOLIO IS A SHOWCASE OF ...

ARTISTRY, SPECIAL SKILLS, AND PROCESS ...

RAFAEL JAEN

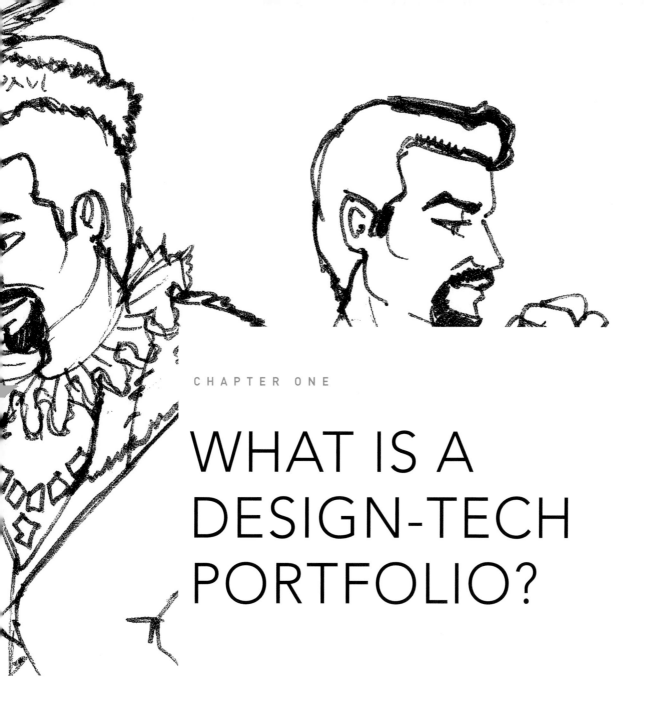

CHAPTER ONE

WHAT IS A DESIGN-TECH PORTFOLIO?

A *design-tech portfolio* is a well-planned, portable case of documents and visual representations of procedures, conceptions, and materials related to various projects. All these items are carefully organized so that when the portfolio is presented to others, it can serve different functions:

1. It can serve as a showcase for the artistry, special skills, personal style, volume of work, and artistic process of a designer or a technician.

2. It can be used as a reference archive in which the designer or technician features the processes that led to ingenious design solutions.

3. It can work as a storybook that emphasizes the individual's history, professional growth, and versatility.

Well-executed portfolios showcase a volume of work, processes, special skills, and personal style. Well-executed portfolios can open doors to new opportunities and create winning situations, such as gaining entry to graduate school, obtaining a desired job, or reaping accolades.

The process of developing and maintaining a design-tech portfolio is not different from the process that takes an idea from a two-dimensional drawing to the tri-dimensional product or that takes a concept from original rendering to realized production on the theatre stage or set of a film. To create an effective showcase, designers and technicians need to include conceptual ideas, the process by which the idea became a reality, and the finished product. They also need to edit materials and organize layouts in a way that best features their work.

The Winning Design Portfolio

Each page of the design portfolio tells the story of a specific project. To be effective, each layout must include a wide range of aspects that speak about the special skills and personal style of the designer; the project resource allocation and budget distribution; and the collaborative process with the director and the company. In the next few pages we'll look at a few sample page choices as a way to introduce some effective practices. We'll continue to look at more samples and go into more depth in later chapters.

Show Case

In the following pages, we see samples of various designers and technicians; they include drafting and superb photos. We start with Kristin Hayes, who won the 2007 KCACTF Region 1 Barbizon Award for Excellence in Lighting Design. Hayes says: "In showing my larger portfolio to a number of people, I found that there were a number of professionals who wanted to concentrate solely on my photographs and paperwork and regarded the research pictures as extraneous and distracting. Thus I created a smaller, more portable portfolio (8½ × 11 inches) that has the same photos and reduced plots, with shorter descriptions and no research pictures. This document was created using Microsoft PowerPoint, which allows me to reprint pages easily if I need to send a small sample of my work to a prospective employer. Also, it means I have the start of a digital portfolio!" (See Figures 1.1a through 1.1d.)

FIGURE 1.1A

Award-winning lighting designer Kristin Hayes starts each new project layout with a title page.

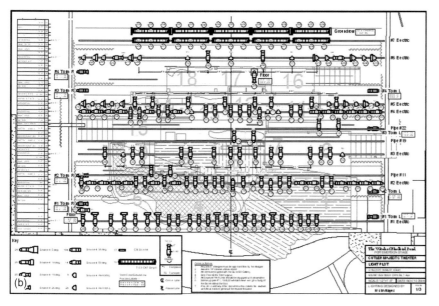

FIGURE 1.1B

Hayes includes drafting samples that can give the viewer a sense of the scale and complexity of each project. She also has actual-size drafting in the portfolio's back pocket.

FIGURE 1.1C

Hayes includes excellent photos to showcase her lighting design approach.

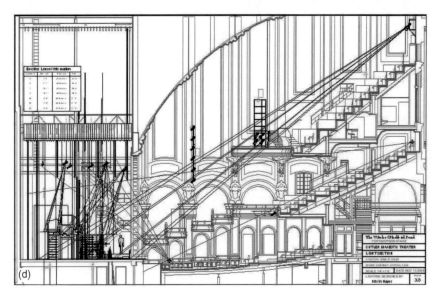

FIGURE 1.1D

Hayes includes sections that clearly show the variety of angles used in her design. Her drafting meets U.S. Institute for Theatre Technology (USITT) industry standards.

Costume designer Jessica Champagne-Hansen creates storyboards that tell the story (from the costume design point of view) of *The Shakespeare Stealer* by Gary Blackwood. She won the 2004 ACTF Barbizon Design Award for Region I. Champagne-Hansen's layout shows her inspirations and notations, as well as the realized designs (Figures 1.2a through 1.2c).

Scenic designer Janie E. Howland favors a *hard portfolio*. She has received many awards, including the IRNE Award and the Elliot Norton Award. She was also a founding member of CYCO SCENIC, a successful NE production company. Howland explains: "By 'hard portfolio' I mean a portfolio with separate pages as opposed to an electronic portfolio." Her first sample is for the show *Assassins* at the Lyric Stage Company of Boston, directed by Spiro Veloudos. The overall

inspiration for the set was an old-fashioned, wooden rollercoaster combined with a shooting gallery from an amusement park. Included in her portfolio layout are the paint elevation of the floor (Figure 1.3a) and a photo from the show (Figure 1.3b). The images are mounted on black matte board.

Sometimes it is important to combine research, process, and layout technique in a portfolio page to contextualize a design approach. For example, costume designer William Henshaw created portfolio pages for the show *American Tragedy: The Case of Clyde Griffiths*, mounted at San Diego State University in April 1996. Henshaw says: "The premise of this show was that it was yellow journalism; therefore, the renderings were left uncolored and very grainy so as to resemble newsprint and pictures from the 1930s. Preliminary

FIGURE 1.2A

Award-winning costume designer Jessica Champagne-Hansen's *The Shakespeare Stealer* portfolio, page 1: Project introduction, cast photo, and book cover.

FIGURE 1.2B

Champagne-Hansen's *Shakespeare Stealer* portfolio, page 2 (clockwise): Character sketches, including Robert Armin, Thomas Pope, and William Shakespeare. Photos: Pope and Shakespeare, Shakespeare, Armin, and Hamlet.

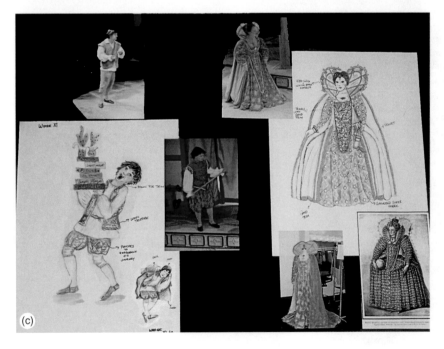

FIGURE 1.2C

Champagne-Hansen's *Shakespeare Stealer* portfolio, page 3 (clockwise): Production photos of character Widge in beige, Queen Elizabeth, Queen Elizabeth's dress on form, and Widge in blue. Production sketches of Queen Elizabeth and Widge.

FIGURE 1.3A

Set design production photo for *Assassins,* designed by award-winning scenic designer Janie E. Howland, at the Lyric Stage in Boston.

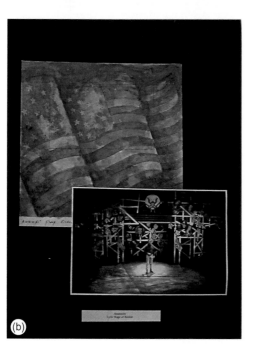

FIGURE 1.3B

Howland's scenic portfolio page for the show *Assassins* at the Lyric Stage in Boston.

FIGURE 1.4A

Costume designer William Henshaw's costume rough sketch for *American Tragedy* at San Diego State University, 1996.

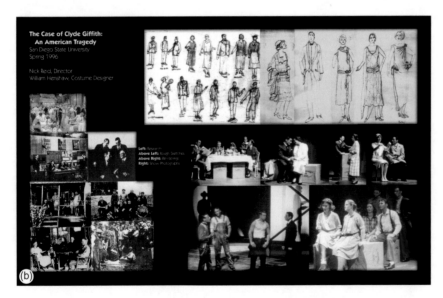

FIGURE 1.4B

Henshaw's final costume design page for *American Tragedy*.

sketches were done all on one page to resemble a layout for a newspaper (Figures 1.4a and 1.4b). Research for the show was presented on boards to give the feel of a newspaper layout."

Some of the design-tech disciplines are more abstract and therefore difficult to explain visually in a portfolio; this is true, for example, of lighting design. To properly present projects for this discipline, good photos showing clear angles, color fillers, and shadows are desirable. They will help emphasize the special talents and sensibilities of the designer. For *The Idiot,* adapted and directed by Alexandre Marine, lighting designer Nicholas Vargelis used white light and sharp angles to add to the high emotional tension in various scenes. The photos in Figures 1.5a and 5b are from the portfolio sequence for this show. To best show his lighting choice, Nicholas uses photos sized to 8½ × 11 inches and printed on quality photo paper.

Nicholas Vargelis's lighting portfolio consists of a series of large (8½ × 11-inch) photographs. The sequences show his range of design for various plays; each show is clearly labeled and arranged by scene. Right after the photos for *The Idiot*, he showcases his atmospheric and soft lighting for the show *Mud* by Maria Irene Fornes (Figures 1.5c and 1.5d). The photos show contrast in Vargelis's design abilities.

Anthony Phelps is a set and lighting designer. He holds a masters of fine arts (MFA) in design from Minnesota State University, Mankato. His professional memberships include United Scenic Artists, the International Alliance of Theatrical Stage Employees (IATSE), and USITT. His portfolio contains what I call a classical storyboard approach that proves very effective for his personal style (Figures 1.6a through 1.6b).

For a sound design portfolio, designer Andy Leviss recommends including one-block diagram samples of the sound system for a show—one, two, or more, depending on the show. "This is the most visual that a sound design portfolio often gets," he says. "It has the benefits of both being very obvious in what it is, even to a nontechnical producer." (See Figure 1.7.)

FIGURE 1.5A

Show: *The Idiot*, adapted and directed by Alexandre Marine. Scene: General Yepanchin's Gift to Nastasya. Lighting by Nicholas Vargelis. Produced at ART Institute for Advanced Theatre Training, June 2004.

FIGURE 1.5B

FIGURES 1.5C AND 1.5D
Nicholas Vargelis's lighting design photo/portfolio pages (showing contrast) for *Mud,* by Maria Irene Fornes; scene 1.6 (The Starfish) and scene 1.7 (What is Lloyd?); ART Institute for Advanced Theatre Training, June 2003.

FIGURE 1.6A

Set and lighting designer Anthony Phelps's portfolio case with storyboards.

FIGURE 1.6B

Phelps's detail photo. With the storyboard approach, photos can be seen without the sheet holders' glare.

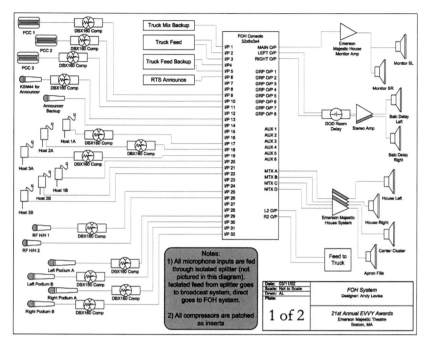

FIGURE 1.7

Sound designer Andy Leviss's one-block diagram sample of the sound system for a show.

SHOW CASE

The Winning Technical Portfolio

Just like the design portfolio, the technical portfolio tells the story of each project, but with an emphasis on the technical aspects, featuring resourceful solutions to achieve the design goals. An effective page arrangement includes a wide range of aspects such as technical drawings, pattern layout, budget allocation, engineering solutions, manufacturing process, fabric treatments, paint chips, and dyed fabric samples. The goal is to feature the special skills and collaboration abilities of the technician. Sometimes, depending on the scale of the project, the designer is also the technician. In this case, the design pages would be separate from the technical pages; they would be used in two separate sections of the portfolio or in two completely different portfolio cases.

Show Case

This part of this chapter features three young technicians in three different areas: technical direction, costuming, and makeup and hair design.

Bill Hawkins is a freelance technical director. He used Auto CAD (a design and documentation software) in the layout and creation of his portfolio; he is well versed in using the software. This tool allowed him to create a full-scale image of each page without the need to physically print, crop, and attach individual photos (Figures 1.8a through 1.8d). Using the software for the purpose of creating his portfolio, combined with his technical drawings and great photos, indicates to an interviewer that he is current in digital applications. This is a great way to make an impression!

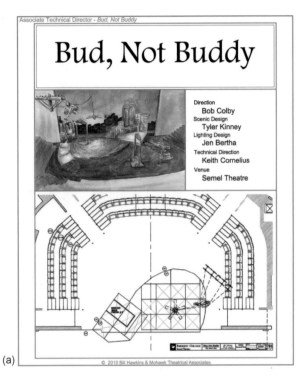

FIGURE 1.8A

Technical director Bill Hawkins's drafting for the platforms of the set for *Bud, Not Buddy*.

FIGURE 1.8B

Bill Hawkins's images of the finished set for *Bud, Not Buddy*. He says: "Perhaps the greatest benefit of designing my entire portfolio digitally is the ability to quickly customize its contents for a particular client or employer."

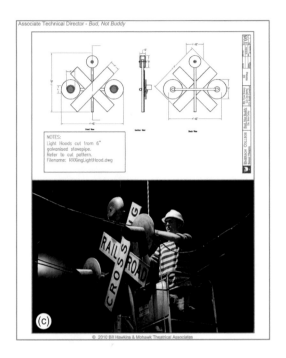

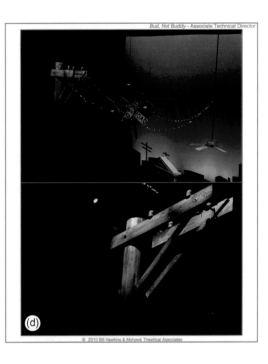

FIGURE 1.8C

Hawkins's drafting and installation image of a railroad sign for the show *Bud, Not Buddy*.

FIGURE 1.8D

Bill Hawkins's detail photos of a railroad hanging sign for the show *Bud, Not Buddy*. Bill adds: "There is also no need for me to scan pages when emailing my portfolio; I just click 'Convert to .PDF' and attach the new document."

Nicole Wilson began her career in costumes at the Pacific Conservatory of the Performing Arts (PCPA), where she worked four consecutive summers as a costume technician. At PCPA she was able to stitch on such shows as *Brigadoon*, *A Little Night Music*, and *Beauty and the Beast*, and she worked as a costume crafts artisan on *Ragtime* and *The Imaginary Invalid*. In Fall 2008 Nicole transferred to Emerson College, where she completed her bachelor of fine arts (BFA) in theatre design/technology in December 2010. While at Emerson she was fortunate to work as the draper on *Esperanza Rising*, *Into the Woods*, and *Light Up the Sky*. Since leaving Emerson Nicole has worked as the draper/wardrobe supervisor on ArtsEmerson's *The Color of Rose*, as the draper on *Dollhouse* at the New Repertory Theatre,

and as the costume coordinator for Boston Children's Theatre's production of *A Year in the Life of Frog and Toad*. Nicole has been honored to work with some of theatre's leading professionals and looks forward to continuing her work in costume technology.

Nicole Wilson's portfolio has some fantastic samples; when I asked her what her favorite project was, she said: "As my capstone project, Emerson Stage's 2010 production of *Into the Woods* was my largest and most exciting project. Working with the costume designer Tyler Kinney, I was able to create pieces that were not only representative of his costume sketches but also utilized eighteenth-century garment-building techniques. I chose Cinderella's gown as the main focus piece for my portfolio." (See Figure 1.9.)

FIGURE 1.9

When talking about the draping of Cinderella's gown, costume technician Nicole Wilson says it is "designed after a late 1700s open gown. I was able to use period undergarments, the hip roll, corset, and petticoat, to create the shape of the gown and utilize this as my draping platform. The pieces for the bodice were draped and patterned, while the underskirt and overskirt were draped on a form. I took process photos every step of the way, not only for my portfolio, but also as reference points so that if I ever have to build another gown like this, I will know exactly how I built it."

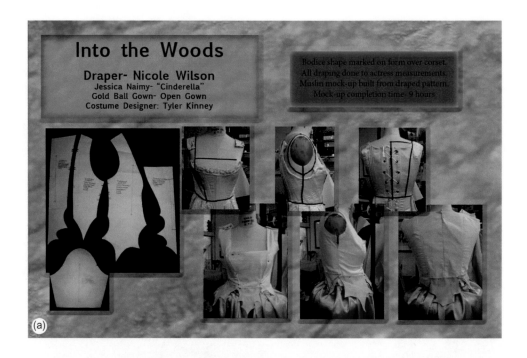

Into the Woods

Draper- Nicole Wilson
Jessica Naimy- "Cinderella"
Gold Ball Gown- Open Gown
Costume Designer: Tyler Kinney

Bodice shape marked on form over corset.
All draping done to actress measurements.
Muslin mock-up built from draped pattern.
Mock-up completion time- 9 hours

(a)

Large hip roll under garment.
Underskirt draped and pleated on form.
Bodice flat lined with coutille.
Seams finished with black seam binding.
Outer edge finished with gold piping from sleeve fabric.

(b)

FIGURE 1.9

(Continued)

Final fabrics and yardages:
Bodice: 1 1/2 yards metallic fashion fabric
Sleeves, over skirt, piping & ruffles- 7 yards poly dupioni
Underskirt & ruffle trim- silk dupioni
Ruffles are 2-to-1 gather
Leaves individually attached to dupioni strips
stitched to underskirt
Final completion time= 26 hours

(c)

Final open gown with built sleeves, scalloped overskirt and 3 tier ruffled under skirt

(d)

Wilson uses the set floor marble pattern as the background of her images. She also includes pattern layout and the costume design sketch for reference.

KJ Kim is a makeup and hair designer. She is a senior undergraduate student from the University of Evansville and graduated in May 2011. She is majoring in theatre design with a minor in fine art. In January 2011, Kim received the USITT Young Designers & Technicians Award in the makeup design area, sponsored by Kryolan Corporation. Simultaneously, she also won first place in the Alcone Company Makeup Design Award of Region III, KCACTF. This is the second year in a row for KJ Kim to advance to national competition. (See Figure 1.10.)

Now that we have reviewed what the final product may look like in a portfolio, we can ask: How do we develop a new (or existing) portfolio, and how do we maintain it?

Henry IV Part 1
Battle Makeup Inspiration

(a)

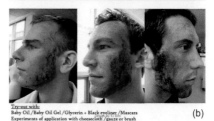

Henry IV Part 1
Battle Makeup Practice

Try-out with:
Baby Oil /Baby Oil Gel /Glycerin + Black eyeliner /Mascara
Experiments of application with cheesecloth /gauze or brush

(b)

Henry IV Part 1
Sweat Effect Practice

Without Makeup ← → With Makeup

Try-out with:
Baby Oil, Vaseline, Baby Oil Gel, Glycerin

(c)

EARL OF WESTMORELAND
IN BATTLE MAKE-UP

FROM *HENRY IV, PART 1*
BY SHAKESPEARE

(d)

FIGURE 1.10

Award-winning makeup and hair designer KJ Kim creates makeup pages that include clear research and clear makeup application directions for the actors and crew, plus final portfolio pages with makeup schematics and production shots. She paints her sketches with makeup.

Base Canvas Finished Rendering

**HENRY IV
IN BATTLE MAKEUP**

FROM *HENRY IV, PART 1*
BY SHAKESPEARE

(e)

AN ATTRACTIVE (PORTFOLIO) PRESENTATION IS NICE, BUT IF THE TALENT AND THE ABILITY ARE NOT THERE, THE PRESENTATION IS MOOT.

MARK NEWMAN

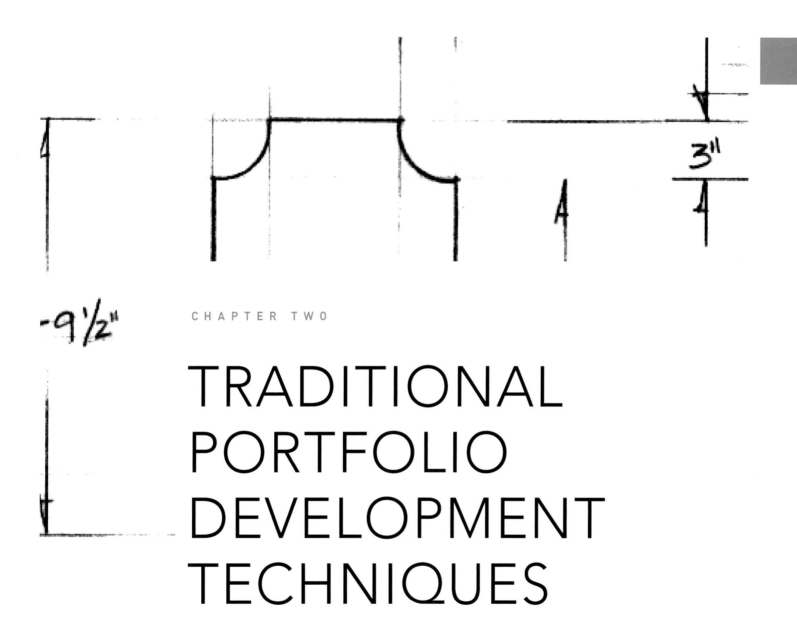

TRADITIONAL PORTFOLIO DEVELOPMENT TECHNIQUES

Planning a design-tech portfolio can be a very exciting project—from choosing a carrying case to the specific layout of each page, it gives designers and technicians the opportunity to show their character, style, talent, and expertise. It can also be a very large and overwhelming task at times. This chapter offers some useful information that can assist in managing this project.

Planning and Creation

Before investing a lot of time and money in a portfolio, the designer/technician needs to define the goals and uses of the portfolio. Will it be a showcase of artistry and special skills or a reference archive? Will it be used to apply for a job or to apply to a graduate school? Will different parts serve equal or different purposes? Will it be carried on a daily basis or only occasionally? Will it hold small documents or large works? How will it be presented? The answers to these questions will clarify the type of case or cases that will be required.

For example, if the body of work is very large in size and volume and the portfolio will be carried occasionally, a large case may be the answer. On the other hand, if the work is large and the portfolio case needs to travel constantly, the designer/technician may consider having a second showcase with reductions of the work or a digital portfolio. Since portfolios come in many styles and sizes (see Figures 2.1a through 2.1c; photos by Eric Cornell), knowing the purpose of a portfolio at the outset will help determine the type of case to choose.

Models, Styles, Dimensions, and Handling

Portfolio cases can be grouped into three categories: binders, presentation cases, and folios. Each one of these can be fitted with a variety of sheet holders that can accommodate different projects. When you're choosing a size, remember that the dimensions given for portfolios, presentation cases, binders, and refill pages are the

(a)

FIGURE 2.1A

A three-ring binder. This very basic portfolio could be used to apply to an undergraduate program.

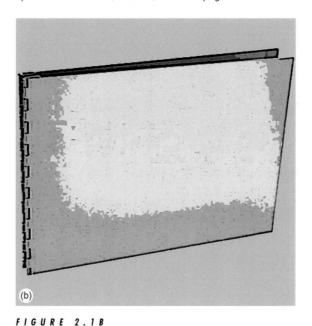

(b)

FIGURE 2.1B

An aluminum case. This type of portfolio could be used by technicians working in hard-hat areas.

FIGURE 2.1C

Leather handles in a classic portfolio leather case.

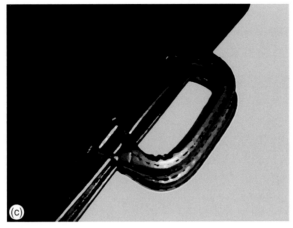

Designers and technicians will find that there are many presentation options in the market today. When you're looking at portfolios, it is important to choose a style that complements the field of concentration and the size of the materials. A steel binder may be great for a tech director, since it suggests that she or he works in a hard-hat area. An acrylic binder may be better suited for a makeup designer or stylist, since the glossy outer material may match the products that he or she uses. In addition, make sure that the size of the portfolio is manageable and that it can fit in an airplane overhead compartment; when you're traveling, a portfolio should never leave your side!

Specifications

Binders Acid-free sheets are recommended to protect artwork, and reinforced rings are a plus for durability. There are many binder varieties, so it is important to do some research prior to purchasing a specific model. Some designers/technicians have different binders for different purposes. The following are some examples of the products available on the market today:

maximum size of the artwork that can be accommodated, not the outside measurements of the case.

Binders are often used for smaller project samplers or for individual project presentations; they are excellent for 8½ × 11-inch workbooks that contain pages of research, diagrams, cue sheets, sketch reductions, budget specs, and the like. Most technicians use binders to organize their projects.

Designers often favor presentation cases because they come in different sizes (that complement the designer's height) and the portfolio pages can be added as needed. A petite person can choose a case that holds 11 × 17- or 14 × 18-inch pages. A taller individual can use a case that holds 18 × 24-inch pages. Designers have to make sure that the portfolio size they choose is not too heavy, that its pages are easy to turn, and that the pages stay put. There is nothing worse than having an unyielding portfolio case with pages falling out during an interview.

Folios are excellent for containing, transporting, and presenting loose sketches and plans. Folios will give an impression of sophistication and organization; they are fancy large folders with ties.

- *Multiring binders.* They can be attractive and sturdy, usually include 5 to 10 sheet protectors, and have 30- to 50-sheet capacity, depending on the manufacturer. They can be covered in leather, vinyl, or fabric. Rings with metal reinforced corners are sturdier. They are ideal for small documents and often-traveling portfolios (see Figure 2.2). Typical measurements include 14 × 11, 17 × 11, 17 × 14, 17 × 22, and 18 × 24 inches.

- *Easel binders.* These types of binders feature convenient spine-mounted retractable handles and allow a horizontal or vertical presentation. They are ideal for on-the-road presentations and industrial designs. They often include 10 sheet protectors and have 30-sheet capacity. They can be found in 17 × 14, 11 × 8½, 14 × 11, and 24 × 18-inch sheet sizes.

FIGURE 2.2

Multiring binders come in various sizes; they can be
covered in leather, vinyl, or fabric.

(a)

- *Aluminum portfolio binders.* These binders are
  stylish and durable, ideal for carpentry, rigging, and
  electrics (refer back to Figure 2.1b). They usually
  include 10 archival multiring sheet protectors,
  zippered black nylon jacket, and a set of screw-post
  extensions. Sizes include 11 × 8½, 14 × 11, and
  17 × 11 inches.

- *Slide-in pocket page portfolio binders.* These are great
  for work that can be included with the main portfolio
  while presenting, but that can also stand on its own,
  such as specific period research and specialty craft
  projects (Figures 2.3a and 2.3b). These binders have
  clear "pocket" pages for an organized, stylish, and
  professional presentation. This type of portfolio is
  ideal for individual project presentation and usually
  contains 24 pocket pages with black inserts. The
  best are acid and PVC free. Sizes vary depending on

the manufacturer; they come in 8½ × 11, 9 × 12,
11 × 14, and 14 × 17 inches.

- *Standard three-ring binders.* These are general-use
  binders for letter (8½ × 11-inch), legal (14 × 11-inch),
  and ledger (11 × 17-inch) sheet sizes. They're best if
  they have interior storage pockets for miscellaneous
  items. Their depth can go from 1 to 3 inches. They are
  ideal for storing organizational data, charts, slides,
  photos, and research (see Figure 2.3c).

In conclusion, there are many varieties of binder. The
desired function will determine the best choice for work
storage and presentation.

Presentation Cases and Folios Presentation cases and
folios can serve multiple purposes. They can be the
main portfolio case or they can be (depending on size) a
presentation aid; for example, they can hold paperwork

(a)

FIGURE 2.3A

A slide-in binder case sample. It opens as a folder and has an elastic clasp at the top.

(b)

FIGURE 2.3B
Slide-in pocket page sheets with group costume sketches for Opera Boston's *Alceste*, designed by Rafael Jaen in January 2005. This type of binder case is great for carrying sketches to design and production meetings.

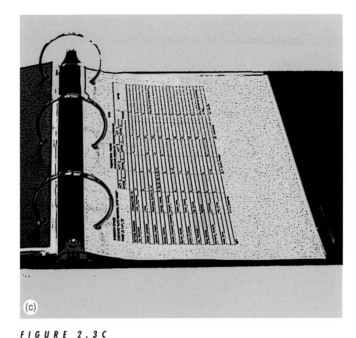

(c)

FIGURE 2.3C

A standard three-ring binder with clear tab dividers. These are ideal for holding and presenting paperwork such as budgets, construction specs, Q sheets, and the like.

for a project in the main case, or they can serve as an individual project carrying case used at a production meeting presentation.

Presentation Cases Presentation cases are the most often used portfolios in the design-tech field and can be found in many styles, from those with a durable vinyl-coated exterior to those with metal covers and soft leather. Many of the varieties found in the market today feature solid construction (reinforced base, metal protective floor bumpers, and industrial-strength zippers) and include inside pockets and carrying handles, adding to their manageability and multifunctionality. Some cases even feature multiuse pockets in their interior for the storage of accessories such as computer disks and business cards. The sheets in this type of portfolio can be part of the carrying mechanism or can be inserts in a separate and removable multiring book (see Figures 2.4a and 2.4b). This is especially important for someone who may have various books

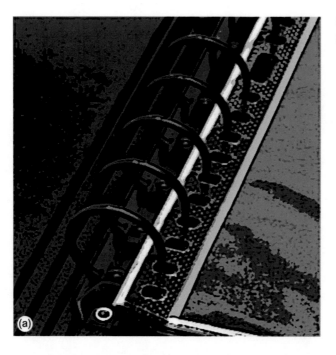

FIGURE 2.4A

Presentation case interior detail; center rings with metal reinforced corners.

FIGURE 2.4B

Presentation cases are the most often used portfolios in the field. The costume sketches in display here are for the musical *Pippin*, designed by author Rafael Jaen, for Emerson Stage in Spring 2004. The sketches were featured in *Entertainment Design Magazine*, ED Designer Sketches Book page, June 2004.

(a)

FIGURE 2.5A

Sample of an easel folio with (fabric) twill tape closures.

but can only afford one case. Most presentation cases include 10 standard archival sheet protectors and have a 25- to 30-sheet capacity. They measure 11 × 8½, 14 × 11, 17 × 14, 22 × 17, or 24 × 18 inches.

Folios Folios are great for hands-free presentations, including industrial designs, museum installations, and designs in other allied fields. These are some recommended styles:

- *Easel folios.* This type of portfolio is designed with an integrated easel stand, which allows easy desktop display. For standard book use and storage, the easel folds away. Covers are often made of durable black polypropylene. They can hold as many as 20 pages. Acid-free and PVC-free pages are best. Usual sizes are 8½ × 11, 11 × 14, and 14 × 17 inches (Figures 2.5a and 2.5b).

- *Oversized expandable portfolios.* For large works, this extra-large capacity portfolio holds up to 25 sheets of 3/16-inch foam board. Zippers open to allow the portfolio to lie flat. They often include two 10 × 13-inch outside zipper pockets, a business card window, two side handles, and a 6-inch expandable gusset. Some have an optional detachable wheel-board for easy transport of heavy artwork. They can expand from 25 × 37 × 6 inches to 41 × 61 × 6 inches.

FIGURE 2.5B

Easel folios are great for hands-on and table-spread presentations. Sketches and paperwork can be stored but are loose for easy handling.

(c)

FIGURE 2.5C

Bamboo laminate, Tera-Cover, and Vista.

New Trends

James Michael Garner, one of my former students, has several years of experience in the fields of technical theatre and broadcasting. Garner has a solid reputation for producing quality work that meets all deadlines and budget requirements. When he learned I was working on a second edition of this book, he sent me an email saying: "This is something I wrote for some students at my old high school that asked about portfolio options. It's only a few pages, but I did mention a couple of new styles that I don't remember seeing in your previous edition. There are new adaptations of the presentation case. They are made by a company called Pina Zangaroo" (see Figure 2.5c).

These are James's descriptions:

- *Bamboo laminate.* This is a contemporary twist on the portfolio that adds an organic element. You could also easily paint your logo on the front of one of these. If you're handy, you could also laminate your aluminum portfolio with something like this if it ever gets scratched up. Bamboo is also naturally ding and scratch resistant. That's why they make floors out of it. Being a carpenter, I think this is awesome.

- *Tera-Cover.* I can only refer to this next portfolio by trade name because I'm not sure how to qualify it. The cover reminds me of Masonite or a clipboard of some sort. It's different and appears durable as well.

- *Vista (snow/onyx/mist).* There are three varieties of the Vista portfolio style, and all are really interesting. The mist is the equivalent of frosted Plexiglas and it diffuses your cover page behind it. The onyx and snow are very contemporary plastic composites that look very clean. While the black onyx is very formal, TDs can use the snow variety as a whiteboard to illustrate concepts for interviewers.

As we can see, there are many presentation cases and folios in the market. They can serve multiple purposes. They can be the main portfolio case or they can hold paperwork for a project (in the main case). They can also be used as an individual project carrying case at a production meeting presentation.

Inside the Case: Supplies and Materials

The portfolio isn't just the carrying case, of course; the inside organization materials are just as important. The proper sheet holders will enhance the overall look of a presentation, the manageability of the display sheets will ease the handling of materials, and the durability of the materials will ensure that you have a healthy and long-lasting showcase for your work.

Multiring Refill Pages

There are a number of types of multiring refill pages:

- *Laser archival.* These are high-quality, super-clear, nonstick, polypropylene sheet protectors that can prevent color alteration and transfer. They are highly recommended for digital images. They are often sealed on three sides with reinforced, perforated multiring binder edge and contain acid-free black paper inserts. Sizes: $11 \times 8\frac{1}{2}$ inches to 24×18 inches.
- *Clear polyester archival.* Clear polyester sheets often come with deluxe black acid-free insert paper and standard multiring perforations. They are recommended for digital images and all laser

copies and will not lift ink or toner off artwork. Sizes: $11 \times 8\frac{1}{2}$ inches to 18×24 inches.

- *Polypropylene archival.* These are heavy-duty, welded polypropylene multiring sheet protectors of archival quality 0045 polypropylene. They are unplasticized, heat resistant, and chemically stable. They come with black acid- and lignin-free paper inserts. Both plastic and paper pass the Photographic Activity Test (PAT) and meet all American National Standards Institute (ANSI) requirements for archival storage. Sizes: $11 \times 8\frac{1}{2}$ inches to 17×11 inches.

Three-Ring Binder Sheet Protectors

Similarly, there are a variety of sheet protectors designed for three-ring binders:

- *Sheet protectors.* When you're using a standard three-ring binder, top-load sheet protectors are best if manufactured of heavyweight polypropylene for crystal-clarity, safety, and extra strength. They're sealed on three sides and contain prepunched holes for standard three-ring binders. They come in varieties such as top loading, side loading, quick load (two sides are open), and foldout sheets. Sizes: letter ($8\frac{1}{2} \times 11$ inches), legal (14×11 inches), and ledger (14×17 inches) (Figures 2.6a and 2.6b).
- *Storage pages.* For photo and slide archival purposes, four mil polypropylene pages are recommended; they provide high clarity for superior presentation and are suitable for long-term storage. They can be used with standard three-ring binders and are PVC free. They can be bought in packages of 25 pages. Size sheet cap: 2×2, $3\frac{1}{2} \times 5$, 4×5, 4×6, 4×7, 4×11, 5×7, and 8×10 inch slides.
- *Tab dividers.* Useful to separate projects by sections and by categories. They come with insertable tabs and

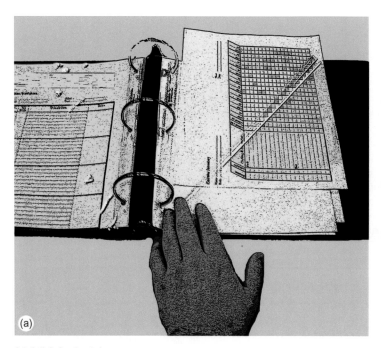

(a)

FIGURE 2.6A

Sheet holders come in many varieties. Quick-load sheet holders are very practical when paperwork needs to be removed and restored repeatedly.

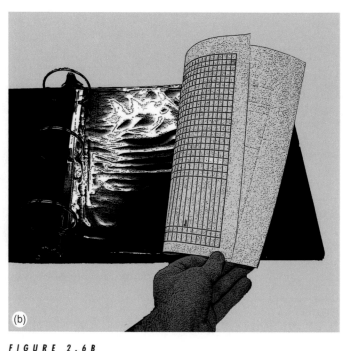

(b)

FIGURE 2.6B

The 11 × 17-inch ledger size foldout sheet holders are very practical for larger documents, charts, CAD printouts, and the like.

blank white inserts. They can be found in traditional eight-tab packs or big-tab five-tab packs. The inserts in the big-tab packs provide 50% more printing space for tab titles than traditional insertable tab dividers. The tab inserts can be created using an inkjet or laser printer (see Figure 2.6c).

In conclusion, there are many available portfolio refill pages and sheet protector options that are designed for multiple uses. The right choice can add pizzazz to a portfolio presentation.

Specialty Layout Materials and Supplies

The materials and supplies needed to put a portfolio together and create the desired layout include sheet protectors, tab dividers, résumé paper, matting boards, double-sided tape, specialty glues, paper-cutting gadgets, computer printouts, labels, and more. The following are some important aspects to consider in choosing these materials:

- *Durability*. The best material choices are acid free, PVC free, and heat resistant to preserve the work and to prevent lifting or transferring the color onto the sheet holders. Acid-free double-sided tape is great to hold down photos and avoid curled edges. Rubber cement is also recommended for art applications where easy and damage-free removal of adhesive is desired. It will not shrink or swell

FIGURE 2.6C

Tab dividers aid in separating parts of a project or categorizing and organizing paperwork.

paper fibers, so it will prevent the adhered surface wrinkles that often occur when other glues are applied.

- *Safety.* When you're using paper-cutting gadgets, it is important to observe manufacturers' instructions and use the instruments that provide personal confidence in their proper use in order to avoid personal injuries and work damage. If you're using n-hexane–or n-heptane–based adhesives such as rubber cement, make sure to follow hazardous waste disposal guidelines. There are comprehensive guidelines at the U.S. Environmental Protection Agency (EPA) website: www.epa.gov/osw/hazard/recycling/.

- *Legibility.* Background paper, matting boards, labels, and résumé papers should not compete with nor detract from the project information on display. In choosing among any of these, it is also important to take into consideration the fact that the paper will have to be photocopied and the work will have to be legible in the copies.

- *Versatility.* Depending on the complexity of the project and the number of parts on display, the materials you choose need to allow flexibility in the presentation. Ask yourself: Is the project going to be taken out of its sheet holders? Does the project have multiple components that need different portfolio cases? Does the project include small inserts such as reviews, programs, or the like that may not need a full large page? Do all the components need to be bound, or do some need to be free for handling purposes?

Where to Find Specialty Materials and Supplies

Larger cities may give the designer/technician the option to visit an art store in person and speak to an informed salesperson if needed. When this is not an option because of geographical location or a busy schedule, the Internet is the best way to access a very diverse market with many products. Experience dictates that it is best to do research first and then shop. Sometimes after identifying a source on the Internet, a designer/technician might want to dial the company's customer service number and ask questions about their products directly.

These are some companies with Web catalogues, presented in alphabetical order:

AllArtSupply.com: Features portfolio cases and carrying devices; www.artresource.com/portfolio_cases.html

Charrette: Carries art supplies and portfolio cases, folios, and archival sheets; www.charrette.com

Colours Artist Supplies: Located in Canada; www.artistsupplies.com

Dick Blick (formerly Art-Store): Ideal for art supplies and portfolio cases, folios, and archival sheets; www.dickblick.com

Digital Art Supplies: www.digitalartsupplies.com

Madison Art Shopping: www.madisonartshop.com

Office Depot: Office supplies and layout materials; www.officedepot.com

Pearl Fine Art Supplies: www.pearlpaint.com

Portfolios-and-Art-Cases: All kinds of portfolio cases and hard-to-find sizes; www.portfolios-and-art-cases.com

Rex Art: www.rexart.com

Staples: Ideal for basic three-ring binders, standard sheet protectors, office supplies, labels, and so on; www.staples.com

Utrecht Art: www.utrechtart.com/

Remember that there are many art stores on the Web, and sometimes if a deal seems too good to be true, it probably is. Check your local yellow page listings for nearby locations and the Internet for specials and discounts in various stores. If you are on a deadline, don't rely on the Web only when you're ordering specialty items; it is always best to call a store's customer service number to check on stock availability, product specifics, and delivery timing. Sometimes stores will refer you to another vendor that may carry something more suitable to your needs. Always do your research first!

Basic Strategy to Get the Right Materials

To make good choices, we need to consider the type of materials we will include in our portfolio. We also have to identify what case is appropriate for our concentration. A makeup portfolio case made out of onyx may look cool, but an aluminum case may work better for a lighting designer or tech director. When in doubt, choose a classic black portfolio case. Here are some helpful tips for obtaining the materials that will work best for you:

1. Check what other experienced folks in your specific field are using.

2. Review your materials and look for size trends. This will influence the size of the portfolio you choose.

3. Try various sizes at an art store; check how well you can handle the case.

4. Look at the sheet inserts. Do they come apart easily? Do they seem fragile? Are they too shiny? These are all considerations that can detract from your work.

5. Does the case have a place to hold résumés and business cards?

6. Does it have a back pocket to carry extra materials such as ground plans?

Show Case: Notes About Printers

by James Michael Garner

When it comes to reputation for personal computer print quality, Canon, HP, and Epson are certainly the leaders in innovation. However, these printers often come with quite a price tag. I have owned printers from all three of these manufacturers as well as several from Lexmark, Xerox, and Kodak, but for me, the all-time, hands-down winner is my current MFC-6490CW model from Brother.

Brother MFC-6490CW With Wireless

Brother often gets a bad rap for being "cheap, therefore it must not be of good quality." I like to think, however, that this model and its cousins, the 6490CN, the 5890CW, and the 5890CN have been built cheaply, efficiently, and with minimal compromise in terms of overall quality. (I own both the 6490CW and the 5890CN, which kind of gives me the entire spectrum.) Many manufacturers design something and then build it cheaply, which causes a whole series of problems, but all four of these Brother printers have been streamlined in their construction so that they use all the same parts, which cuts costs at the factory but ensures a good product. Brother allows you to customize the size of your printer based on your budget limitations.

When it comes to print quality, I happen to think that the 6490 offers superior clarity and color reproduction. Now, if you want to have a printer solely for printing photographs and graphic presentations, you are talking about a very big monetary investment in something that has only one use and an undetermined lifespan. So, if you are only doing a single presentation of your work, you may just want to have your images printed by Kinko's. As for me, I am always updating paperwork and creating new presentations, so purchasing a printer has seemed the logical choice.

The reason I like the Brother printer so much is that it can produce good-quality images but costs only around $200 new (I got mine for $75 on eBay). The other bonuses are that it has wired and wireless network capabilities, and it's an all-in-one printer for office tasks, so it has your standard fax, scanner, and printer integrated in one device as well. One cool thing you can do is send a fax to your printer wirelessly so you don't have to print and then scan it.

Product Review: Brother MFC-6490CW

And speaking of scanning, the 6490 has an 11×17-inch scanner bed! It also has two paper trays so you can print 11×17-inch borderless pictures or documents (it prints to the edge of the page) from one tray and legal or $8\frac{1}{2} \times 11$-inch documents from the other one (or have two trays for one or the other).

The ink is also cheap, with its four-ink cartridge system that allows for more economy and better quality. Today it costs more to buy ink per volume than it does penicillin, vodka, or oil. The Brother brand ink cartridges cost only about $15 each, and you can buy a double-capacity black ink cartridge as well.

To cut costs, I tested the device by printing some of my pictures with the bargain brand inks that you can buy on eBay for $3 each, and to my surprise, the quality was still pretty good. In fact, many of my portfolio pictures were printed with this bargain ink, which saved me tons of money. But don't think that because I am advocating the purchase of bargain products that I don't have high standards, because this is not true. I have a high bar for the work that I produce, and I feel that this solution has met and exceeded that bar. If you want to play it safe, I often recommend that you purchase name-brand black ink and bargain brand color inks, because cheap black ink sometimes comes out tinted blue or red. Another way to cut costs even more is to purchase ink systems that allow for high-capacity cartridges that you never have to replace. Just refill them. I personally don't like to deal with the hassle of refilling ink so I simply buy mine.

Another way I have saved money is by taking those empty $3 bargain ink cartridges and recycling them at my local Staples. They give you a $2 gift certificate in the mail for every cartridge you bring in. It's almost like free ink!

You will notice that the overall rating of this printer is in the three-star range on websites such as CNET. However, the reason for this (and you can check this yourself) is that the overall rating is depreciated because of skewed reviews by people who "don't like the buttons" or don't know how to set up their networks. One review stated that due to licensing, Brother will only allow you to network a total of two computers to the printer and you have to buy a $60 license to increase the number of users. For one thing, if this were true and you were working in an office setting, the cost you save on ink and the printer itself would offset that investment. Second, this statement is purely incorrect. I have two printers like this set up on my home network with four computers and they can all print to the 6490 simultaneously. Another qualm people have with this printer is that it's big. One thing you have to realize is that if you want something that will scan 11 × 17 inches, it has to have a footprint that's at least 11 × 17 inches.

The few actual downsides to this printer are that it does not have automatic paper size detection and that it does not do duplex printing (you can pay an extra $100 if you want the option to do duplex with the MFC-6890CDW printer). If you do want to have portfolio-quality images, the printer will print more slowly, but you can adjust the print speeds depending on what you are printing.

In theatre, I can see TDs using the 6890CW to print 11 × 17-inch plots for construction drawings. Also, props artisans would be able to scan original posters, texts, and other items to make reproductions of them for stage use. Costume and scenic designers can use the scanner if they need to digitize renderings for use in digital portfolios or if they need to provide dramaturges with samples to use in larger displays. The bottom line is that if you are purchasing this printer solely to use as an 11 × 17-inch scanner, it's well worth the money, since standalone scanners of this size cost a minimum of $150 and can reach into the thousands of dollars.

So that's my two cents' worth. You can take it or leave it, but I'm in love with my Brother printer, and I don't care who knows it!

P.S.: You can also print directly from your CF/SD/XD/ Memory Stick cards as well as anything with a USB interface.

In this chapter we have established some basics. We now have information that can help us choose a portfolio case, and we have information that can help us start to get some necessary supplies.

Next, we have to answer the questions: How do we pick the work to be featured in the portfolio? How do we develop an effective showcase?

WORKBOOK

Chapter 2, Development Techniques
Workbook: What carrying and display
materials would I like to use to put
together a portfolio?

DESIGNERS ... SHOULD BE ABLE TO DRAW—FREEHAND, NOT JUST IN

PHOTOSHOP—DRAFT, DEAL WITH COLOR, AND UNDERSTAND COLOR BOTH IN

LIGHT AND PIGMENT.

DAVE TOSTI-LANE

CHAPTER THREE

THE EFFECTIVE
SHOWCASE

In previous chapters we established that a portfolio is (a) a showcase of the artistry of a designer and a technician, (b) a reference archive that features processes and design solutions, and (c) a storybook that emphasizes the individual's professional growth and versatility. In this chapter we will add a new aspect to the discussion by exploring the portfolio as a marketing tool that has specific goals.

General Considerations

The audience for which your portfolio is intended can define your portfolio. A portfolio used to apply for graduate school may be different from a portfolio used to get a professional design job; a portfolio used to apply for a technical job will differ from the one used by a designer. Each goal will have a different set of variables that the individual must consider. To be successful in putting together a portfolio, it is important to get information regarding what a portfolio reviewer will be looking for and plan accordingly. Once the uses of the portfolio have been defined, the next step is to plan the organization—beginning, middle, and end—of the work to be displayed. The order and display of the parts need to be well thought out, contain comprehensive materials, and communicate clearly. This part of the process will help you choose the most appropriate work, layout materials, and sequences.

Organizing the Body of Work: Beginning, Middle, and End

The Beginning

The beginning refers to the portfolio introductory page. It may include a résumé, an identification page, an opening title page, a table of contents, and so on. The identification page is especially important if your portfolio is being reviewed when you are not in the room; for example, some colleges review portfolios without the applicants being present. Some designers/technicians prefer portfolios that have a front pocket so that they can store résumés, brochures, and other similar items for this very purpose.

David C. (Kip) Shawger, Jr., is the immediate Kennedy Center/American College Theater Festival National Design vice chair. He is a native of New Jersey who received a BS degree in drama from Nebraska Wesleyan University and a masters of fine arts (MFA) degree in design from Bradley University. He is an award-winning designer with over 300 design credits and 30 years of experience in education, community, professional theatre, television, and film. Shawger has a very well-organized portfolio; his opening page sets the tone of the presentation with CD cases, workbooks, résumé, and business cards. The work is presented in a clear and sophisticated way right from the start (see Figure 3.1).

FIGURE 3.1

Kip Shawger's portfolio opening page holds his résumé, CD (digital) samplers, workbooks, and business cards.

The Middle

This middle of the portfolio is the main body of the designer/technician's work and is organized by project. It should be versatile and support the goals of the portfolio. It is best to organize each project with its own beginning, middle, and end, to help tell your story. The layout should include sketches, models (or other 3-D items created for the production), and photos of the realized project. It is also helpful to include programs, reviews, and some process photos. In some cases—when the portfolio has multiple purposes—it is important to separate projects with title pages or tab the different parts (see Figures 3.2a through 3.2e). Typical subdivisions (by categories) of the middle body of the portfolio include these:

- *Venue.* Includes traditional venues such as theatre, television, film, and video. It also includes allied fields and newer venues such as industrials, concerts, art installations, museum installations, and virtual productions.

- *Production.* Musical theatre, children's theatre, music video, industrial design, Shakespearean drama, dance theatre, virtual scenery, novelty or theme parks, comedy, commercials, and so on.

- *Type of work.* Produced shows, class projects, conceptual projects, design and/or technical projects, allied fields, installations and/or exhibits, and the like.

The End

This last part of your portfolio can bring in two different aspects. It could be the last aspect of a project's layout, or it could be the end of your showcase. The layout of the last section of a project wants to have

(a)

FIGURE 3.2A

Kip Shawger's portfolio layout for his set design of *Adding Machine,* produced at Ball State University's Mainstage for the 1997–98 season.

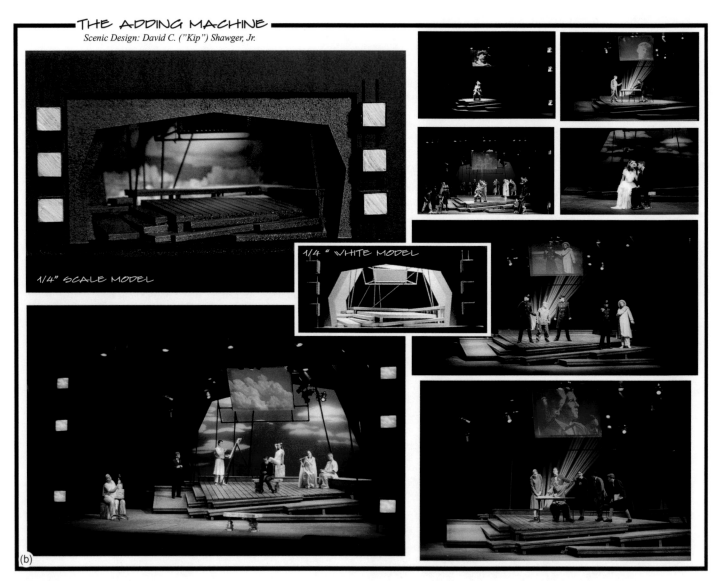

THE ADDING MACHINE

Scenic Design: David C. ("Kip") Shawger, Jr.

1/4" SCALE MODEL

1/4 " WHITE MODEL

(b)

FIGURE 3.2B

Kip Shawger's digital layout for his set design of *Adding Machine*.

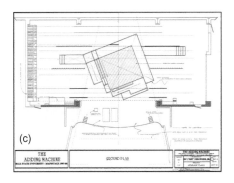

FIGURE 3.2C

Proper labels and keys with important show information, such as name of the play, venue, sketch detail, and so on, are always necessary to help inform the reviewers (and the presenter). Shawger's ground plan for his set design of *Adding Machine*.

FIGURE 3.2E

Good quality photos of the finished product or project helps tell the story from beginning to end. Shawger's production photo of his set design of *Adding Machine*.

FIGURE 3.2D

Including images of a process such as a model gives the reviewer a sense of the scale of the production and skill range of the presenter. Shawger's production photo of his color model for *Adding Machine*.

details that best feature the individual's contributions (Figures 3.3a and 3.3b). The last pages of a portfolio showcase should include one or various smaller projects "to be remembered by." The back pocket is also at the end of the portfolio but is not necessarily featured. It holds various samples of reference and support materials that can be used to show other aspects of the projects, such as extra sketches, drafting, budget specs, or flowcharts.

Presenting Visual Content: Page Layout Options

The visual content of a portfolio can be organized in different ways to best feature the work. Just as with a play, each "scene" has to be integrated with the total "arc" of the work. Start with an opening page for the portfolio and a starting page for each sequence.

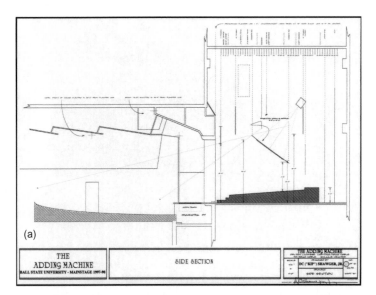

FIGURE 3.3A

Kip Shawger's digital scenic section for his set design of *Adding Machine*, produced at Ball State University's Mainstage for the 1997–98 season.

FIGURE 3.3B

Kip Shawger's digital photo for his set design of *Adding Machine*, including scenic projections.

Opening Page

The beginning page serves as an introduction of the designer/technician and also as an introduction of the work featured in the portfolio. It needs to be clear and direct; it sets the stage of the presentation. It can be as simple as an identification page, a project page, or a place to hold a résumé and/or business cards (see Figures 3.4a and 3.4b).

The next step is deciding how to tell the project's story. Consecutive pages need to maintain the same layout direction to guide the viewer's eye. This also helps prevent what I call the "lazy Susan effect"; there's nothing worse than a revolving portfolio! When you're planning the page sequences, it is important to remember to avoid featuring horizontal and vertical pages next to each other; viewers prefer a continuous flow. It is also best to avoid displaying different projects next to each other, so there isn't any confusion as to what the reviewer is looking at. Sometimes it is also important to include reviews and feature articles (from major publications) to emphasize the scale and impact of the project. Remember that all projects need to be clearly labeled and have proper keys with the name of the production, number of the sketch, scale, name of the character, and so on, depending on your

FIGURE 3.4A

Set designer Brian White's portfolio opening page. To keep things consistent, White uses his stationery color for the portfolio labels and adds an image from one of his best projects. He is currently a freelance scene designer in Houston. His recent awards for scene design include the 2007 Kennedy Center American College Theater Festival (KCACTF) Scene Design Fellowship to the Eugene O'Neill Theater Center in Waterford, Connecticut, and the 2007 KCACTF Region VI Barbizon Award for Scene Design Excellence.

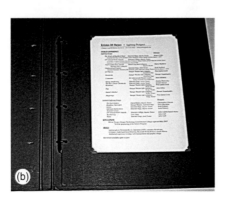

FIGURE 3.4B

Lighting designer Kristin Hayes opens her portfolio with her résumé; this practice can be used by people in all disciplines. Hayes is currently a freelance designer in the New England area. Recent awards include the 2008 KCACTF Scene Design Fellowship to the Eugene O'Neill Theater Center in Waterford, Connecticut, and the 2008 KCACTF Region I Barbizon Award for Lighting Excellence.

concentration. Finally, planning the number of projects breaks you need will help determine how many extra pages to get for a particular portfolio (see Figures 3.5a through 3.5h).

Horizontal Layout

A well-organized portfolio showcases projects in logical and entertaining sequences. For a horizontal layout, plan to display the work in left-to-right order and include concept statements, research, designs, and process images.

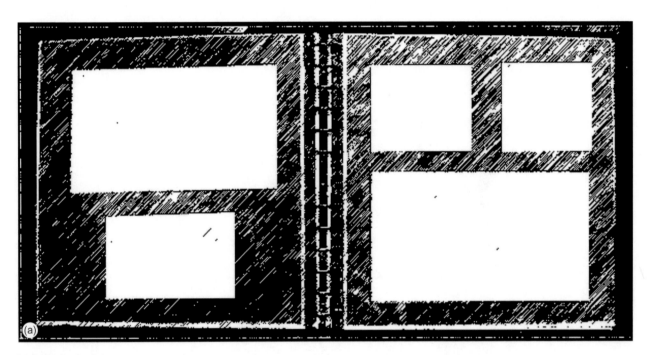

FIGURE 3.5A

Horizontal layout schematic. Plan positive and negative spacing. Sometimes it is indispensable to include concept statements, research, and process images.

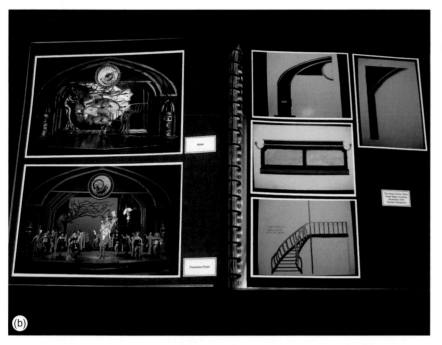

FIGURE 3.5B

Set designer Brian White's horizontal layout sample for *The Rocky Horror Show*, Texas State University, 2006. The concept statement is included earlier in the portfolio pages.

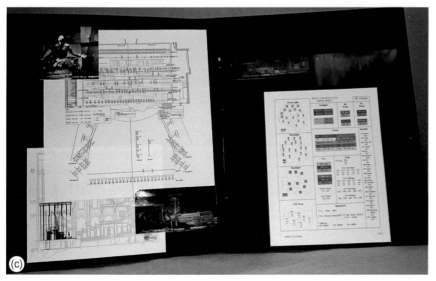

FIGURE 3.5C

Lighting designer Kristin Hayes's horizontal layout sample for *The Witch of Blackbird Pond*, Emerson Stage, 2006. She includes the light plot, section, color choices, and specific production images related to lighting specials.

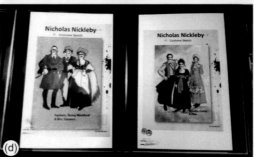

FIGURE 3.5D

The author's horizontal layouts for *Nicholas Nickleby*, Lyric Stage Company of Boston, 2010. In this case the sketches are in a slide-in binder portfolio case, one sketch per sleeve. The images represent four consecutive pages. This is an easy way to present the costume designs to a production team when space is limited.

FIGURE 3.5E

The author's horizontal layout for *The Duchess of Malfi*, Emerson Stage, 2004. From left to right this layout includes concept images, research, costume counts, sketches, swatches, and production images. The swatches are placed on the outside of the plastic sleeves so that viewers can touch and feel the fabrics.

FIGURE 3.5F

Vertical layout guidelines. Keep consecutive pages with the same orientation; order items from left to right and from top to bottom.

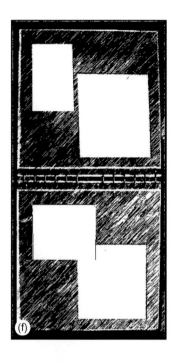

Vertical Layout

Always keep consecutive pages with the same orientation; to help the viewer in handling your portfolio. For a vertical layout, it is best to organize items left to right and from top to bottom.

FIGURE 3.5G

Glen Anderson's portfolio page, vertical layout sample. Design layout for an 11 × 17-inch portfolio featuring scenic design for *Waiting for Godot*. Glen holds an MFA in scenic design from the University of Florida, Gainesville. At the 2007 KCACTF Glen was awarded the Barbizon Excellence in Scenic Design Award. He is a member of USITT and participated in World Stage Design 2005 in Toronto.

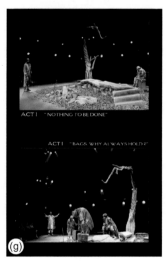

FIGURE 3.5H

The author's costume designs for the musical *Pippin*, displayed in a vertical layout. Produced by Emerson Stage and directed by Stephen Terrell.

Inserts: Adding Conversation Pieces

There are other materials to consider in planning layouts, such as key research, process pictures, and spec information. These can be included as inserts or as loose reference materials and can become "conversation pieces." To create interest, smaller sheets can be added within a project. To add theatricality, transitions can be created (with smaller page inserts) to reveal new parts of a project. These smaller sheets can hold photos, newspaper articles, research, and so on. Foldout pages can be added to present smaller aspects of the project to create interest, as in a play within a play. Always make sure that the sheet holders you choose are compatible with the portfolio case you're using. The goal is to add an element of surprise, variety, and flexibility to the display. In addition, make sure that the layout helps make the portfolio pages more manageable (see Figures 3.5i through 3.5K).

FIGURE 3.5I

Page inserts add surprise, variety, and flexibility to the display. They can be a half page or any other size that best works with your layout.

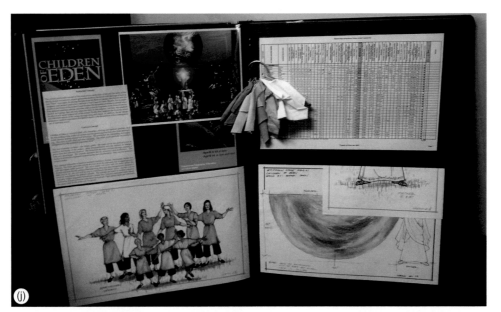

FIGURE 3.5J

The author's costume design layout for *The Musical Children of Eden*, produced by Emerson Stage and directed by Leo Nicole, 2001. At first glance, it seems to be two pages. The upper right features the complicated costume plot with tracking of "quick changes."

FIGURE 3.5K

The author's costume design layout for *The Musical Children of Eden*, produced by Emerson Stage and directed by Leo Nicole, 2001. The upper-right page turns to reveal sketches and costume craft details.

FIGURE 3.6A

FIGURE 3.6A

Scene from *A Little Night Music,* produced by the Lyric Stage Company of Boston in September 2004. Director: Spiro Veloudos; scenic design: Christina Todesco; costume design: David Cabral; and lighting design: Karen Perlow.

Featuring Best Artwork, News/Media Reviews, and Photographs

Reviewers are like critics: They are accustomed to seeing and ranking many portfolios. They will have many questions and high expectations. Featured artwork needs to be clearly labeled, fixed in place, and organized. Drafting, blueprints, and CAD drawings need to be a readable size. Photographs (digital and otherwise) need to be true to stage color and should contain detail. Research and reference materials should include their sources and titles. News and media articles should include dates and title pages. Show programs, reputable production company brochures, and show posters or postcards can be part of the layout and add status to the presentation. The goal is to give reviewers as many contexts as possible so they can understand at a glance the scale and style of the work that you are presenting.

Karen Perlow has been a freelance lighting designer since 1986. She is an instructor at the Massachusetts Institute of Technology (MIT) and a 2003 Independent Reviewers of New England (IRNE) winner for best lighting design. In her portfolio she includes sequences of large photographs that clearly demonstrate a wide range of design ideas executed for each of her shows (see Figures 3.6a through 3.6f). For some scenes Perlow needed to create an expansive sense of space; in others she needed to create an intimate feeling while

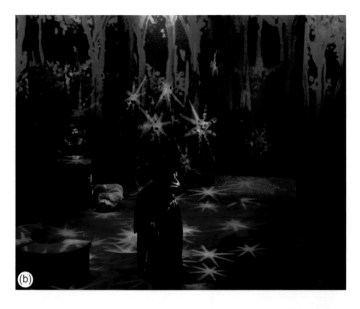

FIGURE 3.6B AND 3.6C

Scenes from *A Little Night Music,* produced by the Lyric Stage Company of Boston in September 2004. Director: Spiro Veloudos; scenic design: Christina Todesco; costume design: David Cabral, and lighting design: Karen Perlow.

FIGURE 3.6F

Scapin, New Repertory Theater, April 2004. Director: Rick Lombardo; scenic design: Janie Howland; costume design: Francis McSherry, light design: Karen Perlow.

FIGURE 3.7

The author keeps various examples of unusual projects in his portfolio's back pocket. This page belongs to a project for a muralist. "I had to dress actual doctors from the Mass General Hospital [MGH] in Boston to reenact an 1846 tumor removal surgery commemorating the first use of ether as anesthesia. The muralist Warren Prosperi created a life-size mural at the MGH Ether Dome using the images and videos from the reenactment." February 2004.

accommodating different upstage playing spaces. In each photograph the composition creates a sense of environment and mood, integrating playing areas and coordinating color palette.

Back Pocket: Research and Organizational Paperwork

There will always be materials that seem superfluous or productions that have more sketches and graphics than others will. If a project has a lot of material that the designer deems important, it can be saved in the portfolio back pocket. The back pocket usually contains reference materials such as extra research, technical information, photos, and design and technical solutions for specific projects that didn't fit or couldn't be featured within the main body of your work. The materials in the back pocket also need to be organized and labeled clearly (see Figure 3.7).

Back-pocket materials can be used as conversation pieces if the interviewer wants more information about a specific skill (such as hand-drafting) or a particular type of project (say, styling for a paper print). If the designer or technician has a large body of work, the back pocket will only include highlights of archival materials. These archival materials need to be catalogued and filed properly so they can be used (if called upon) for installations featuring samples for educational, marketing, and/or exhibition purposes. For technicians, sometimes a simple three-ring binder can contain all back-pocket support materials.

The Designer and Technician's Archives

As the years go by and sample work is accumulated, it is important to file and catalogue your projects. In the academic world these files can be used for promotion and tenure; elsewhere they can be used as teaching tools or reference materials, submitted as written articles for a magazine, and used at artist retrospective exhibits and installations.

To illustrate this aspect of portfolio archiving, I reached out to my former classmate and colleague John Iacovelli, an accomplished award-winning designer who has many nominations and an Emmy Award to his name.

Iacovelli has done theatrical set designs for Broadway and regional theatre productions; art direction and production design for TV and film; and art direction and production design for video and industrials. Some of his impressive career credits include set design for many Broadway productions, including *Peter Pan*; art direction for TV shows, including *The Cosby Show*; production design for *Resurrection Boulevard* and *Babylon 5*; art direction for the film *Honey, I Shrunk the Kids;* and industrial installations for the Summer 1996 Olympics and Disney.

The 2004 USITT Design Expo featured John Iacovelli's work. In his display he featured recent work for theatre, TV, and film. He organized his archival materials to show process, samples, and final designs. The presentation materials had a beginning, middle, and end, and he demonstrated that portfolio archives could be a traveling installation! (See Figures 3.8a through 3.8g.)

Marketing and Networking: Identifying Portfolio Requirements by Venue

In this section we focus on college application procedures, higher education organizations that offer specialized services and scholarships, institutes, and unions. Before pursuing any venue it is of the utmost importance for the individual to do in-depth research into the best

FIGURE 3.8A

Designer John Iacovelli's exhibit, USITT Design Expo 2004; wall display.

FIGURE 3.8B

Designer John Iacovelli's exhibit, USITT Design Expo 2004; design plans and an actual set piece.

FIGURE 3.8C

Designer John Iacovelli's exhibit, USITT Design Expo 2004; set models wall.

FIGURE 3.8D

Designer John Iacovelli's exhibit, USITT Design Expo 2004, the Emmy Award—a recognition of his artistry and fantastic body of work.

FIGURE 3.8E

Sample detail photo from John Iacovelli's exhibit, USITT Design Expo 2004; set for the TV show *Ed*, producer NBC/Viacom, various directors.

FIGURE 3.8F AND 3.8G

Sample detail photos from John Iacovelli's exhibit, USITT Design Expo 2004. *Vincent on Brixton*, producer: The Pasadena Playhouse; director: Elina deSantos; scenery design: John Iacovelli; costume design: Maggie Morgan, lighting design: Leigh Allen.

opportunities available for his or her specific level of skills and temperament. Some requirements are universal and some are specific to the venue.

College Applications

Portfolio requirements vary depending on the program for which the student is applying. Undergraduate programs may have more emphasis in artwork and general theatrical experience, whereas graduate programs will be looking for more area-specific and in-depth production work. When planning a portfolio to submit with a college application, it is important to obtain the specific requirements of each school; most of them will conduct reviews without the applicant present. Most colleges will also look for examples of artwork as well as both nonrealized projects and realized production work. Usually the artwork requirements will include samples such as drawings, paintings, models, sculptures, and so on. Photographs of such artwork can be included; the scale of the project needs to be noted on each photograph to help differentiate among the projects—for example, a large mural from a postcard.

Theatrical projects include samples such as rough and final sketches, materials and swatches samples, blueprints of drafting and/or CAD (digital drafting) samples, model samples and/or photographs, light plots and Q sheets, production photographs, and the like. Some colleges will ask for a digital portfolio (samples on a CD); others will require an actual portfolio case. Each design/tech area will require specific samples. The area of scenic design often requires scale models (or photos), scale ground plans and sections, and examples of architectural sketches (furniture, interior details, and so on). It is important to organize these samples by script or play. The area of costume design often requires sketches with fabric swatches, period research, and technical detail drawings. Concept plates, fashion-style sheets, and samples of built garments may be required

as well. It is important to organize these samples by script or play. The area of lighting design often requires a concept statement about ideas for the projects and their execution, which sometimes includes inspirational photos, research, or color drawings. It also requires a light plot (computer and drafting), full paperwork, and production photographs. It is important to organize these samples by script or play.

A successful portfolio should be as versatile as possible and contain materials that display multiple skills. The work should be properly labeled and the presentation should be well organized and clear. The same portfolios can be used at venues that include higher education organizations and associated groups that offer professional reviews, scholarships, internships, competitions, and/or professional job placements that will enhance the experience of the participants. There are many of these venues, and they all have websites with updated comprehensive guidelines, clear information, and application procedures. Some organizations worth researching are the University/Resident Theater Association (UR/TA), the Southeastern Theater Conference (SETC), the New England Theater Conference (NETC), the U.S. Institute for Theater Technology (USITT), and United Scenic Artists (USA) Chapter 829. The choice of which one of these venues to pursue depends on the individual's level of skill, location, finances, the membership restrictions, and so on. It is important to research these venues thoroughly before making a decision.

Organizations That Offer Portfolio Reviews

The following summary includes general information on various higher education organizations and associated groups that offer portfolio reviews as part of their services and memberships.

- *URTA (www.urta.com)*. The University/Resident Theatre Association is the largest U.S. consortium of professional companies and educational theatre programs. It provides a variety of services to students, theatre professionals, and production companies. It facilitates access to graduate college scholarships and jobs with professional theatre companies. After following application procedures, paying an application fee, and scheduling a portfolio review, applicants receive support materials that include a copy of the *Directory of Theatre Training Programs* (a complete listing of U/RTA member schools and services) and the indispensable *Guidelines for Portfolio Presentation and Interview Procedures*. The *Guidelines* booklet has answers for most questions related to the setup and organization of the portfolio review. The requirements are similar to those listed earlier in the college application section.

- *SETC (www.setc.org)*. The Southeastern Theatre Conference is one the largest and most active regional theatre organizations in the country. Open to a national audience, it focuses on providing theatre experiences of the highest possible standards. Schools must be institutional members for students to enter. This conference offers design professional critiques at design competitions at both the undergraduate and graduate levels. Adjudicators are well-known, acclaimed designers. Specific details for entry can be found on the website under "Student Guidelines." Scene Design Award minimum requirements include ground plan in specific scale, color sketch, model, and/or painter's elevations, plus a statement of the designer's approach. Other items to include: research materials, preliminary sketches, full drafting package including ground plan, elevations, section, and detail drawings, and photographs if realized. The Costume Design Award minimum requirements include color costume sketches (each sketch must be swatched), statement of the approach to the design, research materials, preliminary sketches, a costume plot, plus photographs if the design was realized. The Lighting Design Award minimum requirements include a light plot drawn using USITT standard symbols, plus a dimmer/control schedule, magic sheets, instrument schedule, hanging section (scenic designer's is acceptable), photographs of realized production (graduate level), and a statement of the approach to the design. Other materials include research materials, preliminary sketches, cue sheets, and storyboards.

- *NETC (www.netconline.org)*. The New England Theatre Conference is an organization dedicated to providing its members with professional services, career development, and playwright recognition awards in the theatre arts. It serves Connecticut, Maine, Massachusetts, New Hampshire, Rhode Island, and Vermont. NETC conducts theatre auditions annually for positions in summer and year-round professional theatres. Positions include actors, singers, dancers, designers, technicians, and production staff. The participating companies range from Equity and non-Equity summer stock to Shakespearean and Renaissance festivals, musical theatre, children's theatre, revues, and many others. Tech and staff interviews are conducted to fill the many positions available in these fields. Every applicant also receives a complete list of all participating producers and their season, and every producer receives the résumé of every applicant. Membership is required.

- *USITT (www.usitt.org)*. The U.S. Institute for Theatre Technology, Inc. (USITT), is the association of design, production, and technology professionals in the performing arts and entertainment industry. USITT promotes the advancement and development of the knowledge and skills of its members by sponsoring and sharing information about new technologies, research, and educational programs; safety, industry standards, and ethical practices; and exhibits, conferences, and networking opportunities. The organization also recommends awards, grants, and fellowships to recipients through their various committees. During their yearly Conference and Stage Expo, USITT Commissions sponsor special in-depth review sessions for individuals to discuss portfolios, résumés, and careers with professionals in specific areas. These sessions are open to undergraduate, graduate, and working designers and technicians. They last 30 minutes and are facilitated by professional volunteer members from various disciplines.

- *USA Chapter 829 and IATSE (www.usa829.org; www.iatse-intl.org/index_flash.html).* United Scenic Artists and the International Alliance of Theatrical Stage Employees, Moving Pictures Technicians, Artist and Allied Crafts of the United States, its territories and Canada are labor unions representing technicians, artisans, and craftspeople in the entertainment industry, including live theatre, motion pictures, television production, and trade shows. Membership provides many benefits, including retirement plans, credit unions, and health benefits. Becoming a member of USA is a rigorous process and requires different types of exams. TRACK A is for designers with at least three years of professional, not academic, experience. The Exam is a 20-minute

interview during which various judges review the applicant's portfolio and some required samples. Applicants who fail to be recommended after this interview may consider the TRACK B Open Exam or the Apprenticeship Program. It is advisable to do everything possible to present your portfolio to its best advantage. This way the judges will be able to best assess a candidate's range of knowledge, experience, and qualifications. The panel consists of six designers. Flat-table presentations are favored for easy handling of materials. Portfolios should include Main Project documentation (as prescribed in the application for each discipline), rough drawings/sketches, models, color renderings, complete drafting, storyboards, location photos, research or reference materials, production photos, and/or videotapes. The website mentions that "It's much better to have all the documentation for one or two projects than bits and pieces of two dozen projects." Depending on time, judges may be also interested in assessing organizational skills and flexibility. They can discern these skills by viewing production paperwork such as show bibles, organizational paperwork, budgets whenever possible, process-related photos, and/or shopping lists.

In this chapter we explored some portfolio development techniques and organization as well as networking and marketing venues. Next: What does the final product begin to look like? What do experts in the field recommend?

List projects that you would like to feature in the beginning, middle, and end of your portfolio.

_____

_____

_____

_____

_____

_____

YOU SHOULD INCLUDE ... THE STEPS YOU TOOK WHICH
REFLECT YOUR THINKING AS WELL AS YOUR WAY OF WORKING.

PETER BEUDERT

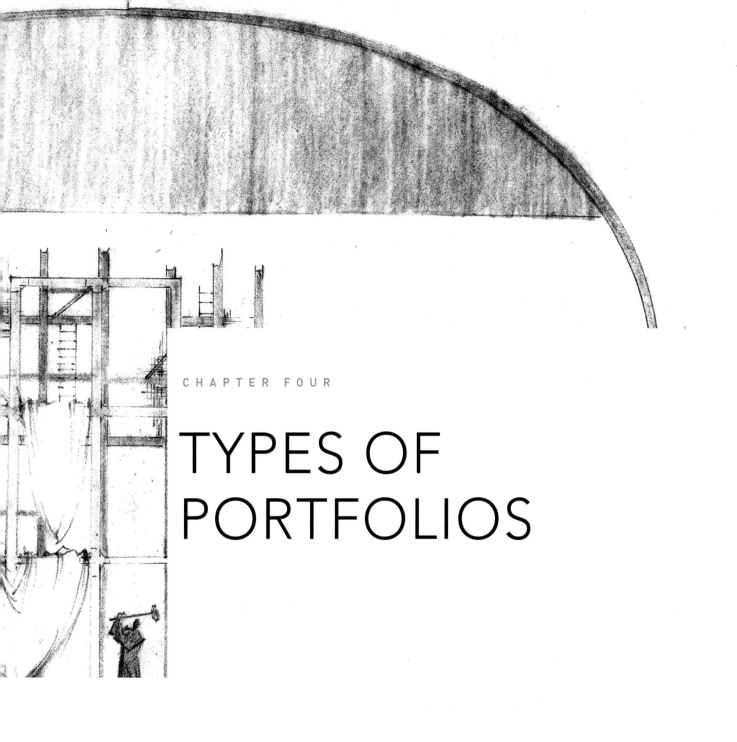

CHAPTER FOUR

TYPES OF PORTFOLIOS

In October 2004, *Entertainment Design* magazine featured an article called "Avoiding a Portfolio Imbroglio." Mark Newman, the magazine's managing editor, conducted interviews and wrote this very comprehensive article, paying careful attention to the expectations described by various design-technology experts about different types of portfolios. The comments included in his article help illustrate what reviewers in different areas of concentration look for and best respond to. This chapter includes Mr. Newman's findings as well as feedback and samples from colleagues who contributed to this book.

Avoiding a Portfolio Imbroglio

by Mark A. Newman

(reprinted from *Entertainment Design*, October 1, 2004)

"Who am I anyway? Am I my résumé?" So goes the lyric from the opening number of *A Chorus Line,* sung by an aspiring triple-threat. For aspiring theatre designers, the answer to the lyric is yes … and no. Design faculty at top colleges can easily see through the gloss of a slick portfolio. An attractive presentation is nice, but if the talent and the ability are not there, the presentation is moot.

In the Fall 2004 issue of the *U/RTA Update,* U/RTA executive director Scott Steele noted that portfolios are partly about concealing weaknesses. But a designer's strengths should not be buried for the sake of presentation. A portfolio that is all "bells and whistles" keeps university design recruiters from seeing what really exists in the student's mind, what gifts the students truly have, or even where the real talent deficits may hide.

Know-How

For example, if you cannot adequately represent your designs by taking pencil to paper, you already have an uphill battle. "I'm looking for art skills traditionally called 'visual arts,' which is problematic in the American educational system in terms of training designers," says Richard Isackes, chair at the University of Texas, Austin, and a set designer. "Most candidates have been theatre majors in their institutions, which seems completely appropriate, but the skills of a theatre designer really start with skills of a visual artist." He added that some of the best designers he has seen have come out of architectural programs.

"Far and away the most important skill to me is drawing," Isackes continues. "Drawing is a learned skill. It is not a skill that I can teach at the beginning of a graduate training program along with all the other things that need to be taught in terms of learning how to design for performance."

Isackes is particularly interested in students who have adequate experience in figure drawing because he believes that is where one really learns to draw. "A basic understanding of perspective, drafting, and two- and three-dimensional work is also essential," he says. "There are fundamental classes that are taught in most college art departments where they can get these skills. If they know how to draw, I can teach them how to make a model; I can't teach them if they don't have basic skills."

Drawing is also imperative from a lighting design point of view, especially examples of hand drafting, which should not be ignored just because computer drafting is available. "You can't be a lighting designer without the ability to hand-draft," says Bill Teague, a professor of theatre at the University of Alabama who teaches both lighting and technical theatre design. "It's a skill you just have to have. You can hire someone to do the computer renderings."

Scenic, costume, and lighting designers need to show an impressive command of the visual media, according to Dave Tosti-Lane, chair of the Performance Production Department at Cornish College in Seattle. "They should be able to draw—freehand, not just in Photoshop—draft, deal with color, and understand color both in light and pigment," he says. "Lighting designers should be able to represent their ideas graphically and be able to communicate a lighting idea to someone who does not speak the language of the designer, which is really the key for all designers: find a way to translate your ideas so that people who think differently than you can understand them."

A student's portfolio should not only present their capabilities but also the direction they hope to pursue. "I don't respond well to a student's portfolio that is so broad that they set themselves out as a jack of all trades, which is not realistic in terms of what the industry is," says Peter Beudert, a set designer and the head of design and technical production at the University of Arizona. "I encourage students to have as much specificity as possible in terms of where they think their strengths are or what they want to work on in grad school. That tends to be one thing that some students don't achieve too well."

The Right Stuff

It is also important to not only show your final work but how you got to that point. "Show process, show process, show process," is Tosti-Lane's mantra. "Don't just show pretty pictures, but try to show the progression from research through sketching, through rough model or fabric swatches, through final design and photographs of finished work," he says.

Beudert echoes this sentiment and adds that it's just like having to show your work in an algebra class. "The resulting beautiful image that demonstrates their work can be achieved in a lot of different ways. The artistic impulse that got them there is critical," he says. "You

should include casual sketches and a finished product, as well as notes taken during the process that reflect how you got where you're going, particularly as we see more and more digital portfolios. The steps you took which reflect your thinking as well as your way of working are as revealing as anything else."

Teague also likes to see how potential lighting design majors achieve their finished rig. "It doesn't matter to me if you tear up a Rosco swatch book and tape it so it becomes a backlit slide, but I do like to see the colors represented graphically," he says. "I also like to see cheat sheets and hookups. A lot of that gets lost today. I really like to see realized work, obviously. Good photographs of the finished product are pretty important."

Teague feels it is advisable to keep the narrative to a minimum. "I don't know that a long, windy statement of purpose is necessarily important, but a paragraph or two about their approach to the show would be okay," Teague says. "It's important to know what impact your colleagues' work had on your lighting. What other designers did and how you responded to them is not a bad thing to include, but not for every piece in the portfolio."

Beudert says that it helps him understand how the student's design process works if there is an accompanying statement of purpose with certain projects. "If they put into words what they thought about the design or work process, that indicates a process of synthesis that is important for someone going to graduate school," he explains. "Graduate school is, after all, an academic environment, and success in graduate school requires that kind of [writing] ability. If you choose to go to grad school, you can't forget about the academic aspect."

Buy the Book, CD, or Website

It probably goes without saying that the contents of your portfolio matter a lot more than the context, but your presentation should be somewhat aesthetically pleasing without being "slick." "It's nice to be neat and well organized," Isackes says. "Some of the most exciting students I've seen are not particularly neat or well organized, but I do look at neatness and tidiness because that's not an unimportant value."

Although Cornish does not offer an MFA, Tosti-Lane and his colleagues are heavily involved in coaching their students in proper portfolio preparation for graduate school. "We generally suggest that they arrange their portfolio with realized productions first and paper projects after, though exceptions are made when classroom work is particularly stunning," he says.

The first step that Tosti-Lane and his colleagues take in portfolio prep is having students buy the pages first rather than purchasing an expensive carrying case. The students use the pages to experiment with the best way to present their work. The next step is all about layout and deciding what goes first, second, etc., and labeling everything properly. Finally, during their last semester, students have their last public portfolio review where they present their portfolios to the entire department (faculty and students). "We also invite guests including production managers and artistic directors from local companies, other designers, and various other potential employers," Tosti-Lane says. "Students often wind up getting work from these presentations, and their portfolios are generally excellent."

Then there is the issue of whether you should have a portfolio at all, at least in traditional terms. Many students are putting their portfolios on CD, DVD, or websites. Teague is a big fan of multimedia portfolios, if, for nothing else, sheer convenience. "I think you'd be crazy not to use a website or a CD," he says. "I can see everything I need to see from a CD and it's just so convenient." He added that hand-drawn work can be easily scanned and computer work can just be saved.

Tosti-Lane is very comfortable reviewing work on a website or CD—he recently received a DVD from a BFA candidate—but he says that designers should not rely on just a multimedia portfolio. "If they have a really good presentation on CD or a website, then they can probably make the decision to go smaller with their paper portfolio, but there are still enough potential employers and grad school evaluators out there who are computer challenged," he explains. "If anything, I might lean toward either website or DVD at this point—DVDs are easy to make and more and more people have DVD players at home." He added that he would advise a student using a DVD portfolio that they might also do a simple QuickTime and Windows Media version and carry them on a CD, in case the reviewer doesn't have a computer with a DVD drive.

DVDs, CDs, and to some extent Web portfolios can work especially well for a sound designer because they have the capacity to introduce time-based events. "The danger is always that you'll wind up presenting to someone who just doesn't have the gear to play back your presentation," Tosti-Lane says. "I suppose the fallback is to always bring something that you can play it on—laptop, portable player, etc. But do not commit yourself solely to this technology; always have a real, honest to goodness, hold-it-in-your-hand-and-turn-the-pages portfolio."

A digital portfolio does, however, give a professor an instant insight into a student's ability, and Beudert likes being able to get that first impression of a student's work. "However, I always need to see the real thing at some point because I think there's an awful lot a digital portfolio can mask," he says. "It's easier to oversell your work in a digital portfolio. I would certainly take in a student after having only seen their work in a traditional portfolio, but I can't say the same is true with only a digital portfolio." He added that sound designers in particular can benefit from a mostly digital portfolio but that he needs to see how visual artists draw, paint, and draft, even if it is only in CAD.

"I think it is quite telling how students present their work," Beudert continues, "although some students may not be terribly well coached. However, when you speak with a student you try and establish a connection to their work. I prefer to encounter a student who has an artistic investment in their work but their skills may need improvement, and that's what graduate school can do. The reason you're going to school is that you want to learn more. If you were perfect, there'd be no need to go to grad school, and that's less of an interest to me."

Beudert added that he has seen portfolios that are, in a word, fantastic, and he encourages those students to skip graduate school altogether. "Quite frankly, what are they going to get out of three years in school when they probably need to spend that time working in theatre, whereas other students need that environment and could benefit from grad school [in order to improve their design skills]. What graduate school can't do is create a passion that isn't there."

Everybody Says Don't!

Even MFA design faculty have their pet peeves. Here are a few missteps to avoid when assembling your work for review:

- Leave out your professors' projects, no matter how much you helped.

- No basic scene-painting projects. Everyone has those.

- Leave out bad, sloppy, or illegible work or drawings (duh).

- Don't put in too many photos of the same type of show. Demonstrate variety.

- A neat portfolio will not disguise a lack of ability. But don't be haphazard or sloppy, either.

- No reviews, certificates, or letters of recommendation, but do keep these things handy (in a pocket or a folder).

- Only include projects you truly believe in.

- Make sure each project is clearly labeled.

- Do not include any bowls of candy or other snacks at a portfolio review; it won't make anyone like your work more.

No Techie Left Behind ...

Just because you are pursuing an MFA as a stage manager, technical director, or sound designer does not mean you should relegate your portfolio to a simple résumé and transcript. You should also be well versed in the various technical languages as well as have a commitment to collaboration. But just like everyone else, you need to show your work, processes, and finished product.

- *Sound designers.* Sound designers should be able to sketch out a visual representation of their speaker location in a set, so be sure to include speaker diagrams, equipment lists, checklists, cue lists, etc. Be able to communicate your ideas as an artist, not just your equipment choices and the physical layout of the system. "Your research probably needs to be even more thorough than the other designers', because many people will not be used to thinking of sound other than in terms of specific cues, volume, and so on," says Tosti-Lane. It is also recommended to include a CD of carefully prepared examples, along with a method for playback (laptop, CD player with headset, etc.).

- *Technical directors.* TDs need to show that they are more than the just person who builds the sets. Show that you are a master of many skills but especially adept with collaboration, organization, and graphic presentation. "A good TD can make everyone else's work so much easier, but a lackluster TD can make everyone's life difficult," Tosti-Lane says. Realized projects are really key for a TD's portfolio, as well as carefully documented examples of how the process was moved forward by your proactive efforts.

- *Stage managers.* Demonstrate your organizational drive; communicate just how comfortable the director, design team, and actors will be under your hand. You should show an understanding of all the various skills, but you need not show proficiency in each one. However, you should include your drawings and your work in at least one design area. Also, be sure to have at least one complete prompt book and examples of the forms you used to give an idea of your methodology. "They need to convince the reviewer that they can communicate with everyone on the team and that they know how to deal with the difficult people as well as the pussycats," Tosti-Lane says.

The Basics

In the professional field, a winning portfolio would contain a combination of traditional visual representation as well as contemporary technology. The goal is to demonstrate the individual's capability to communicate ideas visually. Some projects can be presented in traditional ways through renderings, perspectives, and production photos; other projects may need to be contextualized with period research, process photos, and digital multimedia.

A professional interviewing for a job should assume that directors and producers will look for the talents and expertise that best match a designer/technician to a specific project. They may be interested in the individual's capability to abstract from descriptive pieces in a script and use metaphors for a conceptual piece, or they may be looking for someone who is excellent at research and style sheets for a historical piece. It is important that the designer's work can show variety of skill and process.

Design-tech portfolios need to show a good understanding of perspective, drafting, and two- and three-dimensional work in addition to having clear and impressive layouts. Each discipline may rely on specific formats due to the nature of the work; but some projects may require nontraditional approaches. For example, a lighting project for a dance-theatre piece may need color renderings to clearly show the director the lighting design style for the piece. Another instance would be a costume design for a special-effects creature; this may require drafting or sections to explain how the actor wears and handles the mechanics of the garment.

Show Case
The Specifics: Scenic, Costumes, Makeup, Lighting, Sound, and Allied Fields

Scenic Design

Projects in a scenic design portfolio can include concept and inspirational art sources, research and style sheets, specialty materials sources, drafting such as ground plans and sections (traditional and digital), innovative ideas and solutions, perspectives and elevations (traditional and digital), swatches and material samples, photos of model and process, and photos of final set and performance for fully realized projects.

Brian Prather is a MFA graduate of Brandeis University. His scenic work includes the premiere production of *Fuente* for Barrington Stage Co., the premiere of *My Heart and My Flesh* for Coyote Theatre at Boston Playwright's Theatre, *First Love* for StageWorks Hudson, and *Thief River* for Barrington Stage Co. I enjoyed working with him and had an opportunity to observe his work (firsthand) for the production of the musical *Working* for Emerson Stage at the Cutler Majestic Theatre (see Figures 4.1a and 4.1b). His portfolio pages for this project help illustrate some of the comments discussed in Mark Newman's article.

Costumes

Projects in a costume design portfolio can include concept, research and cut sheets; preliminary sketches (if process is key to the project), color palette, and finished sketches; and construction notes, garment detail drafting, and fabric/trims swatches. If a project has crafts, then fabric paint and distress samples would be needed. Amanda Monteiro, one of my former students at Emerson College, did successful layouts for nonproduced (class) projects, paying close attention to the materials in display. For the opera *Rigoletto* (see Figures 4.2a and 4.2b), she included her research plates and watercolors.

The costume design portfolio would also include photos of finished garment and performance for realized projects. My friend and colleague Donna Meester says: "For large shows, particularly those with identifiable groups, one way to organize the presentation is by groupings of such groups (see Figure 4.2c). These pages,

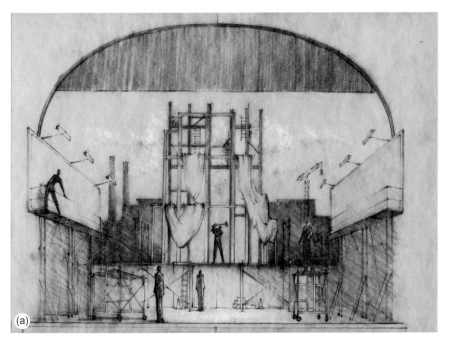

FIGURE 4.1A
Brian Prather's sketch detail. Notice the excellent quality of his hand drawing. This skill will set him apart in an interview.

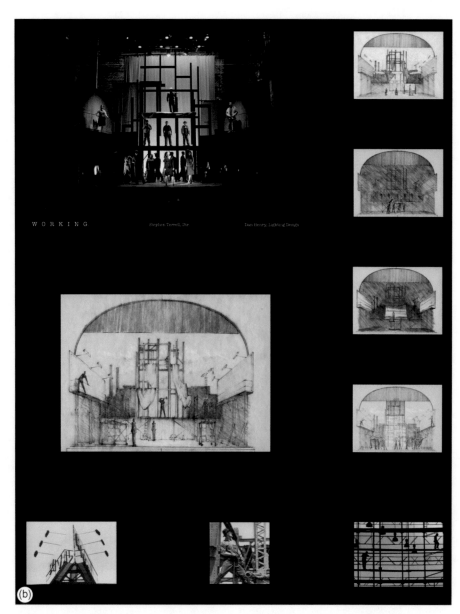

FIGURE 4.1B

Brian Prather's scenic portfolio page. It includes, from top to bottom: A photo of the realized production of *Working the Musical,* produced by Emerson Stage in April 2004 at the Majestic Theatre in Boston, various sketches/perspectives of different scenes, and some research photographs used for inspiration.

FIGURE 4.2A
Costume designer Amanda Monteiro's concept and research plates for the opera *Rigoletto*.

FIGURE 4.2B
Amanda Monteiro's watercolor sketch of *Rigoletto*, the title character in the opera.

when found in a portfolio, can be presented with the research and photo pages with the painted sketches next to the group they belong with [see Figure 4.2d]. Another presentation would be to have all of the research/photo pages together followed with the complete set of sketches. Don't feel compelled to include one sketch per page. If more than one fits, use the space!"

Makeup and Hair

KJ Kim is a student at the University of Evansville. I met her while adjudicating projects for the KCACTF III Festival XLIII, on January 4–8, 2011, at Michigan State University in Lansing. I was very impressed by sketches she presented. Her work has also been exhibited at the USITT 2011 Young Designer and Technicians exhibit and the USITT Costume Commission Student Leadership

Initiatives. KJ uses digital software to create face canvases and makeup schematics. She includes clear instructions, or what I call the *makeup recipe*. She also sometimes paints the schematics with actual makeup (see Figures 4.2e through 4.2h).

Lighting

Bill Teague, a professor of theatre at the University of Alabama who teaches both lighting and technical theatre design, states in Newman's article: "Drawing is also imperative from a lighting design point of view, especially examples of hand drafting, which should not be ignored just because computer drafting is available. You can't be a lighting designer without the ability to hand-draft," he says. "It's a skill you just have to have. You can hire someone to do the computer renderings."

FIGURE 4.2C
Donna Meester's portfolio page for *Twelfth Night,* produced at the University of Louisiana, Monroe. Page layout includes a group sketch with notes and fabric swatches.

FIGURE 4.2D
Meester's portfolio page for *Twelfth Night.* Page layout includes, sketches, research, and production photos.

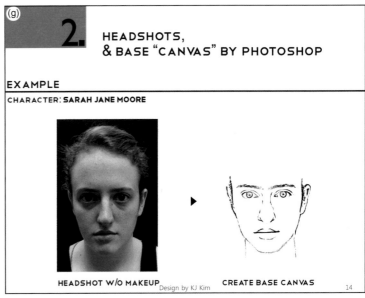

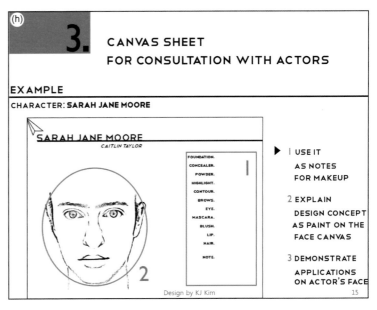

FIGURES 4.2E, 4.2F, 4.2G, AND 4.2H

For her portfolio, KJ Kim uses PowerPoint to create slides that feature a step-by-step process of makeup design and application. These slides are then printed on quality paper and placed in a portfolio case (see Figures 4.2i through 4.2k).

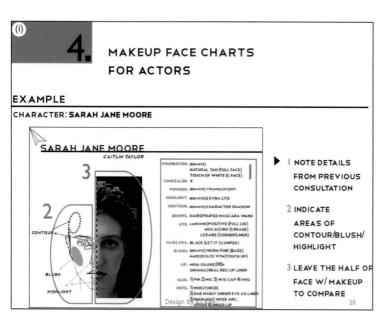

4. MAKEUP FACE CHARTS FOR ACTORS

EXAMPLE

CHARACTER: **SARAH JANE MOORE**

▶ 1 NOTE DETAILS FROM PREVIOUS CONSULTATION

2 INDICATE AREAS OF CONTOUR/BLUSH/ HIGHLIGHT

3 LEAVE THE HALF OF FACE W/ MAKEUP TO COMPARE

5. HAIRCUTS, WIG /MUSTACHE/SCAR TRYOUTS

EXAMPLE

CHARACTER: **SARAH JANE MOORE**

WIG TRY OUT

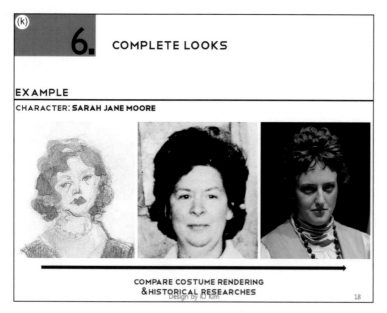

6. COMPLETE LOOKS

EXAMPLE

CHARACTER: **SARAH JANE MOORE**

COMPARE COSTUME RENDERING & HISTORICAL RESEARCHES

FIGURES 4.2I, 4.2J, AND 4.2K

KJ Kim prints PowerPoint slides and puts them in her portfolio case. For *Assassins*, she persuaded the director of the project to use her makeup and hair design skills to assist the actors with their character transformations. She says: "The actors were grateful to have the makeup schematics to look at as part of their preparations every night before the performances."

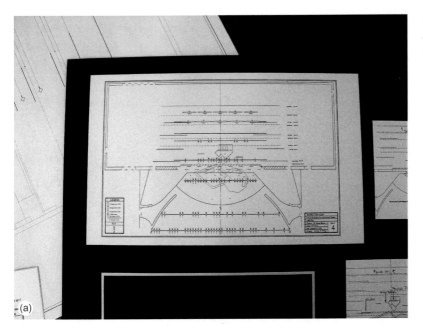

Projects in a lighting design portfolio can include light plots and sections, cue sheets, samples of special effects, technical paperwork (as needed), and photos of final design and performance for fully realized projects. Depending on the project, they could also include inspirational research photos, drawings, or watercolor washes on a set elevation as well as color gel swatches. Anthony Phelps (featured in Chapter 1) has worked as associate technical director at Harvard University. His portfolio pages illustrate some of these points (see Figures 4.3a through 4.3c).

Sound

Projects in a sound design portfolio can include design concept narrative (as needed), sources research, cue sheets, microphone pack plots, and CD samples. Sometimes it is helpful to show photos of key moments from a fully realized production, with sound cues added to them. Freelance sound designer Andy Lewis says: "A good example of a divider page for a show should

include a number of production shots—a good way to add visuals to a portfolio for a nonvisual design medium [see Figure 4.4a], a couple of "eye candy" shots of the FOH [front of house] sound system, a brief description of the show and what its design entailed, and a listing of what documentation from the show is included in its section of the portfolio."

Andy Lewis also says that a project should include "a sample page from the bid specifications that were sent out to potential bidders for the show's rental package [see Figure 4.4b]—useful for producers to view your ability to communicate the gear you need in a clear fashion, regardless of whether they're interviewing you for a show that will be bid or just one that will be stocked from an in-house shop."

Lewis also includes block diagrams of the sound system for each show (see Figure 4.4c): "One of two, in this case (although many shows will have lots more); this is the most visual that a sound design portfolio often gets. It has the benefits of both being very obvious in what it is,

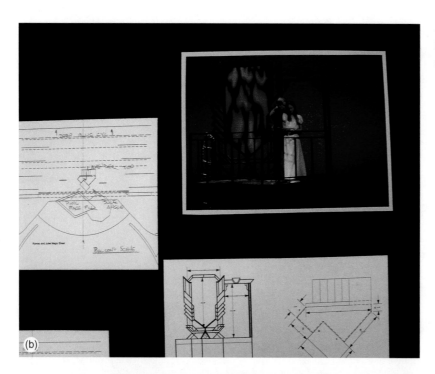

FIGURE 4.3B

Phelps's photo sample: Detail shot of the set and lights for *Romeo and Juliet* showing the detail of the balcony.

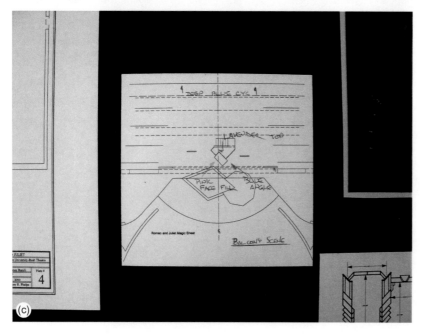

FIGURE 4.3C

Phelps's magic sheet sample: The photo shows a small lighting magic sheet on a portfolio plate for *Romeo and Juliet.*

FIGURE 4.4A

Sound designer Andy Lewis's example of a divider page for one of the shows featured in the portfolio.

FIGURE 4.4B

Sound designer Andy Lewis's sample page from bid specifications that were sent out to potential bidders for a project.

FIGURE 4.4C

Sound designer Andy Lewis's sample of a block diagram of the sound system for a show.

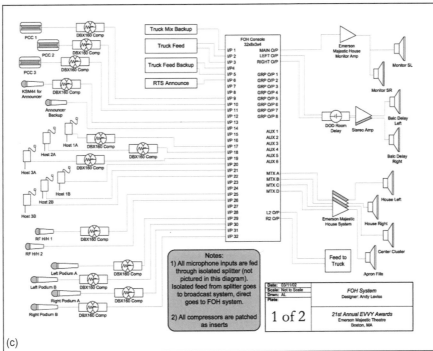

FIGURE 4.4D

Sound designer Andy Lewis patch sheets used to actually set up and cable the show when loading it in the theatre.

					06/06/2005 12:43 AM
	FOH Patch for 22nd Annual EVVY Awards				
	Andy Leviss, Sound Designer/FOH Engineer				
	Input Patch				
Ch	Description	Snake Ch.	Splitter Ch.	Notes	
1	Kick	C1	-		
2	Snare	C2	-		
3	Overhead Left	C3	-		
4	Overhead Right	C4	-		
5	Bass	C5	-		
6	Rhythm Guitar	C6	-		
7	Lead Guitar	C7	-		
8	Harmonica	C8	-		
9	Keys	C9	-		
10	Vox 1	Y-E6	22	Y'd from H/H A (18)	
11	Vox 2	Y-E7	23	Y'd from H/H B (19)	
12	Vox 3 (Drummer)	C10	-		
13	Ben/Shira Backup	E1	41		
14	Vanessa/Dave Backup	E2	42		
15	Seth/Chachi Backup	E3	43		
16	Evie Backup	E4	44		
17	Sarah Backup	E5	45		
18	Handheld A (Red)	Y-E6	22	Y'd to 10	
19	Handheld B (Yellow)	Y-E7	23	Y'd to 11	
20	Ben/Shira	E8	24		
21	Vanessa/Dave	E9	25		
22	Seth/Chachi	E10	26		
23	Evie	E11	27		
24	Sarah	E12	28		
St1	FX A Return				
St2	FX B Return				
25	Piano Bass	E13	15		
26	Piano Treble	E14	16		
27	Podium Automixer				
28	PCC 1	E15	6		
29	PCC 2	E16	7		
30	PCC 3	E17	8		
31	PCC 4	E18	9		
32	PCC 5	E19	10		
33					
34	Announcer	E20	17		
35	Announcer Backup	E21	18		
36	Playback Feed	E22	50		
37	Podium Left - Tall	E23	30	Direct Out to Automixer	
38	Podium Left - Short	E24	29	Direct Out to Automixer	
39	Podium Right - Tall	E25	32	Direct Out to Automixer	
40	Podium Right - Short	E26	31	Direct Out to Automixer	

(d)

work so much easier. On the other hand, a lackluster technician can add challenges to the process and make everyone's life difficult. Realized projects with technical drawings are a must in a technician's portfolio. They should also include carefully documented examples of how the process was moved forward by proactive efforts.

Technical portfolios should include project management-related paperwork such as work orders, budget specs, yardage specs, supply inventories, plots, cue sheets, labor specs, and lists of vendors. They would also include technical drawings (traditional and digital) such as pattern drafting, sections, and elevations. The technicians would execute these drawings to show their skill level and their ability to solve particular design challenges on paper. It is also important to have reductions of the original design drawings or research next to photos of the final product. This comparison helps demonstrate the technician's ability to translate original designs from paper to the stage.

even to a nontechnical producer, as well as generally just looking impressive."

"These are part of the patch sheets [see Fig. 4.4d] used to actually set up and cable the show when loading it in the theatre," Lewis says "They actually contain much the same information as the block diagram, but in a format that's easier to reference for the purposes of setting up the console and running cables; the idea here is to show that in addition to actually designing the system, you can translate the information into a way that's easy for the crew working for you to set it up quickly and without confusion."

Specialized Technicians, Crafts, and Allied Fields

Technicians, crafts, and allied field professionals need to show that they are more than "just" the person who builds or rigs the final product. In the professional world, a good technician can facilitate matters and make everyone else's

Show Case
Costume Technician

A costume technician's work involves the performance of a variety of duties in making and altering costumes and accessories as well as operating, maintaining, and repairing related equipment. This job also includes determining the materials and supplies to be purchased and supervising and coordinating the work of others.

Costume technician Nicole Wilson is a fantastic costume draper. I have seen her mock up dresses for period shows, modern dress, fantasy projects, and musicals. She is a consummate perfectionist and avid researcher; she is also pragmatic and time conscious. Originally from the West Coast, she now resides in Massachusetts. For her portfolio Nicole chose a PowerPoint layout that she in turn printed in 11 × 17-inch landscape format (see Figures 4.5a through 4.5d).

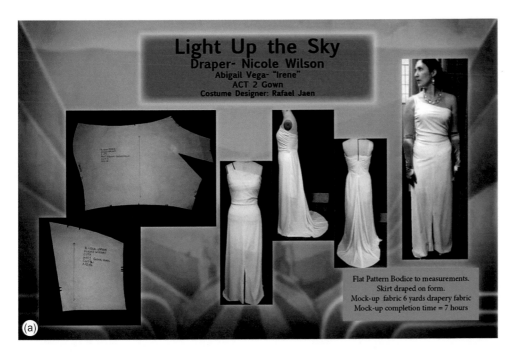

Light Up the Sky
Draper- Nicole Wilson
Abigail Vega- "Irene"
ACT 2 Gown
Costume Designer: Rafael Jaen

Flat Pattern Bodice to measurements.
Skirt draped on form.
Mock-up fabric 6 yards drapery fabric
Mock-up completion time = 7 hours

(a)

Final fabrics and yardages:
Bodice & understructure- 1 yard metallic fashion fabric
Skirt- 4 yards silk taffeta
Hip drape- 1 yard metallic fashion fabric
Trim- 5 yards sequins
Final completion time = 16 hours

(b)

FIGURES 4.5A AND 4.5B

Costume designer Nicole Wilson makes sure that each project's portfolio pages include process detail images and the finished product. She also adds notations on fabric yardage plus findings and time specs as part of her displays.

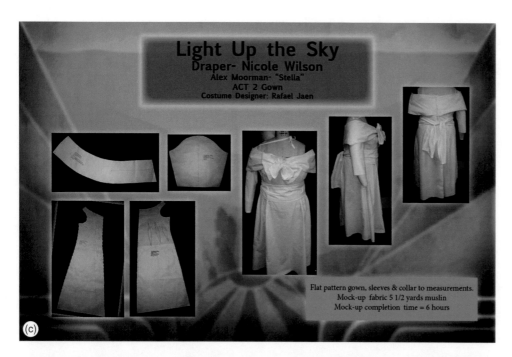

Light Up the Sky
Draper- Nicole Wilson
Alex Moorman- "Stella"
ACT 2 Gown
Costume Designer: Rafael Jaen

Flat pattern gown, sleeves & collar to measurements.
Mock-up fabric 5 1/2 yards muslin
Mock-up completion time = 6 hours

(c)

FIGURES 4.5C AND 4.5D
For Wilson, the 11 × 17-inch (ledger size) sheets are ideal because they can hold plenty of sequential horizontal information and they can fit into an easy-to-handle presentation case.

Gown with off the shoulders collar, sheer sleeves and darted waist

Stella X2

Final fabrics and yardages:
Gown- 5 1/2 yards satin
Collar, sleeves, belt & bow- 4 yards embroidered organza
Self-lined with spiral boning for structure.
Horsehair hem
Final completion time= 18 hours

(d)

Technical Director

Anthony Phelps was the associate technical director at Harvard University. He was also the founder and executive editor of the renowned magazine *The Painter's Journal*. Phelps's portfolio has a variety of technical drawings, sketches, and production photos that illustrate his talent and capabilities in each show that he has worked on (Figures 4.6a through 4.6c).

For a graduating student pursuing new jobs or entry into a grad school, the portfolio has to show skill, technology knowledge, and superb organization. Andrew Kirsch was one of the students I had the opportunity to coach. His is a very good sample of a well-balanced technical director portfolio; it shows that as a technician he is able to solve problems and make fantastic things happen. (See Figures 4.7a through 4.7g.)

By the Book, CD, or Website: The 21st Century Multimedia Portfolio

A multimedia portfolio can include both a traditional and an electronic portfolio. Today's digital software allows designers and technicians to produce portfolios that can be printed as traditional books, saved to a DVD, or uploaded to the Web. For example, PowerPoint slides can be printed from a CD; screen grabs from a website can also be printed. I am a big fan of multimedia portfolios as long as the formatting is neat and they include strong content, clear process, and good production images.

FIGURES 4.6A, 4.6B, AND 4.6C

Technical director Anthony Phelps uses black mat boards for his display instead of portfolio sheet holders. The paperwork includes drafting, technical drawings, spec sheets, and shopping lists. Each storyboard includes research, sketches, and production photos. He also includes scenic art in his technical portfolio.

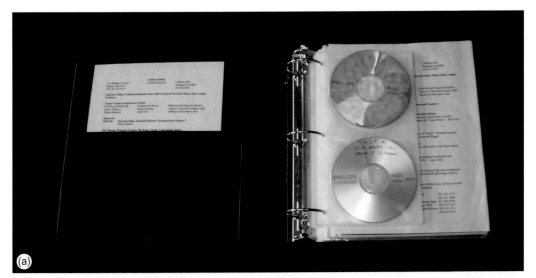

FIGURE 4.7A

Technical director Andrew Kirsch's portfolio opening page. Notice how he includes digital information and a résumé at the start.

(a)

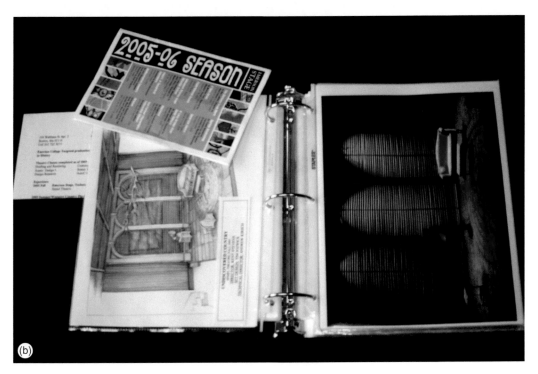

FIGURE 4.7B

Andrew Kirsch's first project is one of his strongest; he starts with a bang! These pages feature sketches, drafting, CAD drawings, shopping lists, technical detail, process, and final pictures for the production of *Undiscovered Country*, produced by Emerson Stage in 2005. Director: Kent Stevens; sets: Timothy Jozwick; costumes: Angela Markman; and lights: Kristin Hayes.

(b)

FIGURES 4.7C, 4.7D, AND 4.7E

Notice the use of fold-out pages and inclusion of technical solutions. Andrew was in charge of solving and rigging three large blinds that covered three large arches during different scenes.

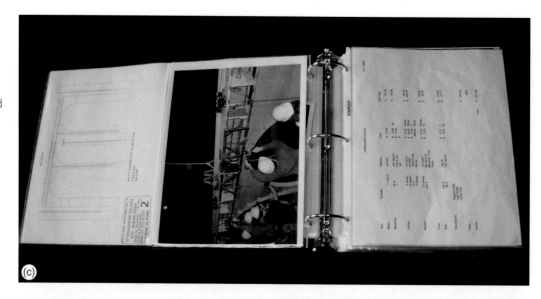

(c)

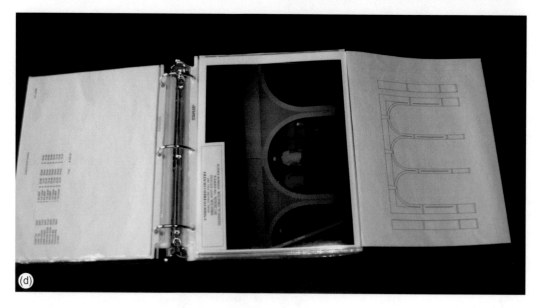

(d)

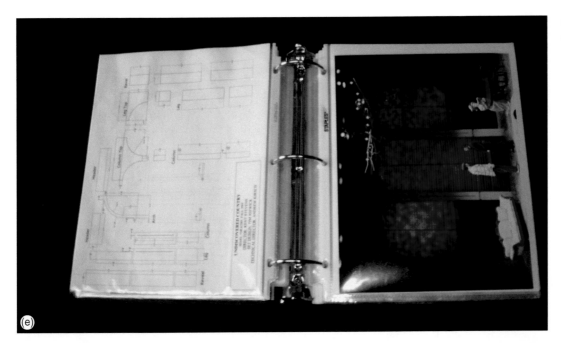

FIGURES 4.7C, 4.7D, AND 4.7E

(Continued)

(e)

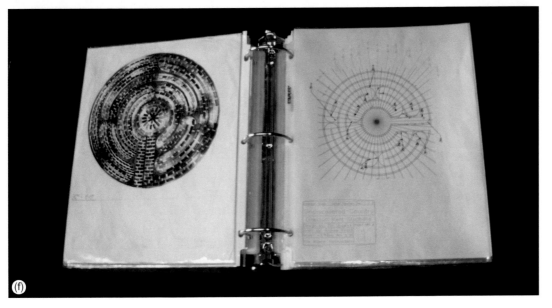

FIGURES 4.7F AND 4.7G

Andrew Kirsch also had the challenge of figuring out the scale labyrinth path of the floor plan design. These pages show how the original set design translated to a CAD plan as well as showing the floor in process and the finished product.

(f)

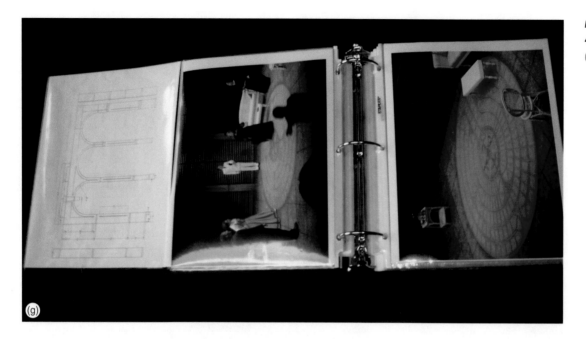

(g)

Show Case
Properties

Joanna (Joa) Stenning currently lives and works as a freelance properties designer in Boston, though she considers Western Massachusetts her home. She has been working for ArtsEmerson in Boston and is in the process of applying to graduate programs.

Stenning says, "The hardest part of the process is choosing the content of each project and the order in which you choose to display that content."

Stenning took her traditional portfolio and made it digital right away upon graduation. She says: "I think it's incredibly important in this day and age to have an online portfolio. Once a job interview is over, a potential employer has the ability to look back at the work you've displayed as many times as he or she likes. It's also extremely beneficial when applying for jobs that are out of state or at least out of traveling range. Employers

who are browsing the Web can easily access your work and can also gauge your level of professionalism and how you present yourself. I've had numerous employers contact me because they saw the link to my portfolio in my LinkedIn profile and were impressed with what they saw. It's a whole new level of marketing and saves time for both employers and potential employees." (See Figures 4.8a through 4.8d.)

Production Design

For folks working in film and television, the rules may be a bit different. To shed some light on this subject, I turned to my colleague and friend, production designer Amy Whitten. Whitten and I collaborated on the PBS/WGBH *American Experience* series *God in America* in October 2010.

Whitten says: "I have been in the film and video business since 1992. I began my career thinking that I would ultimately become a producer. In 1997 I had an on-set epiphany and knew that my heart belonged to the

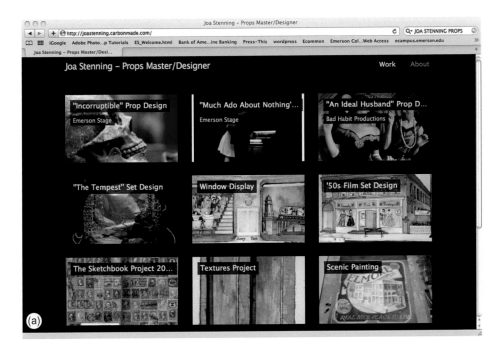

Joa Stenning has this to say about her online portfolio: "The Carbonmade .com portfolio builder is a really simple, inexpensive, and user-friendly option for busy students like myself. The hardest part of the process is choosing the content of each project and the order in which you choose to display that content. Otherwise, this site takes you through every step necessary to complete your portfolio. I appreciate that the site gives you an option to advertise whether or not you're available for freelance work, as well as an 'About Me' section so that viewers are given a personality to match with the work they see." Stenning includes process images for most projects in order to feature her skill set.

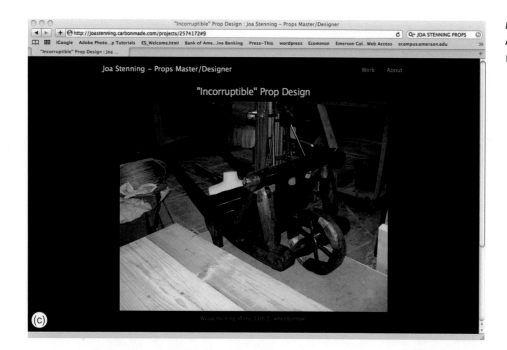

Art Department. After a time, I accumulated enough videotapes and photographs of my work to make myself a portfolio. Working in such a highly visual medium, it was necessary to have something to show potential clients what I could do, especially as a novice stylist." (See Figures 4.9a and 4.9b.)

Whitten continues: "While I knew a portfolio was an essential element of marketing and promoting oneself, I discovered there were challenges in keeping an up-to-date hard copy version most people were accustomed to using at the time. For one, it was expensive: Paying someone to edit a reel together; the cost of stock; the cost of printing images; mailing it out, including return postage to get it back; having multiple copies on hand; changing all those copies when it was time to include new work. Orchestrating these different components was time consuming as well as space consuming. Yards of shelf space were dedicated to VHS tapes, padded envelopes, and binders.

"In 2005 a friend offered to make me a website, and I jumped at the chance to go digital. It made so much sense! I could clear up valuable real estate in my office. My website would be available 24 hours a day. It was free to send someone the link anywhere in the world. I could have photos and videos in one place. With the click of a mouse, clients could look at different aspects of my creative skills. I could easily show, not just tell."

She continues: "S. G. Collins, filmmaker and the designer of my website, and I both believe that the style of one's website is an extension of oneself and one's personality. At one point he said he wished he had things that I touched for work. I responded by scanning different tools and items I used in my job, including a used paintbrush, a hammer, some buttons, and a tiny pair of my grandmother's scissors. The background textures came from some of my photographs and notes I made to speak from at a production design class. I am able to keep my résumé as a PDF on my site, as well as my contact information." (See Figures 4.9c and 4.9d.)

Portfolio Photos

I recently caught up with Kirk J. Miller, a recent college graduate. He is a lighting designer, director, and programmer working in theatre, dance, live events, television, and film. Based in New England, he is also a freelance theatre and event photographer. Born in Connecticut, he now splits his time between Boston and Los Angeles. Those of us who have been lucky to work with Kirk have in their possession some really good production photos. Since good photographs are an indispensable part of every design-tech portfolio, I asked Miller if he could share some words of wisdom about photographing one's work. He provided some samples from different productions, including dance, comedy, and drama. He says that what makes a good portfolio photo is equal parts "framing, subject matter, exposure, and good luck!"

FIGURES 4.9A AND 4.9B

Amy Whitten's portfolio opening page and page with menu.
The textures and vivid colors speak to Whitten's field, as do her
strong sense of style and *joie de vivre*. I love that these pages
could be printed to make a hard-copy portfolio.

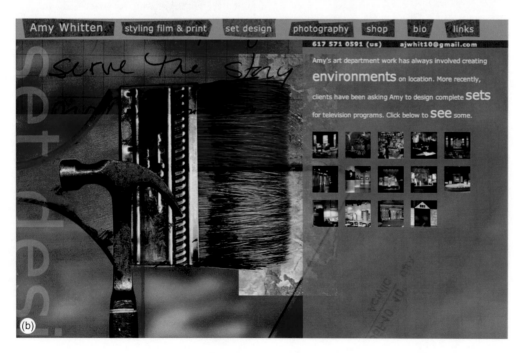

FIGURES 4.9C AND 4.9D

Amy Whitten's final words of wisdom: "If you are building your own site from scratch, there are a few things I would recommend: Be aware of how large your files are, especially the videos; it shouldn't take forever for your page to load. Also check out how your site looks on different browsers and different computers. While things have become more standardized over the years, not every browser supports the same files, and not every user has the same programs. Finally, I strongly advise against using music on your site, unless it is relevant to what you do, i.e., you're a musician or vocalist. It may be just my pet peeve, but I find it distracting from the overall experience of someone's site if I'm searching for the mute button!"

The Best of Masterpiece Theatre, with Derek Jacobi. WGBH television special. Directed by Bob Comiskey.

Holmes. Stills styling for package designs.

What Makes a Good Portfolio Photo: Framing, Subject Matter, Exposure, and Luck!

An Interview with Kirk J. Miller

Rafael Jaen: Did you always have an interest in photography?

Kirk J. Miller: I wouldn't say that I've always been interested in photography. I have, however, always had an interest in visual imagery; that's what inspired me to pursue a career in the field of lighting design. My interest in photography came about when I realized I needed to start capturing my own work as a designer.

RJ: What got you started taking production photos?

KM: Knowing I'd need to capture my work for a personal portfolio, I purchased a camera, thinking I'd just have one around for when I designed a show. A friend saw me with a camera, assumed I was a photographer, and asked if I could take photos of their upcoming show. I agreed, not fully knowing what I was doing or how the photos would come out. The photos came out well, my friend was happy, and I ended up falling in love with production photography.

RJ: What makes a great production photo?

KM: There are many things that make a good photo: framing, subject matter, exposure, and luck are a few. While photographs are just the blink of an eye, you can read so much from just a single frame. A great production photo is one that says something. It captures emotion, intent, character, and story—all in a well-framed image. [See Figures 4.10a and 4.10b.]

RJ: What kind of camera do you prefer and why?

KM: I personally shoot with a Canon 7D. However, when it comes to Canon vs. Nikon vs. another brand, it's all about personal preference. Shooting with a digital single-lens reflex (DSLR) is what makes the difference when it comes to production photos. A DSLR allows the photographer to adjust all settings of a camera. The ability to calibrate aperture, shutter speed, and focus quickly is invaluable when you're trying to capture the perfect shot in only seconds.

RJ: What is your biggest challenge when taking photos?

KM: In the theatre, the photographer's biggest challenge is uncertainty. The lighting is changing, characters are moving, and action can escalate and resolve in only seconds. It's exhilarating because it's live and you've got to capture the moment, but success is in the preparation. With a DSLR, there are always many lens options, some more expensive than others. Having a zoom lens with a low f-stop is one step toward good production photos. Many times when shooting in low light, the photographer battles between the image being too dark or the image being brighter, yet blurry. A lens with a lower f-stop (for example, f2.8) allows more light into the camera. More light allows the photographer to shoot with a faster shutter speed. This combination ensures that the image will be of proper exposure without sacrificing the crispness of a good photo. [See Figures 4.10c and 4.10d.]

RJ: What do you look for when you're taking photos?

KM: As a designer, I'm aware that the characters seen on the stage are but a fraction of the personnel it took to make the production happen. While it's my job to capture the characters, their actions, and their emotions, I keep an eye on design. I look for a photo that displays scenic elements, props, costuming, and the character, all under beautiful light. While every element cannot

FIGURE 4.10A
A well-framed image can capture a moment's emotion.

FIGURE 4.10B
A well-framed image can help tell a story.

FIGURE 4.10C

Proper exposure will help keep the image crispness and produce a good photo.

FIGURE 4.10D

Kurt Miller says: "More light allows the photographer to shoot with a faster shutter speed. This combination ensures that the image will be of proper exposure without sacrificing quality."

FIGURE 4.10E
Rehearsal photo featuring light angles and hue.

be present in all of the photos, I make an enormous effort to ensure that everyone will have a piece for their portfolio when the dress rehearsal has finished. [See Figures 4.10e and 4.10f.]

RJ: In general, what type of photo do you think works best for a portfolio?

KM: The best photo is one that displays your work best. As a theatrical designer, you're a collaborator on a project where there are many pieces of the puzzle. Many times it's the process and communication that yield the greatest results. A photo that represents a designer's work in collaboration with the other aspects of the show is priceless. You want to ensure that you have photos that represent your work alone as well as ones

FIGURE 4.10F
Rehearsal photo featuring light angles, costume, and hair and makeup details.

showcasing the project as a whole. It's great to have photos that show process as well. A photo that can be compared to your concept and research to show the translation from paper to stage is one you don't want to be without.

Now that we have reviewed some specifics about what to include in a portfolio concentration, what are some of the things to avoid? What new technologies do we need to be aware of?

WORKBOOK

What is my portfolio concentration? What work do I need to include in my portfolio? What works do I need to collect in order to plan my layouts?

HAVE STORIES THAT TELL SOMETHING ABOUT YOU AND YOUR APPROACH TO
DESIGN AND COLLABORATION...FOR EACH IMAGE YOU SHOW.

JOHN PAUL DEVLIN

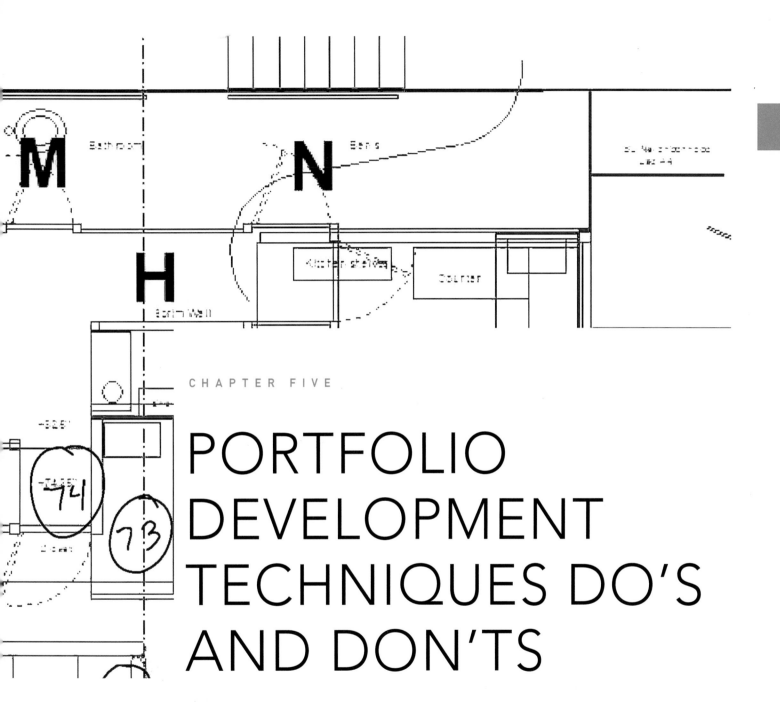

CHAPTER FIVE

PORTFOLIO DEVELOPMENT TECHNIQUES DO'S AND DON'TS

Experienced professionals and seasoned academicians agree that there are common guidelines to consider in developing a portfolio. Although there are no hard-set rules, some standards do apply. This chapter looks at some commonly accepted practices and some practices to avoid. I'll call these the do's and the don'ts of portfolio development.

Portfolio Development Do's

The process of developing a design-tech portfolio is not different from the process that takes an idea from the drawing table to the final product on a stage. Successful portfolio development takes clear vision, commitment, and hard work.

Most reviewers will say that a portfolio must be put together in such a way that it answers questions specific to its goals. A portfolio prepared for graduate school will meet different expectations from one used to apply for jobs as designer or technician in regional theatre. Donna Meester, assistant professor in the Department of Theatre and Dance at the University of Alabama, has reviewed many portfolios while serving as the design chair for the Kennedy Center American College Theater Festival (Region VI, and design vice chair for Region IV). She recommends making the individual's goals the focus of the portfolio. "You may be a fantastic technician," she says, "[but] if you are looking for more design opportunities, focus on the design work that you have done. You can include your technical experience later. Whatever you focus on [in your portfolio] is what the interviewer will see as what you are most interested in." There are some pointers for students as well when they do not have produced shows to present. In such cases, Meester recommends: "Begin the portfolio with the strongest class projects ... [and] don't forget art classes. Photography classes produce work that shows a good eye as well. If the portfolio is full with produced work and design-tech class projects, don't be afraid

to have art projects at the end of the portfolio or in a separate binder."

The project sequences, support materials, and general organization of the book are important, too. They will assist in conveying the individual's capabilities. "Do start with your strongest produced work. Do only show work that you feel confident about," says Kitty Leech, who is on the faculty at New York University's Tisch School of the Arts Drama Department. Leech has reviewed hundreds of portfolios while chairing the Costume Design Exam Committee for the United Scenic Artists Local 829 (a committee she has served on since 1987) and chairing the Young Master Award committee for the Theatre Development Fund's Irene Sharaff Awards. She states that it is important to "be able to talk about the work from a number of different points of view: concepts, process, budget .... Do try to include a piece of promotional material (a program or flyer, not reviews) as well as a minimum of one or two sketches and production photographs for each production being shown. Do show class projects, but at the end, not at the beginning of your presentation." Donna Meester adds, "Organization, organization, organization! 'Nuff said. Detail, detail, detail! More to say here! Good design relies on attention to detail. A portfolio is no different. Starting with the sketch, lettering should be neat, edges should not be ragged, pastels need to be fixed, etc. Sketches, swatches, research should be affixed to the page neatly when put in the portfolio. While many like to present their portfolio in chronological order, the reverse may be more effective. There is no rule saying that a portfolio needs to be in any type of chronological order. I like to see the strongest (and produced) work first and then move on to weaker projects. It is nice to end with a bang!"

Final touches are important, so featured artwork needs to be clearly labeled, fixed, and organized. "Employers will equate your attention to detail in all of your work with the level of detail you put into your portfolio, so pay attention to detail. That means use a ruler, don't eyeball. Layout and design of the portfolio pages is as important as the work on the page. Keep the principles of design in mind when planning your page layout and your rendering plates. It is another opportunity to exhibit good design choices." This advice comes from Kristina Tollefson, who served as the vice commissioner for communication for the Costume Design & Technology Commission of USITT. Pattern layouts, traditional drafting, blueprints, and CAD drawings need to be a readable size. Photographs need have good resolution and be true to stage color; it is also important to include photos that contain detail. Research and reference materials should include their sources and titles. News and media article should include dates and title pages. The goal is to give the reviewers enough contexts so they can, at a glance, understand the scale and venue of the work that you are presenting.

Good Practices Checklist
by John Paul Devlin

John Paul Devlin earned an MFA in drama and an MA in history from Syracuse University as well as a BA in history and communication arts/theatre from Allegheny College. He is an assistant professor of fine arts at Saint Michael's College in Vermont, where he specializes in scenic and lighting design and serves as technical director during the academic year and resident designer and production manager for the Saint Michael's Playhouse during the summer. John has 70 professional scenic, light, and properties design credits among his 170 designs. He served as chair for design, technology, and management for the KCACTF Region One and is a member of the National and New England section of USITT, active in the Education Commission. He shares some good practices about portfolio presentation:

Have stories that tell something about you and your approach to design and collaboration prepared for each image you show. These stories should reflect positive experiences and demonstrate your skills—and a little humor is often appreciated. Often interviewers will ask questions about what they are looking at; be prepared to answer a range of questions that may allow you to "strut your stuff" a little more. It is useful to have a short list of character traits you want to emphasize and tie some examples from your portfolio into those specific traits.

Spend time being fussy with your images. Neatness and consistency do count here, and sloppy labels or presentations that fall apart are embarrassing for you in the moment and indicative of shoddy work. Make sure your labels are professional in appearance and appropriately mounted. Check spelling on all written work! Don't misspell anything. Your work tells a story too and can reflect well on you or poorly (regardless of the aesthetic values of the finished product).

Select images that demonstrate the process, not just the final projects. Most employers or schools are interested in seeing how you work through a project (as well as the final results). So, having beginning sketches and finished drawings as well as images of the project on stage help (see Figures 5.1a through 5.1c). In many cases, you will have class projects that were not realized; you are not alone! Save those projects and use them to demonstrate your skills.

Be very selective. It's far better to have two or three very good projects in the portfolio than to have many more mediocre ones. People will remember both the great work and the really not-great work, so work to eliminate the latter. Weed out your portfolio from time to time; keep new works readily available and remove old pieces to your own archive (don't discard them, since you may find a good chance to use them in the future).

Show a variety of work. Take and keep pictures of all that you do. Do your homework on the company, department, individual, or job you are applying for, and assemble

FIGURE 5.1A

John Paul Devlin says: "Select images that demonstrate the process, not just the final projects." For the show *The Spitfire Grill*, Saint Michael's Playhouse, 2004, Devlin designed sets and lights. In regard to this model, Devlin says: "The show *Spitfire Grill* began with one set of ideas and morphed into a very different look. If you look at the image of the model, you will see a framed structure that housed the grill itself. There are also cut drops surrounding the stage."

FIGURE 5.1B

Devlin says: "The director and producing artistic director arrived at a different starting point after a long discussion, and the resulting design is much stronger. The framed house was replaced with a space delineated by light and the cut drops were replaced with real tree branches."

FIGURE 5.1C

Devlin says: "Two crushed dichroic filters (thin film color filter) gobos helped to create the 'colors of paradise' moment. Templates spilling across the stage from behind helped to break up the space visually without creating shadows on the performers. Note the moon (sanded acrylic disc) that was side-lit."

your work in a way tailored to their needs. This may also mean you assemble more than one portfolio. If you are using copies of work, get the best copy quality you can afford. This is an investment in your future (and may be tax deductible).

Don't skimp on the portfolio. You are selling a product: your skills. Just as looks count when you are shopping, the package you keep your portfolio in says something about you. It might be a large-format traditional hard-copy portfolio, a small booklet of 4 × 6 inch photos, or a CD with images or PowerPoint presentations on it. Take the time to make the package aesthetically appealing; this takes time and money.

Hang onto materials. Have a folder, drawer, or box into which you put materials you've worked on once you are done using them. Go through the box from time to time to organize the materials. It's much easier to pull together this information into a presentable format if you have it in one place instead of having to go looking for it (or worse, trying to remember that show you did in two weeks three years ago!).

Devlin's white model images and good quality production photos are great samples of what to include in a scenic design portfolio. The images give a director insight into his design process. Devlin adds: "Most employers or schools are interested in seeing how you work through a project as well as the final results."

Portfolio Development Don'ts

If clear goals, good organization, and specific context information are key aspects to consider in developing a successful showcase, then disparaging goals, bad organization, and incomplete information are the bad practices to avoid. What lessens the impact of a portfolio? "Ill-organized materials, incomplete projects, and pages that must be turned a different way for each picture" is William Gordon Henshaw's answer.

Henshaw is a member of USITT whose awards include the Kennedy Center American College Theater Festival Regional Costume Design Nominee, the Bernice Prisk Award for Excellence in Theatrical Costuming, and the Wendell Johnson Award for Excellence in Design. He also considers "too much information spread over too many pages" a distraction from a portfolio's goals. The amount of materials in display and the handling of your portfolio will influence outcome as well. Donna Meester adds: "Do not include the kitchen sink! You may have many projects or many pages per project that you want to include, [but] most interviews have a limited time frame. Include only what is most effective in showing your abilities. If it is difficult for you to eliminate, ask a friend or mentor to help you clean house."

Luckily, a portfolio is an ongoing process, so anyone at the receiving end of feedback can incorporate his or her experience in future planning. April Barlett is a grad student working toward an MFA at Carnegie Mellon in a scenic design concentration. She received a Meritorious Achievement in Scenic Design Award from the Kennedy Center American College Theatre Festival in 2004. She has recommendations that could be useful to any designer and technician; she says, "Don't apologize for anything in your portfolio. If it requires an apology it probably doesn't belong in it. If your pictures don't look good, it doesn't matter how good [the production] looked in real life. Become your own photographer."

Five Observations on What Isn't Good Practice in Presenting a Portfolio
by John Paul Devlin

Assistant Professor of Fine Arts John Paul Devlin specializes in scenic and lighting design and serves as technical director during the academic year and resident designer and production manager for the Saint Michael's Playhouse during the summer. Devlin has excellent points to share regarding what isn't good practice when one is presenting a portfolio:

Don't answer questions with answers you "think" are right for the situation; be yourself. The folks on the other side of the table don't want to hire based on a false impression. Conversely, you should also have some questions prepared for your interviewers. They need to fit you as much as you need to fit them!

Don't be late or unprepared unless you're brilliant, in which case tardiness may be overlooked. (And don't assume you're brilliant—truly brilliant people generally don't assume they are.) If you are late, apologize. Once. And be sincere.

Don't arrange photos, images, or layouts in your portfolio so that folks have to keep changing the format or spinning the book, especially with big portfolios. Do treat each page as a design opportunity in itself. Even simple things like font choices say something about you as a designer and artist (see Figures 5.1d and 5.1e).

Never take a cell phone call unless you've explained in advance that you are expecting a *very* important call (as in someone's dying, giving birth, or arriving from Europe). Make sure your cell phone is off; honestly, you won't dematerialize! If you are fortunate enough to have a shop working on a show you've designed and they're at a critical point in construction, try calling them just before your interview is scheduled to begin, explain you'll be out of touch for one or two hours, and answer whatever questions they might have before you go into your interview.

Don't look at your watch or a clock (again unless you've explained that you have a very important engagement to keep); the interview is the most important thing you are doing right now and should absorb all your concentration. If you're looking at the time, you're telling the interviewer that you really don't want to be there and consequently really don't want the position.

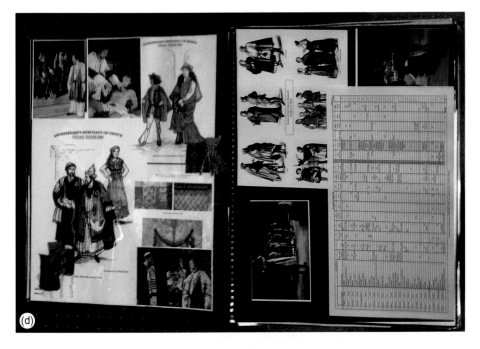

FIGURE 5.1D

Devlin says: "Don't arrange photos, images, or layouts in your portfolio so that folks have to keep changing the format or spinning the book, especially with big portfolios. Do treat each page as a design opportunity in itself. Even simple things like font choices say something about you as a designer and artist." *Note:* These sample pages are from the author's portfolio; they have been doctored to illustrate John Devlin's point. It is best to have consecutive pages going in the same direction.

FIGURE 5.1E

Devlin says: "Do treat each page as a design opportunity in itself." I personally avoid using bright construction paper to frame sketches or photos. Backgrounds are best when used discreetly (1/8-inch frames) and as long as they match the actual environment of the production. Tricks like this one detract from the work rather than emphasize its worth. *Note:* These sample pages are from the author's portfolio; they have been doctored to illustrate this point.

Now that we have gained awareness in regard to good practices and things to avoid in developing a portfolio, how do we prepare ourselves for presentation and marketing?

_____

_____

_____

_____

_____

_____

AND HAVING HAD THAT NEW IDEA, HAVE YOU HAD ENOUGH TIME ... TO SKETCH

OUT THAT NEW IDEA AND RISK CHUCKING THE PREVIOUS, ALMOST TOTALLY

APPROVED SCHEME?

CARRIE ROBBINS

CHAPTER SIX

THE EFFECTIVE DIGITAL PORTFOLIO

We can all agree that in today's world, digital technology helps create new pathways that enable easy sharing of artistic ideas, research, and design. It can also facilitate communication and speed up problem solving. An e-portfolio, also known as a *digital portfolio,* is one such pathway, but it is important to understand that it doesn't replace the traditional case with original artwork. A digital portfolio's practicality is what makes it appealing; user-friendly websites are easy to maintain and CDs are easy to copy, change, carry, or mail. Digital files make it easy to share information with fellow designers, technicians, directors, producers, managers, and school program administrators. Even so, some may question whether digital technology is a necessary expense in terms of money and time. Others may challenge its value in comparison to foundational abilities such as drafting, rendering, painting, and the like. The intent of this chapter is to explore how the design-tech process is enhanced through the use of digital files and how the traditional methods and the new methods can complement each other to achieve better results. It also looks at practical matters, such as what digital portfolios are for, what information is important to keep, and how that information should be stored. It is important to note that a digital portfolio will open many doors when it is used in combination with other marketing tools such as résumés.

I turned to Carrie Robbins, one of my mentors at New York University (NYU), for information about computer use in theatrical design. Carrie Robbins knows; she has designed costumes for more than 30 Broadway shows and many operas, films, and TV programs. She has received multiple Tony Award nominations, has been a Master Teacher of Costume Design at NYU for more than 25 years, and is a pioneer in the use of digital technology to produce sketches. It is amazing to realize the kind of visionary that Carrie Robbins has always been. Her article, "Theatre Designers and Computers," published in *Theatre Design & Technology*, Vol. 38, No. 4 (Fall 2002), illustrates still-relevant things to consider when you're using computer technology in the design-tech process.

Theatre Designers and Computers
by Carrie Robbins

We're all familiar with the arguments on both sides of the debate about using computers in the design studio. Some designers lament the mechanical look of pictures created with computers; Why, they ask, should I spend thousands of dollars on computer hardware and software and spend countless hours learning to do something that I can already do quite well using simple, inexpensive tools like paper, charcoal, pencil, and watercolors? Other designers argue that drawing and painting software is very sophisticated these days and capable of producing renderings every bit as expressive as hand-painted ones. I am one of the growing number of designers who use computers in almost every aspect of their work. Of course, a hand-drawn, freehand sketch can never be duplicated by a machine, and I really do miss the physical sensation of a pencil biting into a fresh sheet of paper, but working in the digital realm gives me some capabilities that I never had before.

Working with Collaborators

All theatre design evolves—sometimes swiftly and easily. But more often it takes many rough starts to conceive something that everyone likes—the director, the choreographer, the writer, the producers, the stars. There is never enough time to draw, redraw, and rework, especially if you must start from scratch on each sketch. Or have you ever had a new idea late in the process? And having had that new idea, have you had enough time, or even what I call psychic energy, to sketch out that new idea and risk chucking the previous, almost totally approved scheme? Have you thought to yourself, "This new idea may actually be a much better solution, but how long will it take me to get it to the point where it is presentable to a team of nondesigners who (rightfully) need help visualizing an idea?" And so you don't mention it.

Or do you use your sketches to help yourself visualize the color of the gown you're designing? You paint it blue, but wonder how it might look in a different shade. If only you had the time to paint another option to see for yourself. But you're out of time and must get the sketches to the shop.

Or you're working with a director who demands a bright fuchsia dress. You spend many hours making the best fuchsia dress you can. The response when you show the dress to the director—which you might have anticipated—goes like this: "Well, I know I said fuchsia, but actually I think, on reflection, and now that I see it, peach would be better." This has happened to me, and I have been quite annoyed. I paint slowly, and as I fumed, all I could think about was how much more time it was going to take me to produce a sketch that I could even tolerate looking at for the length of the build. (It's my nemesis that I care too much for the sketch itself. I want everyone to see a fully realized sketch because I think it helps them, if only as an inspiration. Besides, creating a detailed sketch involves making a decision that is vital to people who will build the costume.) Now changes are not so traumatic in the digital realm. Changing fuchsia to peach is literally just a few clicks away, and I remain a happy camper.

I have found that I make costume decisions more clearly if the colored ground I'm using for my costume sketches is similar to or connected somehow to the dominant color of the set. I believe it is easier for directors to make informed judgments about clothes if they can see them relative to that ground. So, when I hear that the set designer has changed the background colors of the scene, I love being able to revise my ground color with a few clicks. I also love being able to paint light over dark without having

to spray-fix the dark tone or put a thick layer of some nonbleed glop over the area I want to change, or paint the new, lighter section on a different piece of paper and meticulously cut it out with my surgical scissors so that the patch doesn't show, then glue it into place. Only Maxfield Parrish does this trick undetectably!

I have yet to find a look or a medium I can't mimic fairly accurately using standard computer painting software—oil, charcoal, transparent or opaque watercolor, chalk, marker. I often find myself creating effects that I never would have thought of when I was working traditionally. I love this kind of graphic surprise—the happy accident. Besides, if I want to draw on a piece of paper, I can still do that whenever I want.

If you're a set designer working with a director who truly has trouble visualizing space and you don't have time or money for assistants to make clear scale models, mightn't it be useful to sit at a computer and show such a director various layouts of furniture, walls, and doors, each on its own layer so that it can move independently anywhere onstage or disappear with a click? How cool is that?

If you're a set a designer needing to revamp a gaggle of sketches quickly, and you don't want to give away half your fee hiring a sketch artist for the job—or if you're on the side of that old argument about the efficacy of having another person do that work, who believes that the person doing a major portion of the sketching is the person doing the designing—then learning enough about the computer just to make those revisions or variations might be well worth investigating. Pushing oneself up and over the computer learning curve is really not so awful.

Relearning and Learning for the First Time

Relearning how to draw using a computer probably isn't for you if you aren't the kind of person who enjoys "going back to school." However, it is true that once you learn one program, learning how to use other ones is much easier. Basic computer-drawing skills—using the mouse, using a graphics tablet and a stylus, getting used to looking at a computer monitor while you draw—are applicable to all the drawing and painting programs you will eventually use.

I know that some computer artists are quite skillful drawing with a mouse, but I am not. I use a Wacom graphics tablet because using the stylus (they come cordless now) is fairly similar to working with a pen or pencil. In fact, most drawing programs are able to take advantage of pressure-sensitive technology built into graphics tablets, allowing you to make thick, heavy lines or light, thin ones, depending on how hard you press with the stylus.

My students at NYU's Tisch School of the Arts, Department of Design for Stage and Film, have talents that often only emerge while they're learning to use computer. Some students of costume design who never considered it possible to draw the simplest of rooms in decent perspective have created amazing spaces within two weeks of learning Photoshop. Set designer students who normally shy away from drawing figures have produced wonderfully sensitive portraits in Painter. And lighting design students who often have difficulties with both figures and freehand perspective have created persuasive environments as well as impressive figures. All the students I've worked with have created sophisticated work in no more than two or three weeks of targeted study per program (see Figures 6.1a and 6.1b).

When I teach computer drawing or painting, I limit our work in each software program to only what's most important for the specifics of theatre design, which I guesstimate might be as little as 15% of each program's full capability. We cover three programs—Photoshop, Painter, and Illustrator—and I let the students decide which, if any, is most comfortable or useful for them in design work once they complete the course. I stress that

FIGURE 6.1A

Patterned Room Color & Texture Study 1, by student designer Jennifer Paar. Notice the use of inventive patterns to create a mood.

FIGURE 6.1B

Patterned Room Color & Texture Study 2, by student designer Jo Winlarski. There is potential in every bit of this study. Sampling allows the designer to keep sharp computer skills by making selections, filling, copying, and so on.

our goal is to learn to use these new tools artistically, not just technically. I also remind them that even though learning how to use computers requires logical and somewhat technical thinking, eventually they will feel proficient and will be able to concentrate on creating works of art.

New Capabilities and New Uses

When designing the cloths for the musical *Rags*, I wanted to create fabrics that were printed with images associated with immigrants: photos of people at Ellis Island and ships, lists of names on ships' manifests, and the like. Hand painting these images would have been prohibitively expensive for the production at Papermill Playhouse, but I was able to acquire authentic images, arrange them to suit the patterns of the cloths, and then have them printed on an inkjet fabric printer (see Figures 6.2a through 6.2c).

Image research is an essential part of designing any show. With the help of image acquiring and editing software such as Photoshop, the designer can collect pictures from many (*heavy*) books and other sources to create a collage of research for use in discussions with directors and other designers (see Figures 6.3a and 6.3b). The days of dragging suitcases full of source materials to meetings, fumbling for the right pages where the yellow stickies have fallen off, are *gone*.

Conclusion

The beauty of the integration of computers into our work as designers is that we can show more options and make more revisions in much less time than we ever could before. While it's true that a good drawing, whether in the computer or on a piece of paper, takes the same amount of time (possibly a little longer in the computer until you get used to how to do it), the ability to make changes swiftly using the computer, without your drawing looking scrubbed over, is simply wonderful. It frees you to contribute many more ideas than ever before.

We are seeing only the tip of the iceberg as far as the artistic uses of computers. I believe that if you give a smart, talented person a new tool, he or she will figure out what to

FIGURE 6.2A

Rags, Painted Lady, by C. Robbins, using Painter and Photoshop. *Rags* (study for an Immigrant Woman), Papermill Playhouse, 1999.

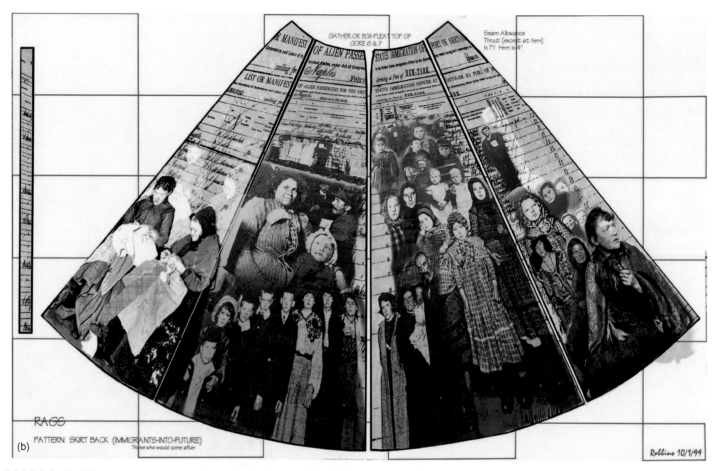

Within the image: GATHER OR BOX-PLEAT TOP OF GORE 6 & 7; Seam Allowance Thrust (except at hem) is 1"/ Hem is 4"; RAGS; PATTERN: SKIRT BACK (IMMIGRANTS-INTO-FUTURE) Those who would come after; (b); Robbins 10/1/99

FIGURE 6.2B

For the musical *Rags,* C. Robbins used computer-assembled graphics printed onto fabric (using an inkjet printer) achieving a hand-painted effect. Period research is superimposed on several gores off a skirt.

do with it. I intend to keep practicing and, hopefully, getting better. If you have discovered new ways to create your art with the help of the computer, please let me know.

What Is a Digital Portfolio; What Is It For?

A digital portfolio can be considered a communication facilitator and a marketing presentation tool. With today's technology, it isn't unusual to find established

and aspiring designers and technicians who are scanning their hand-drawn work and saving JPEGs in their computers and Flash drives. These in turn can be used for Web archives, photo slide shows, CDs, and websites. CDs are easy to carry, easy to copy, and easy to mail, and their contents can be posted on the Web. Websites and photo slide shows can be shared via a link. The result is a presentation that is accessible, practical, and convenient for sharing one's work. Many producers

FIGURE 6.2C
Sample garment for the musical *Rags* using inkjet-printed fabrics.

FIGURE 6.3A
Research cut sheet by C. Robbins for *Tallulah Hallelujah*, starring Tovah Feldshuh.

and directors can preview the work of a designer/technician from a website, a CD, or an email PDF file, which can lead to interviews.

It is important to remember that some specialties may benefit more than others from digital presentations. For example, a sound designer can introduce sound cues and scenes in real time. In preparing for a presentation that includes digital components, we also have to remember that some potential employers and grad school interviewers may not have the newest computer software; designers and technicians preparing a digital component should always plan to bring the equipment—a laptop or portable player—to play back their digitalized work.

We also have to remember that most producers, directors, and colleges still prefer seeing how visual artists draft, draw, and paint. Many may also want to look at real color and texture samples. Most agree that a digital portfolio is an effective way of complementing a traditional portfolio presentation and not a way to replace it. Of course, this trend could change in the future.

Given the fact that digital technology is used for portfolio presentation today, what do we need to know in order to create a digital portfolio?

What are some of the considerations that
I need to look at prior to developing a
digital portfolio? How would I use that
portfolio?

THE IMPORTANT THING IS TO CREATE CONGRUENT ELEMENTS THAT CAN BE UNDERSTOOD AS ONE INDIVIDUAL'S BRAND.

RAFAEL JAEN

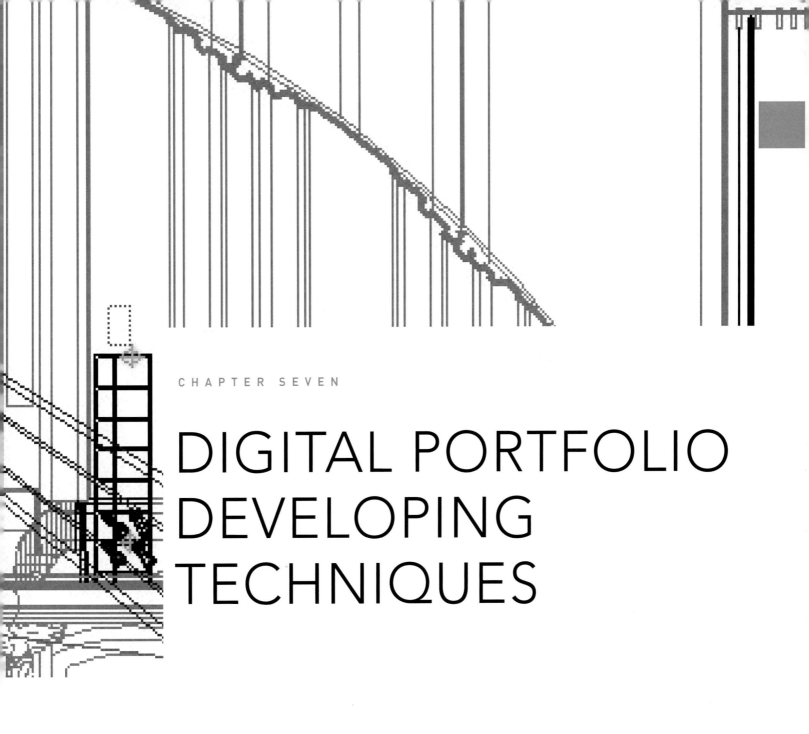

CHAPTER SEVEN

DIGITAL PORTFOLIO DEVELOPING TECHNIQUES

Computers and the Internet are effective resources that allow designers and technicians to share their expertise, communicate ideas, and seek out new career opportunities faster. For these reasons, CD samplers and Web pages can be used in addition to the traditional portfolio case. To create an effective digital showcase, designers and technicians need to be aware of available software, use proper graphic design principles, and learn about social media. Social media has become a far-reaching (and mostly free) marketing tool for communication, networking, collaboration, and multimedia sharing.

In this chapter we'll look at graphic design principles and branding applied to digital design; software applications and CD showcases; and websites, Web archives, and multimedia sharing. We will also look at social media for marketing purposes.

Graphic Design Principles and Branding

There are some key graphic design elements to consider in designing a digital portfolio. They include the color scheme, fonts, and the background design; organizational parts such as columns, rows, and multimedia links; and headings such as banners with logos, contact information, and tabs.

The color scheme can be monochromatic, analog, or complementary, depending on the type of contrast the individual wants. It can also include textures and gradations of color.

Multimedia platforms are used to add animations, videos, and interactivity to websites. One of the most used platforms is Adobe Flash Professional. Flash content may be displayed on various computer systems and devices using Adobe Flash Player, which is available free of charge for common Web browsers.

Tabs, images, and text can include hyperlinks to connect to other sites on the World Wide Web or within a presentation—in other words, they can have a Web address embedded in them so that when you click on the image or the text, they'll open a new window linked to a movie trailer, a link to a press review, or a photo slide show.

Elements such as banners and logos can be found in most marketing parts; for example, a résumé can have a banner with a logo that matches the website banner and logo of the designer or technician. The important thing is to create congruent elements that can be understood as one individual's brand.

Individual branding is the process whereby individuals' careers are self-packaged and marketed as brands. This branding includes special talents, body of work, and personal style—aspects that will leave a uniquely distinguishable impression with prospective employers. This type of branding often involves the application of one's name to the works that one is producing in a particular field. The use of brands containing personal logos and banners continues to gain in popularity as a tool through social networking sites such as Facebook, LinkedIn, and Twitter.

In designing an individual brand, it is important to look at one's body of work as though it were a design for a production. There are questions you can ask yourself in order to get inspiration and clarity. Sometimes it helps to go to a museum or take a walk in nature to check what grabs our attention. Here are some sample questions to help you come up with ideas:

1. What gets your attention in regard to color, shapes, distinctive areas, environment, lighting, and the like?

2. What geometric shapes get your attention: curves and squares, color themes, positive/negative balance?

3. How does the arrangement of space draw you in? What is the scale, and how do transitions work— slow, fast?

4. What arrangements are easier to remember? What is their design unity, their direction?

5. Are there colors and textures that most often get your attention in regard to background and foreground? Why? Is there a contrast?

The answers to each of these questions can translate into graphics that you find useful for Web design.

Show Case

(a)

(b)

FIGURE 7.1A

Molly Trainer has designed costumes for Boston area theatres since 1984 including New Repertory Theatre, Lyric Stage Company, Gloucester Stage Company, Boston Theatre Works, the Súgán Theatre Company, and others. She is a frequent guest designer at Salem State Theatre. A graduate of Northeastern University, Molly studied photography at the University of the South and design at both The School of the Museum of Fine Arts and The School of Fashion Design in Boston. Molly has designed a marketing package for herself; it includes stationery, business card, CD, and fold-out brochure. All these elements can be printed on a home computer system.

Notice that the main element of Molly Trainer's brand is the prominent logo. Trainer limits the use of various fonts to two in order to give the eye a rest between transitions; she also favors a monochromatic palette with light gradation. She drew the color and light inspiration from a visit to the Museum of Fine Arts in Boston. Notice that there is a general consistency in the use of color and graphics; all variations accommodate the scale of the particular brand element. For example, the business card uses more color than the stationery page, but they are still part of one unit. Molly used Photoshop to edit the shapes and color variations and the light gradation.

FIGURE 7.1B

Ellen Jaworski is a production designer who has a broad range of experience designing for live talk shows, standup comedy, award shows, and sitcoms. On her website she writes: "Not limited to scenic design, however, Ellen's experience encompasses costume, lighting, and make-up design for television, theatre, and social events. Passionate, driven, and dedicated, Ellen is determined to meet the client's needs while delivering a design she is proud to call her own." Ellen Jaworski's brand includes great textures, high contrast, and vivid colors. Knowing Ellen, these elements make sense and give a sense of her style. Her marketing pack includes a website, business card, stationery, and an 8½ × 11 portfolio sampler with 12 pages. This sampler is a PowerPoint saved as a PDF. It can be saved as an email attachment, on a CD, or as a hard pack.

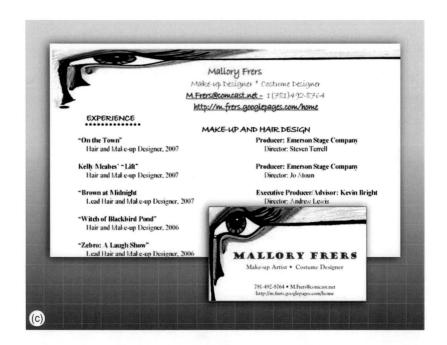

FIGURE 7.1C

Mallory Frers is a freelance make-up artist and costume designer. She says: "There are only so many things you can do in order to make a business card one of a kind. They all have the same information on them and they all serve the same purpose. To make mine stand out to people, I decided to create my own logo. My individualistic design symbolizes my design style as well as my personality. By using this same logo on my résumé and on my brochure, I have created an identity for myself on paper."

FIGURE 7.1D

Bill Hawkins is a freelance technical director. Bill markets his freelance project management and theatrical construction business as Mohawk Theatrical Associates. In regard to branding, he says: "I chose the Mohawk Theatrical Associates logo because it visually tied the business's brand to my own image. Elizabeth Breda, a scenic designer and colleague, created the Mohawk insignia for me. Using research photos that I brought her, Elizabeth was able to create several versions of the logo. After much discussion and some revision the design was finalized. I then redrafted the final design in Auto CAD. I used Auto CAD to digitize the logo because, as a technical director, I am well versed using that software. Additionally, having the logo as a .DWG file allows me to easily insert it into my drawings or scale the logo to fit on a truck, van, or business card. I also used Auto CAD in the layout and creation of my portfolio. This allowed me to create a full-scale image of each page without the need to physically print, crop, and attach individual photos to my portfolio. Perhaps the greatest benefit of designing my entire portfolio digitally is the ability to quickly customize its contents for a particular client or employer. There is also no need for me to scan pages when emailing my portfolio; I just click Convert to .PDF and attach the new document."

Software Applications and CD Showcases

Nowadays personal computers have compatible system programs that allow picture viewing in folders with thumbnails or as a slide flow. People who are new to the technology need not worry if Information Technology Department staff or computer technicians aren't available; most software programs come with tutorials and Web links to provide user help. What is important is to take the time to experiment and practice. Creating a digital portfolio can be as simple as taking digital photos of an existing portfolio and saving them to a CD. This is the first step for anything digital: to save everything electronically!

Electronic portfolios showcase the individual's abilities and style; they are user friendly and the information in them can be maintained dynamically over time. CD showcases are e-portfolios; the information in a CD showcase can be saved in a laptop as well and used for interview purposes. Some users prefer the directness of a simple folder with superb images.

Show Case

Janie E. Howland is a scenic designer and member of United Scenic Artists Local 829. She is also an Elliot Norton Award winner (1997) and founding member of the CYCO SCENIC production company. She says: "I used to carry around a large portfolio case with images mounted onto black matte board pages. There were approximately 15 pages. Now I have an electronic portfolio. I carry my laptop computer and show producers a slide show of about 30 images of my work, and I leave them with a disc that includes my résumé, the images, and the articles that have been published about me and my projects (see Figures 7.2a through 7.2c). I still present them with a printed copy of my résumé."

Antigone - Concord Academy

(a)

FIGURE 7.2A

This image is a scanned slide from the *Antigone* produced at Concord Academy High School, Concord, Massachusetts, directed by David Gammons. The Plexiglas panels create a "sacred space" outside the palace that has been boarded up and protected with barbed wire during the war in which the two brothers have killed each other. Scanned photo for use in Janie E. Howland's digital portfolio.

MAIDEN'S PRAYER - HUNTINGTON THEATRE STUDIO 210

(b)

FIGURE 7.2B

This image is a scanned slide from *Maiden's Prayer*, produced by the Huntington Theatre in Studio 210, directed by Scott Edmiston. The set represented the fragmented memory of the "perfect" childhood. It was scattered with shadow boxes inspired by Joseph Cornell. The boxes contained the frozen objects of childhood, the family estate, the perfect green grass of the back yard. Scanned photo for use in digital portfolio.

SWEENEY TODD - SEACOAST REPERTORY THEATRE

(c)

FIGURE 7.2C

This image is a scanned slide from *Sweeney Todd,* at Seacoast Repertory Theatre, directed by Spiro Veloudos. It is a unit set in a thrust theatre with 4-foot upstage of the proscenium walls. The set combines the many locations required by the script with the barber shop chair that dumps customers through a trap door in the floor onto a slide and into the pie shop oven. The paint style was inspired by Gustave Doré etchings of London.

PowerPoint and Adobe Portable Document Format (PDF)

The Adobe Portable Document Format (PDF) is the native file format of the Adobe Acrobat family of products. The goal of these products is to enable users to exchange and view electronic documents easily and reliably. To improve performance for interactive viewing, PDF defines a more structured format than that used by most PostScript language programs. PDF also includes objects, such as annotations and hypertext links, that are not part of the page itself but are useful for interactive viewing and document interchange.

For formal presentations such as portfolio samplers or a slide show for a specific project, PowerPoint is recommended. Microsoft Office PowerPoint enables users to quickly create high-impact, dynamic presentations while integrating workflow and ways to easily share information. The software comes with various layout options; images and text can be imported into a template, saved to CD, and then can be presented as a slide show. The slides in a PowerPoint presentation can be saved as JPEGs and in turn can be uploaded to a Web photo archive and become a Web album. If you know how to use Microsoft Word you'll find that using PowerPoint is intuitive. You can define and save your own custom slide layouts, so you no longer have to waste valuable time cutting and pasting your layouts onto new slides or deleting content on a slide with the layout you want.

With PowerPoint, creating professional, unique presentations can be easy. The software offers multiple tools for keeping slide content clear, well designed, and professional. The software also offers many layout and design options that can be customized. When you're planning to use PowerPoint, it is key to create slides that get the viewer's attention, choosing your graphics carefully and treating each one of the frames as a portfolio page. We need to use the space on our slides effectively, so only include elements that contribute to the points we want to make, and choose images that serve a purpose, such as drafting, research, sketches, or photos that best display our ideas. Presentations created with PowerPoint work just like the frames in a filmstrip.

Show Case

I use PowerPoint to create slides for each show that I design. I choose from existing templates, which can be adapted with different text boxes and color schemes. Each slide becomes an individual sketch that can be printed in large format. In addition, saving a PowerPoint as JPEGs allows the individual to upload the slides to Web photo albums such as Flickr for easy viewing via a web link (see Figures 7.3a through 7.3d).

PowerPoint presentations can also be saved as PDFs that can be emailed (see Figure 7.3e). The PDF conversion is recommended so that the design scheme and fonts don't get altered when you're switching to a computer different from the one on which your presentation was created.

FIGURE 7.3A, 7.3B, 7.3C, AND 7.3D

PowerPoint and Flickr Web Archive samples for the show *Boston Marriage*, produced by New Repertory Theatre, 2010, Boston. Director: David Zoffoli, costumes by Rafael Jaen.

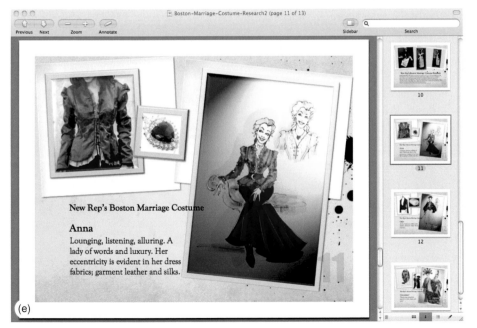

FIGURE 7.3E

A PDF conversion is recommended so the PowerPoint design scheme and fonts don't get altered when you switch to another computer. Production: *Boston Marriage*, New Repertory Theatre, 2010, director: David Zoffoli, costumes by Rafael Jaen.

Photo Editing Software

Sometimes images need retouching; this is where photo editing software such as Adobe Photoshop Creative Suite is highly recommended. This software is ideal for photographers, graphic designers, and Web designers. It delivers features such as automatic layer alignment and blending that enable advanced compositing.

In purchasing Adobe software, it's important to consider obtaining InDesign as part of the suite. Adobe InDesign is a page-making software that enables designers and technicians to create very sophisticated and professional-looking layouts. InDesign provides precise control over typography as well as built-in creative tools for designing and publishing documents for print and online or mobile devices.

Show Case

Tyler Kinney is an outstanding set and costume designer for theatre, film, and television. He is the recipient of the prestigious KCACTF Barbizon Award for Excellence in Set Design Region 1, 2011 (see Figures 7.4a through 7.4e).

Websites and Web Archives

Web pages are becoming the marketing norm in our digital world. To reach many people with different levels of computer skills, it's best to keep things simple by retaining consistent color schemes and templates. Websites need to be maintained and up to date; having a template makes that process much less time consuming. Templates let you just plug in content rather than starting from scratch each time. In addition, the layout and links must be easy to follow so that viewers can easily access the files in display and get the information they need.

The Adobe Photoshop Creative Suite also includes Macromedia Dreamweaver. This is a professional HyperText Markup Language (HTML) editor for designing, coding, and developing websites, Web pages, and Web applications. Whether you enjoy the control of hand-coding HTML or prefer to work in a visual editing environment, Dreamweaver provides you with helpful tools to enhance your Web creation experience. The visual editing features in Dreamweaver let you quickly create pages without writing a line of code. You can view all your site elements or assets and drag them from an easy-to-use panel directly into a document. Many Web design platforms on the market offer components that are compatible with the Adobe software; this way design elements can be uploaded into a template and adapted to create an original and unique look.

FIGURE 7.4A

The images show a sample layout that set and costume designer Tyler Kinney put together using InDesign.

FIGURE 7.4B

This is the actual printed version of the InDesign file that Kinney glued to the three-sided board that he presented at the 2011 KCACTF Region 1 Festival.

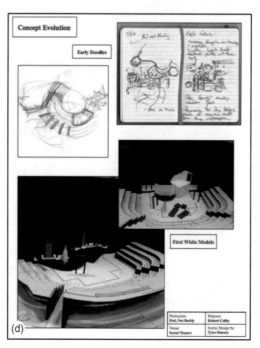

FIGURES 7.4C AND 7.4D

Kinney also uses InDesign to produce workbooks for productions. The featured images include a concept page with visual research, a preliminary doodle, and a white model page.

FIGURE 7.4E

Kinney also uses InDesign to produce workbooks for productions. The featured images include a progress and final rendering page. Workbooks can serve as companion portfolio pieces, study guides, and digital archives. Kinney likes to use spiral-bound workbooks as a durable and professional-looking option.

Show Case

Files that have been saved to computer folders or CDs can be imported to a personal website. "While there are a number of programs that can be used to create the content of a site, Adobe Photoshop is by far my most important tool," says Kristina Tollefson, who served as the vice commissioner for communication for the Costume Design & Technology Commission of the USITT. Kristina finds that Photoshop is extremely easy to use and it offers many shortcuts and tricks to make repetitive tasks (such as resizing photos or preparing image maps of graphic creation) less taxing. She adds that even renderings that are bigger than a scanner bed can be scanned a couple of times and then pieced together. "Photoshop makes piecing the images together pretty simple," she says.

Tollefson is considered a wizard of digital technology by her colleagues. She has an MFA in costume design and technology from Purdue University, is currently an assistant professor and resident costume and makeup designer at the University of Central Florida in Orlando, and is also a member of USA 829. Tollefson and her husband work together on her website (see Figures 7.5a and 7.5b); they are Mac users at home (and PC based at work) so the programs they use are all Mac compatible.

Sometimes taking the time to learn and experiment can pay off. "We don't use any of the What You See Is What You Get (WYSIWYG) programs on the market, like Dreamweaver, to build our Web pages," says Kristina. "My husband Jason got interested in Web design originally and we couldn't afford the software. So, for the

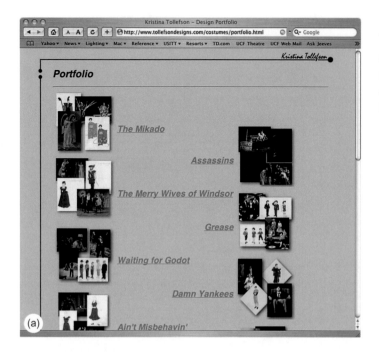

(a)

FIGURE 7.5A

Tollefson's portfolio menu. "This screen capture is the main page of the portfolio section of my site. Its primary purpose is to give viewers instant access to any show in the portfolio. Because I provide a small collage of renderings and production shots, the viewers can better choose which shows are of interest to them. The regular arrangement of the shows is contrasted with the more organic groupings of images for each show, to soften the linear nature of such lists."

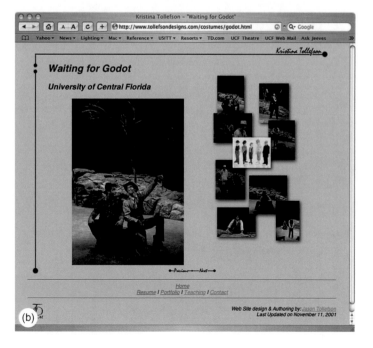

(b)

FIGURE 7.5B

Tollefson's *Waiting for Godot* show in the portfolio. "The layout on the page is exactly the same as the other productions, but because of the collage menu on the right, each production has an individual feel and there is no sense of monotony. The Previous and Next buttons near the bottom of the page allow the viewer to step through the entire portfolio in the order I chose, if they desire, or they can opt to return to the main portfolio menu page and choose any production in any order they wish."

price of an *HTML for Dummies* book, he taught himself the programming language instead. Many people don't realize that Web pages are actually just text files containing specialized instructions, which tell the Web browser (Internet Explorer or Safari, etc.) what to do and how to display information."

Shanna Parks started sewing at eight years old with the help of her mother and grandmother and found her way into a costume shop by age 13. Soon after, she decided to pursue a career in theatrical costuming—first choosing

design but soon discovering her real interest was in construction. Parks completed her MFA at the University of North Carolina at Chapel Hill. Her work experience includes the Utah Shakespearean Festival; PlayMakers Repertory Company in North Carolina; the Oregon Shakespeare Festival; PCPA Theatrefest in California; and the Huntington Theatre in Boston. Her exquisite work was presented as part of the USITT Young Designers and Technicians (YD&T) forum 2011 in Charlotte, North Carolina (see Figures 7.5c through 7.5h).

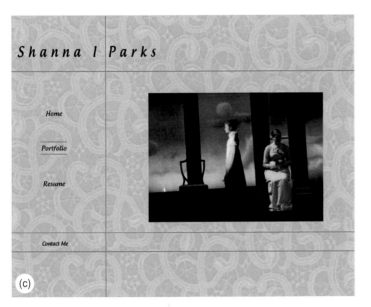

FIGURES 7.5C AND 7.5D

The opening pages of costume designer Shanna Parks's website. The use of a beautiful lace print as a background and the neat arrangement of thumbnail images creates anticipation. Parks says: "As a draper, the detail I can put into my work is one of the most important elements of what I do. When you look at the research or rendering and see that I have achieved the same level of detail and proportion, then you can see that the project is successful."

FIGURES 7.5E AND 7.5F

Parks says: "The Romantic-era bodice has a level of detail in it that needs to be viewed up close—from a distance the puff, buttons, and cording become the important part, but when you click on the photo to make it full screen you can see the real level of detail in the piece. At the same time a full-length image is important to show the overall silhouette of the period and, in this case, if the fullness of the sleeve is successfully balanced with the shape of the skirt."

FIGURES 7.5G AND 7.5H

Park continues: "The Edwardian dress is a favorite of mine since I love working with lace and these lingerie dresses are a perfect outlet for that. This project was also interesting because it allowed me to work on an antique dress form. In the full-length image of this garment, I wanted to show the silhouette—especially the way the skirt falls over the hips and how round the waist looks. These aren't things we can achieve on a modern body, so they are important to this project. The research images for this dress feature two dresses, one that I took the overall line from and another with a square lace yoke more suitable for the lace I was working with. The detail shot shows the lace work in the bodice; I wanted the look and feel of an expensive period French lace."

Show Case
Other Considerations: Choosing a Server

James Michael Garner is no newcomer in the fields of technical theatre and broadcasting. With more than seven years in technical direction and related areas, Jim has a solid reputation for producing quality work that meets all deadlines and budget requirements. He is currently based in the greater Boston and Washington, D.C., areas but is always looking to broaden his horizons by working in other locales. Jim shares his criteria in choosing a website server:

"Getting a job is not just about being good. It is also about networking and getting you and your work "out there." In today's techno-savvy world, a website is the logical choice.

"While the best way to design a website for you can be as unique as you are, the steps taken in building one are generic. You first itemize and prioritize your goals, research potential website carriers, analyze and rank which providers will help you meet your goals, and, finally, make your choice.

"Before I even began my search for the 'perfect' server, I had three specific criteria in mind to maintain a quality online portfolio. I wanted maximum exposure with reasonable cost/time investments and flexibility in presentation.

1. *"Getting maximum exposure.* Since a major reason for having a website is to create a public face for your target audience, you need a site that is readily accessible and user-friendly. This is why it is important to verify that whatever site you create will be properly displayed by all common browsers. To make my site more reachable, I made a point of checking to see that it would be registered with the popular search engines. In my case this was done automatically, but you can also do it directly

through the search engine. Widgets are popular as well because they enable live feeds to your Twitter, Facebook, and LinkedIn accounts. A bonus I like is the ability to create an embedded contact form to reduce the amount of spam that reaches my inbox. It also allows potential employers to reach me without having to open their email accounts.

2. *"Keeping money and time in mind.* As someone with a limited budget, I wanted something economical. However, I didn't want to sacrifice quality for price. For that reason, I purposely avoided the "free" domains that included annoying popups, which would detract from my content. Also, since I am always busy, I wanted a site that would be user friendly for me, the creator. For this reason, I targeted services that offered a selection of free templates that would appeal to my time constraints.

3. *"Flexibility in presentation.* Clearly, you want your website to showcase your accomplishments. This can be achieved in terms of layout, resolution, and volume of graphical elements. Naturally, I wanted to include work that would be visually pleasing and of high caliber. This meant that in addition to having the option of layout templates, as mentioned earlier, I would need a server with the capability of handling everything I would want to upload as well" (see Figures 7.6a through 7.6c).

The solution that Garner came up with was to use Wix .com, a Flash site. He adds: "I personally prefer the look of Flash, but it may not work for everyone. Older computers take longer to view Flash sites, and some don't even have Flash players. (This was not an issue for me, though, since I'd prefer to work for people who have kept current with today's technology.) Another disadvantage of a Flash site is that it limits the number of random hits you might get because of the way search

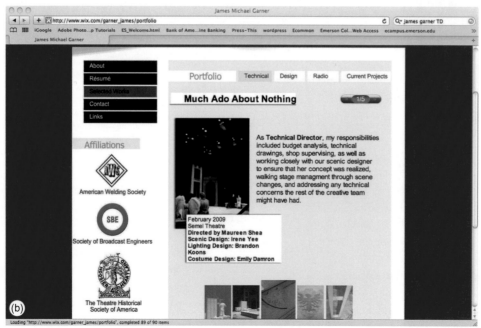

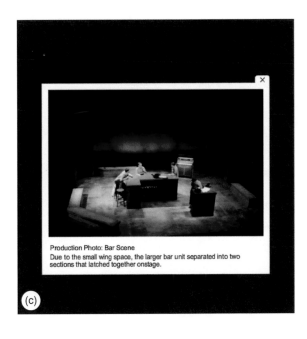

Production Photo: Bar Scene
Due to the small wing space, the larger bar unit separated into two sections that latched together onstage.

(c)

engines scan for keywords. However, if you're like me and happen to share the name of someone famous, searching by name alone is unproductive anyway. (This is also the reason I include my middle name on my website and all business correspondence.) Nevertheless, with Wix I do have the option of upgrading my service to include a private domain that is more recognizable and easier for others to remember. The package I found also includes a service called Google Analytics, which provides demographic info about people who access my site and offers me recommendations on how to better reach potential clients. Of course, we live in the real world. We may not be able to get everything we want in the way of a website. (As I mentioned before, my limiting factors were time and money.) Whatever the case, your best bet would be trying to establish a list of priorities before you actually begin hunting for a host. Fortunately, I was able to satisfy all of my priorities and still keep the setup and operating expenses to a minimum."

Multimedia Sharing and Social Media

Nowadays many sites allow designers and technicians to share audio, images, and video. Multimedia sharing sites facilitate the archiving of projects, sharing of research and/or process, and creation of audio, images/photos, and video samplers. These sites offer sizeable hosting space to post the media directly into your own websites, blogs, and social networking sites.

The site Participatory Media Guidebook (http://pmguide .wetpaint.com/page/Multimedia+Sharing) states that "it takes a lot of storage space to hold onto media files and it takes a lot of bandwidth to share them. If you were to pay for your own hosting and distributing infrastructure for multimedia, it would be very expensive and require a lot of technical expertise to maintain. There would always be a threat of overwhelming your system and causing a crash if too many people attempt to view a video, for example, simultaneously."

Show Case

I use multimedia such as Flickr, Blip.TV, and YouTube to showcase projects; then I use hyperlinks in my website and my blog to connect all entries. I use Flickr the most. What I like about Flickr is that it gives me the opportunity to share images fast in a user-friendly environment. Images can be uploaded, descriptions added, and privacy settings changed, depending on the stage of the process. Figures 7.7a through 7.7d illustrate the possibilities; they are my Web archives for the show *Nicholas Nickleby*, produced by the Lyric Stage Company of Boston in Fall 2010 and directed by Spiro Veloudos.

The production was nominated for an IRNE Award for Best Costume Design 2011.

I also use a combination of social media for communication and collaboration with production teams and communities I work with. These include blogs (Blogger and WordPress), microbloggers (Twitter), social networking (Facebook), and multimedia sharing (YouTube). I use blogs to share detailed information about projects, Facebook to post upcoming projects, Twitter to create buzz, and YouTube to create records and share with the world (see Figures 7.7e through 7.7g).

FIGURE 7.7A

Rafael Jaen's Flickr Web archives. Each set has its own detail page where individual images open to a larger scale.

FIGURE 7.7B

The author's Flickr image set for a specific show. A production team can see the progress of the designs by clicking on a link.

FIGURE 7.7D

With Flickr, the image set can be shared with a production team as a slide show as well. This approach creates a more finished presentation with animation.

FIGURES 7.7E, 7.7F, AND 7.7G

The author uses his blog to "Report on experiences in the world of theatre and film design, digital rendering and Web design, plus costume and fashion design." The samples show blog entries and a hyperlink for the show *Nicholas Nickleby*, produced by the Lyric Stage Company of Boston in the Fall of 2010 and directed by Spiro Veloudos. The first blog reported the design process with sketches and images from fittings; the last one had a hyperlink to a video review of the production, posted at PBS/WGBH.

Show Case

More About Websites: The Allied Field

In many regions across the United States, more and more theatre folks are also working in the film and TV industry, and vice versa. In all instances of design and technology, skilled craftsmanship is allied to advanced technology. I spoke to a group of innovative designers from the United States and the United Kingdom to explore the many opportunities of crossover. Here we showcase Thomas Walsh, president of the Arts Directors Guild; Ann Cudworth, a two-time Emmy Award-winning set designer; Seághan McKay, a Boston-based projection designer extraordinaire; and Rosalind Robinson, a scenic artist who has worked as a professional artist and specialist decorator for more than 30 years in the United Kingdom and abroad.

Thomas Walsh is president of the Arts Directors Guild. He has designed for feature films, Imax/Omnimax, television movies and series, documentaries, Broadway dramas and musicals, and regional theatre. Walsh is the winner of a Primetime Emmy for art direction and an ADG Award nomination for *Buddy Faro* (1998). He is also winner of the 2004 ADG Excellence in Production Design Award for a Single Camera Series for the hit ABC-TV show, *Desperate Housewives* (see Figures 7.8a through 7.8c).

Thom Walsh generously offers the following words of wisdom regarding websites and social media: "The wide array of today's off-the-shelf digital tools must surely be regarded as magical, as they have endowed us with a unique ability to create and communicate both an understanding and an appreciation for our talents and capabilities as never before. The power and potential to network and promote one's work

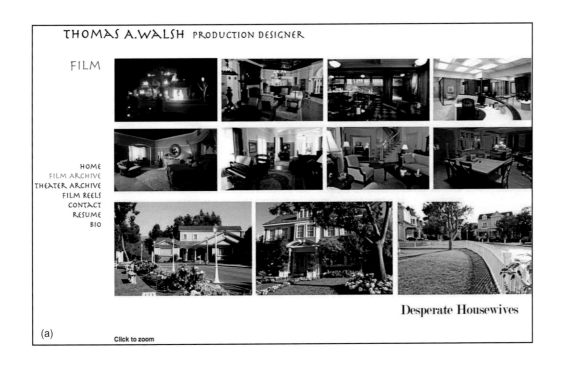

(a)

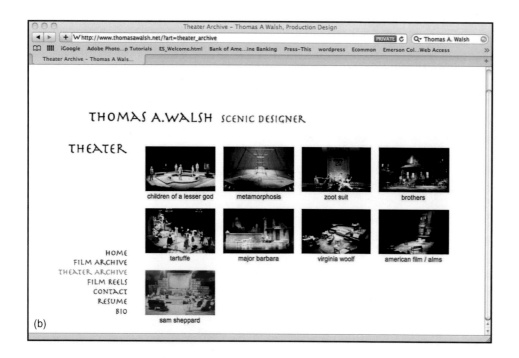

(b)

(c)

FIGURES 7.8A, 7.8B, AND 7.8C
Designer Thomas A. Walsh's website combines a sleek design that relies on clean lines and image strength. He uses consistent boxes and layouts. His portfolio includes work in film, TV, and theatre.

through the use of a dedicated website or the other social networking media such as Facebook cannot be overstated. The startup periods for new narrative film and live performance ventures continues to diminish. The ability to make one's work accessible through the use of these new tools on a 24/7 basis can make a significant difference in how one is seriously considered by a potential employer. With the increasingly global nature of the narrative design industry, the ability to promote one's work or view the efforts of others that you might be seriously considering collaborating with in a visually dynamic and multifaceted manner must be embraced and cannot, nor should not, be undervalued. The freedom and flexibility that my personal website has afforded me has proven invaluable in my abilities to reach out to a far larger audience and potential employment base, one much greater than I could have ever imagined."

Thom Walsh and I share an interest in the crossover between theatre and film; he wrote about this in his "Preparing Narrative Artists and Practitioners for a New Century" article, published by the magazine *Perspectives: The Journal of the Arts Directors Guild*. Thom agreed to let me share the article in which he expressed his thoughts. You'll find the article below.

Preparing Narrative Artists and Practitioners for a New Century (Excerpt)

by Tom Walsh, President, Art Directors Guild

Entry and survivability in today's multifaceted entertainment industry require a much broader spectrum of experiences, and one's academic training can no longer be "theatre-centric" to the exclusion and introduction to all other entertainment, communication, and media practices.

Future designers, performers, writers, directors, producers, artists, and technicians must now be exposed to all relevant entertainment media practices within the span of their academic educations. The theatre is still one of the most effective mediums for laying the educational foundations for narrative practitioners, but it cannot stop there. Young artists face a much different career environment than was encountered by their teachers and mentors. Surviving this new world will require of them a more diversified exposure to potential career paths and opportunities, many of which until recently we're regarded as unique and separate. Providing them with this greater diversity of knowledge and training is essential if we wish them to sustain and excel at their future endeavors.

Technology is providing many bridges between what were once considered unique and separate disciplines, creating convergence where once there were partitions. The Academy's future training and curriculum must become accepting of this reality. The academic syllabus that was established in the 20th century became sorely in need of updating as we entered the 21st century and the digital age. The intellectual and professional barriers that have long separated the performing arts programs from their communications and cinema cousins must finally come down so that the future graduates of these programs can freely derive the richest and fullest spectrum of experiences possible during their brief academic sojourns.

Ann Cudworth is a two-time Emmy Award winner—one for a real set, and one for a virtual set. She has worked professionally in the four realms of set design: theatre, film, television, and virtual reality. For the past 18 years Ann has been a production designer for shows at CBS such as *60 Minutes* and *48 Hours* as well as *CBS News* productions and CBS Evening News Special events. The creation of virtual scenic pieces for the 1994 election coverage started Ann's virtual set design career. Her current work can be seen on projects for *Market Watch* and *CBS News* promotions.

Cudworth shared some words of wisdom when I spoke with her: "For the rare birds in set design who create real as well as virtual scenery, an online portfolio works very well. A small, relatively simple, five- to six-page website that shows images from the designer's completed projects, as well as media clips, is easy to set up, is readily accessible to most Internet users, and will probably cost less than $200 per year to maintain." She continues: "Website domain providers offer templates that allow even the most novice Web designer the opportunity to produce a professional-looking website that can be viewed by anyone at all times (see Figures 7.9a through 7.9c). This is especially useful when the designer is in long-distance contact with a producer and wants to discuss his or her portfolio during a phone chat. All the producer has to do is log on and look at the portfolio. Instant gratification!

"Utilizing the powerful resources of the Internet allows the designer to seek new clients as well as provide information to existing clients, such as preliminary designs and plans while the project is being designed. Furthermore, if the designer is working with a graphic team, the images can be edited, annotated, and reworked jointly simultaneously. All in all, for its cost vs. potential exposure, the Internet is a very effective presentation vehicle."

Seághan McKay is a Boston-based projection designer whose work has been seen at the SpeakEasy Stage Company, the Boston Conservatory, the Brandeis Theatre Company, and others. As a designer, technician, and educator for 17 years, Seághan has been affiliated with the American Repertory Theatre, the Huntington Theatre Company, Blue Man Group, the Commonwealth Shakespeare Company, Brandeis University, Boston College, and others. Seághan also performs as a live

visualist, creating real-time interactive motion graphics for the popular Thunderdome series of club events in Boston. Seághan is lighting supervisor at Brandeis University, where he also holds a position as lecturer in theatre arts.

Seághan says: "I have always been a very computer-savvy person and probably should have gotten into Web design a long time ago. In truth, I never had a reason to create a website for myself, and the thought of learning HTML without a goal in mind didn't seem worthwhile. Recently, however, I reentered the theatrical design world after a long absence, and it became clear I needed something to represent my work. Since I am a projection designer, computer graphics is a large part of my work, so it was doubly important that I show my work in an online way.

"In the end I did not need to learn a line of HTML or CSS to create my site. I used a program called Rapidweaver by Realmac Software, which is extremely easy to learn and to create good results with little prior experience. It can be used very powerfully, however, if you do know what you're doing and want to add some CSS, Flash elements, etc. The user forums on Realmac's site hold a wealth of information about custom themes, third-party plugins, and answers to just about any beginner question you might have.

"Rapidweaver is only made for the MacOS, which is my preferred platform. I also upload video content to Vimeo and can embed these clips into my website very easily. My site has served as a good reference so far when meeting directors for the first time on a new project. Since projection design for theatre is a newly emerging field, there is usually some explanation involved at the beginning of any project with creative teams who have not used the tools before. Having the website available so that directors can view my work before the initial meeting answers a lot of those questions and also fosters new questions about creative possibilities."

He continues: "I have learned that simpler is better when it comes to designing my website. It's important

FIGURES 7.9A, 7.9B, AND 7.9C

Production designer Ann Cudworth's website includes pages for virtual worlds, virtual sets, and real sets. These varied skills set her apart in the market. Her website is high-tech and contemporary.

to remember that the emphasis should be placed on the quality of the design onstage, not on the Web page itself. Naturally the design should be effective and elegant and should express who the designer is. However, visitors to the site will be looking at the content (production photos, video clips, etc.) first and page layout second. Make sure that navigation around the site is very clear" (see Figures 7.10a through 7.10c).

He also offers these words of wisdom: "My advice for students would be to get the best-quality production photos possible. Most company photographers shoot for publicity use, which means close-ups of actors. Designers generally need a wider shot that shows more of the stage picture, so it is best to learn how to do this yourself. Use a good-quality digital SLR camera with a fast (very light-sensitive) lens and a tripod. Blurry or noisy photos will not represent your work very well. If the company holds a designer photo call, use this

opportunity, since you can get the performers to stand still, making for clearer photography."

After studying for a Fine Art degree in London, Rosalind Robinson trained as a scenic artist with the BBC, acquiring the skills of *trompe l'oeil* painting, marbling, gilding, and graining. She has worked as a professional artist and specialist decorator for more than 30 years, producing fine decorations on walls and furniture in the United Kingdom and abroad. She has studied botanical painting in courses at Kew Gardens and the Chelsea Physic Garden and teaches occasional botanical painting classes. She is a member of the Traditional Paint Forum, the Bath Society of Botanical Artists, and the Calne Artists Group.

I asked Rosalind to share some words of wisdom regarding her experience featuring her exquisite work on the web. She says: "Ten years ago I decided to join the rapidly accelerating number of professional artists showing their work online. Not having any knowledge

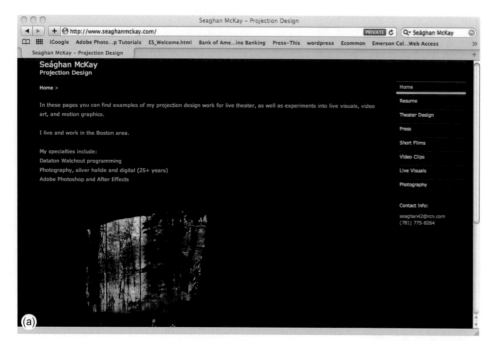

FIGURE 7.10A
Seághan McKay's format includes a clear identification banner and a left column menu.

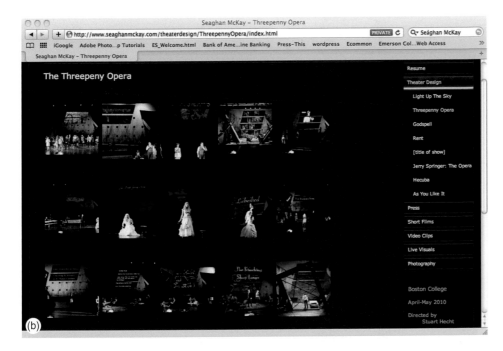

(b)

FIGURES 7.10B AND 7.10C

Seághan McKay's format includes a clear identification banner and a left column menu. The menu is easy to use; each category opens into a new window with the project description and credits. Keeping the information in the same column adds continuity and consistency to the design.

(c)

of website design, I consulted a friend who worked in computing to advise me. Tim Molloy turned out to be a creative and original thinker, and he is responsible for the appearance of my website. Choosing which images to show was a complex process that required an objective second opinion. I work as a specialist painter, muralist, botanical artist, scenic artist, fine artist, and teacher. I decided to feature just the mural commissions and recent theatre work without reference to the other aspects of my professional work, which can be seen by following links to two other sites."

She adds: "It's easy to ignore website maintenance as long as work keeps trickling in. Consequently, my site has changed little in ten years, except for new work being added from time to time. This 'hands-off' approach might have worked in my favor, as the rather retro simplicity of the site marks it out as different from the norm (see Figures 7.11a through 7.11c).

"I think my site has a serene quality. It is an unassuming presentation of my work, where the images speak for themselves—an oasis of calm in the frenetic, wildly interactive world on the Web. The simple scrolling through the selected works is an invitation for quiet contemplation of the details shown, encouraging the viewer to linger. Does it work? Well, having a website is a cheap but completely random way of advertising and displaying work. I have found it very useful as an online portfolio to direct potential clients to in the first instance, cutting down on costly and sometimes unproductive meetings."

She also notes: "A presence on the Web is as essential now as email and a mobile phone, but it hasn't really worked for me in generating new enquiries. After working professionally for 30 years or so, I still find real-time social networking to be the most effective way of generating new business. Belonging to other artists' groups and professional bodies is also a potentially

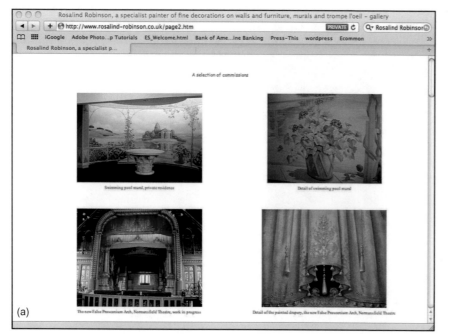

(a)

FIGURE 7.11A

Scenic artist and decorator Rosalind Robinson's website includes a beautiful sampler page with many images and varied projects, including private clients and theatre venues.

(b)　　The new False Proscenium Arch, Normansfield Theatre, work in progress

FIGURES 7.11B AND 7.11C

The emphasis on scenic artist and decorator Rosalind Robinson's website is the exquisite work itself in front of a white background.

(c)　　Detail of the painted drapery, the new False Proscenium Arch, Normansfield Theatre

rich source of new contacts. If you are just starting out, research similar businesses on the Web and note the sites where the style of presentation appeals to you. Armed with these URLs, consult a sympathetic Web designer to set your site up effectively, maximize your exposure, and also give you that invaluable second opinion on choice of images. If, like me, you find it difficult to regularly maintain and update the site, it is worth employing someone to do that for you, too."

As an added comment, Rosalind shares: "Incidentally, I fell completely in love with the creator of my website and subsequently married him. I can't recommend that course of action to everyone, but it has worked for me!"

About Interactive Portfolios

Ryan Fischer holds a BFA in theatre design and technology from Emerson College. Since graduating in 2009 he has freelanced as a lighting designer, theatre electrician, and lighting programmer at notable Boston-area venues, including the Huntington Theatre Company, the Lyric Stage Company, the Zero Arrow Theatre at American Repertory Theatre, the Cutler Majestic Theatre, and the Arsenal Center for the Arts. Recently Ryan also served as the assistant director for the Stagecraft Institute of Las Vegas and as an intern with the Integrated Systems office of Production Resource Group (PRG) Las Vegas.

In regard to interactive websites, Fischer says: "I was motivated to create a portfolio website in the first place because I knew it would be the only way to quickly and effectively reach out to people who didn't know me. Not only would a link to my online portfolio sent in an email create an instant opportunity for someone to view my work, but an online presence would, in itself, be a 24/7 personal advertisement for anyone to find via a search engine. The growing importance of the Internet in business and building a professional reputation only

underscored the fact, for me (particularly as a young designer), that if I was not online I was significantly less likely to be considered for new design work.

"The interactivity of my site (i.e., the incorporation of social media, blogs, etc.; see Figure 7.12a) was inspired by the importance of networking in the theatre industry. Theatre professionals work with others they know because they trust in each other's work; they know the quality of the other's work because of experiences working together. Without any prior mutual work experiences it is very hard for designers (especially new or young ones) to inspire a sense of trust in others who could potentially hire them, which is why we create portfolios. With online portfolios, however, which display photos and other examples of our work, those that view them are missing an important element of the equation that they need in order to hire someone—the human element. Online portfolios don't present like traditional, hard, paper-and-glue portfolios. They don't allow potential employers to walk up to us, look us in the eye, and shake our hand; they don't communicate our personality, our thoughts, ideas, or attitudes. Thus, someone looking for a new potential designer or technician is much less likely to hire someone they 'meet' online over someone they meet in person. Luckily, the Internet has evolved rapidly over the past few years, providing people like us, who market themselves online, tools to tip the balance more in our favor."

"Online tools in the form of social media, blogging, and micro-blogging (see Figure 7.12b) offer professionals with an online presence the chance to communicate with others in a new, informal, personal way, providing potential employers a much more complete picture of the person that they could potentially hire. Let's face it: The next best thing to face-to-face interaction or a phone conversation in terms of getting to know someone is through writing. By writing articles, news, and other

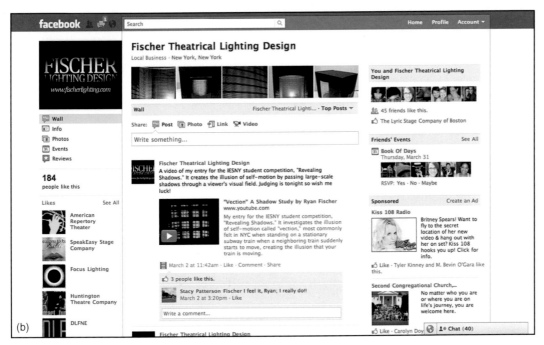

business communications that are all visible in the public domain, potential employers and clients can learn more about us simply by reading what we write. They can learn about our personal philosophies, our abilities and skills, our business interactions, our personalities, and many other nuances that define who we are that can better inform them in taking that first step to contact us. That's the virtual equivalent of getting your 'foot in the door.' Once an employer expresses interest in you, you have all the power in the world to get the job, but if they don't even notice you, or worse, ignore you because you don't have an online portfolio, your chances of employment drop significantly. Why not use all the tools available to us? What is there to lose?

"Fortunately, I have seen many benefits from my efforts in developing a creative, interactive, easy-to-use online portfolio. The most radical results have come from directors local to Boston who have simply found me via a Web search; the biggest-budget, largest-venue design I have landed since graduating was a result of this. Most of the other jobs I have been hired for, which were all design related, were achieved through a combination of my résumé and my website. I always include my Web address on any printed résumé that I hand out at job fairs, conferences, and interviews, and I have had several employers tell me that they made the decision to hire me based on the link they followed from my hard-copy résumé to my digital portfolio. Colleagues and other professionals that I work with have also given me many compliments on my website, and since they all now know where to go to find out what projects I am working on, I have significantly increased my chances of them wanting to connect with me again.

"One of the biggest benefits of maintaining an online presence, however, comes at the end of every project. I simply ask my employer, if they liked the services I provided, to leave a short review of my work on one of my social networking sites, and *voilà*—I have an instant reference and (publicly visible) testimonial for any future employers. I have found that if I want to be successful, I have to leverage the tools I have at every stage of the process in order to maximize the benefits. Believe me, the results speak for themselves."

Final Words: Things to Know When Designing Websites

What Is a Domain Name?

Wikipedia says, "The main purpose of a domain name is to provide symbolic representations, i.e., recognizable names, to mostly numerically addressed Internet resources."

What Are Domain Name Registrars?

Domain name registration and the industry itself are monitored by the Internet Corporation for Assigned Names and Numbers (ICANN), an organization that is responsible for certifying companies as registrars and handling domain names, IP addresses, and domain name extensions. Domain name registrars are companies that are allowed to directly access and modify the database of domain names that have been registered up to the current date; the database itself is maintained by a nonprofit organization.

How Do I Know I Am Buying from a Real Registrar?

To make sure that you are buying from a real registrar, you can always check with the following agencies: Internic, ICANN, and the Better Business Bureau. If you are concerned about your expenses, when choosing a domain host look for companies that are able to offer domain name registration for $10 or less per year. Be aware that there are some companies that offer a free year or two with the purchase of Web hosting. These may be a good choice for you.

What Are Some Recommended Resources for People Starting Out?

These are some of the sites that many professionals say are helpful for both beginners and experienced users alike:

- For business cards, mini cards, brochures, and logos: http://us.moo.com/

- For website templates with free Flash website design: www.wix.com/flash_websites/fish

- For website templates that keep images and videos at the forefront: http://carbonmade.com/

- For both domains and website design (with no Flash): www.godaddy.com/search/domains .aspx?isc=goaf2001ab

- For online backup, file sync, and sharing: www .dropbox.com

- For sending large graphic files: www.yousendit.com

- For CD label templates: www.onlinelabels.com/ templates/blank-label-templates

Now that we have an understanding of how to prepare a digital portfolio, we are ready for an interview. Are there guidelines on how to present it?

A PROJECT SHOULD INCLUDE A SAMPLE PAGE FROM THE BID
SPECIFICATIONS THAT WERE SENT OUT TO POTENTIAL BIDDERS
FOR THE SHOW'S RENTAL PACKAGE.

ANDY LEWIS

CHAPTER EIGHT

DIGITAL PORTFOLIO DO'S AND DON'TS

There are some basic things to remember in planning and executing a digital portfolio CD or a website. Always remember that, above all, the work should represent you and your skills.

CDs, slide presentation, and website do's:

- Save all your projects in digital format.

- Ask for help from your computer wizard friends.

- Learn new software via free tutorials on the Web.

- Save your work (on CD and for email) as a PDF file so that anyone can read it.

- Attach a short written statement and table of contents with your CD, explaining the contents of the portfolio.

- Invest in CD labeling software and supplies for professional-looking labels.

- Choose the best images of completed projects as well as media clips.

- Start your website with a few targeted pages, keeping things simple.

- Plan for easy, inexpensive, do-it-yourself maintenance.

- Look for website domains that offer templates with current options such as Flash slide shows so you can design a contemporary-looking site.

- Label things clearly and add notes as needed for the viewer's instant gratification.

- Add hyperlinks to other sites, including YouTube clips, slide shows, reviews, and the like.

- Keep graphic design elements consistent, including banners, logos, fonts, and background/foreground color and/or textures.

- Update your bio and résumé often.

- Use Web tools such as YouSendIt.com or Dropbox.com to send and share big files with images.

Show Case

Colin Dieck has worked in technical theatre since his days at Bowdoin College. This includes working as a technician during the Edinburgh Fringe Festival and as lighting designer and production manager for Cho-In Theatre of Seoul, South Korea. He now resides in Washington, D.C., and recently served as a venue manager for the Capital Fringe Festival. He has worked with Beau Jest, stage-managing *Samurai 7.0* and both stage-managing and designing lights for *The Remarkable Rooming House of Madame LeMonde* for the Provincetown Tennessee Williams Festival, 2009.

Dieck's portfolio CD consists of a series of slides (see Figures 8.1a through 8.1d). He uses very high-quality images to show how he sees lights and how he creates environments.

**FIGURES 8.1A
AND 8.1B**

Lighting designer Colin Dieck's images
from *The Remarkable Rooming House of
Madame LeMonde* for the Provincetown
Tennessee Williams Festival, 2009.
The light helps create the feeling of a
hot attic; the light angles help isolate
characters.

**FIGURES 8.1C
AND 8.1D**

Dieck's images from *The Angel
and the Woodcutter* for the Cho-In
Theatre (Korea), 2007. He creates an
environment of mystery by using color
contrast, high angles, and side lighting.

Lighting, set, and Web designer Scott Clyve has designed for Broadway, off-Broadway, regionally, and internationally. Scott's wide range of design experience has included such areas as theatre, dance, opera, industrials, and television. Scott is a member of USA Local 829 and holds a BFA from Purchase College at the State University of New York (SUNY).

Clyve chose a simple, well-organized, and sophisticated design for his website in order to present his work with clarity. He has chosen works that best represent his skills and his approach for various venues (theatre, dance, industrials, and so on). (See Figures 8.2a and 8.2b.)

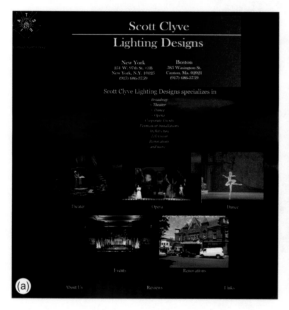

FIGURE 8.2A

Scott Clyve's website homepage showing the simplicity and organization of his Web design.

FIGURE 8.2B

Scott Clyve's *New York City Dance Alliance* detail image. He says: "This is a good image to show when interviewing for an industrial project." This show is the finale to a 22-city multinational tour that took place at the Waldorf Astoria in New York City.

CDs, slide presentation, and website don'ts:

- Label CDs by hand as though you were in a hurry or as an after-thought.

- Email large files that may not make it to the recipient's email mailbox.

- Use low-quality photos on your website or CD.

- Rely on scanning photos; it's best to start with digital images.

- Change pictures by retouching them (color correction) so they look different from the staged production.

- Use low-resolution images.

- Save original PowerPoint presentations in a CD; they may change formatting, depending on the software installed in the viewer's computer. The slides can also be accidentally altered when they are opened using different computers.

- Make the site all about distracting "Flash and splash," with random graphic design choices.

- Make your website too complicated to navigate, with confusing tabs. Too many elements will slow down the website upload time.

- Sacrifice content over Web design; your work has to be the main feature!

- Use design elements that are different from your traditional portfolio and stationery. Remember, you are your own business and brand name.

Show Case

Brendan F. Doyle is a sound designer, engineer, and artist currently pursuing his Master's in sound design at the University of Edinburgh. Doyle says that he uses a combination of portfolios to present his work. Having a combination of a traditional portfolio, a website, and a CD allows him to show off something tactile in person,

show a website from which a PDF can be downloaded, and leave behind a reference CD as a "present." (See Figures 8.3a and b.)

FIGURE 8.3A
This is a doctored sample showing what *not* to do with a CD case presentation.

FIGURE 8.3B
Sound designer Brendan F. Doyle's sample of a well-presented CD case for a production. Notice the attention to details such as the cover and the CD labels.

WE EACH HAVE BETWEEN 7 AND 17 SECONDS TO MAKE A FIRST IMPRESSION,
AND IT TAKES AN ADDITIONAL 18 ENCOUNTERS TO CHANGE THAT IMPRESSION.

STEPHANIE DEITZER (BASED ON FINDINGS FROM JOHNS HOPKINS AND OHIO UNIVERSITY)

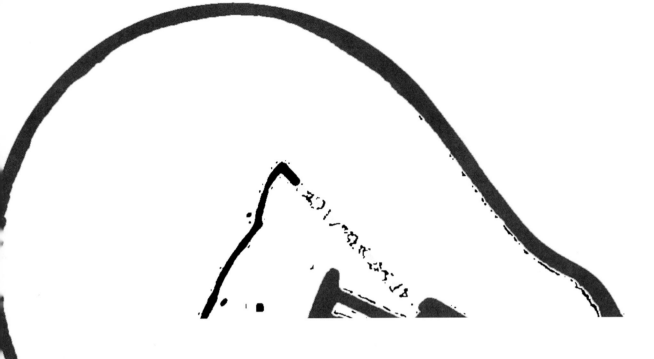

CHAPTER NINE

PORTFOLIO PRESENTATION TECHNIQUES

Leading experts in the field of interpersonal relations emphasize the importance of first impressions to set the communication dynamics of most relationships. During a first interview, designers and technicians are appraised in some specific aspects, so it is of the utmost importance to always be prepared so that you can forge productive collaborations. Good presentation skills can aid this process. In this chapter we'll review some useful techniques.

First Impressions

Stephanie Deitzer is the founder of Style at Work. With her 20-plus years of corporate experience, she empowers clients to dress stylishly, yet appropriately, for business and other life roles where confidence and capability matter—to feel good from the inside out. With her help, clients develop a look that makes them stand out in a crowd, bridges from work to play, and promotes self-confidence.

I asked her to share some key points about first impressions. Deitzer says: "We each have between seven and seventeen seconds to make a first impression, and it takes an additional eighteen encounters to change that impression. In addition to these findings from Johns Hopkins and Ohio University, the following behavioral study results from UCLA's Dr. Albert Mehrabian, professor emeritus of psychology, may surprise you. What you say accounts for only seven percent of an overall first impression you make on someone; the tone and sound of your voice, thirty-eight percent; and how you look, including facial expression, accounts for fifty-five percent. A quick way to remember this is to think verbal, vocal, and visual, with the visual component being most important."

"From a verbal and vocal perspective, when you meet someone, speak clearly and loudly enough to be heard. Will Kintish, author of *We Don't Get a Second Chance to Make a First Impression*, offers further advice in the form of an acronym: SHINE. You should *Smile*, give a *Handshake*, give good *I* (eye) contact, know their *Names*, and be *Enthusiastic*."

Deitzer also asks: "Regarding the visual, what does your appearance say about you? In my practice, I ask each of my clients to choose three words to describe how they would like the world to experience them. I allow one set of words for business and one for personal life. I then suggest that each day before they leave their home, they evaluate the consistency of their appearance, their 'words,' and the desired outcome for their day's activities."

Stephanie Deitzer concludes: "What is the first impression you would like to make? Choose three words that best convey how you would like to be perceived by others. Since people often make assumptions based on limited information, first impressions do matter. If your overall appearance seems well thought out, organized, and current, most people will assume that your other qualities are as well, and they will engage you accordingly."

The Professional and Appropriate Appearance for Portfolio Presentation

When I hear the word *professional* I think of different words with equal meanings, such as *expert, accomplished, skillful, competent, polished, top-notch*, and so on. When I hear the word *appropriate* I think of words such as *suitable* and *proper*. How do these words relate to professional appropriate appearance? I always share three stories to answer this question. First, there was the scene painter; to make ends meet she worked many jobs, so when she had to interview she hardly had time to go home and change her clothes. Second, there was the makeup/hair artist; he was into a Goth style and loved wearing dark nail polish and lots of spiky finger rings. Finally, there was the TD who looked like a supermodel. How did they each dress for interviews? They wore some field-specific garments, combined with some business attire that fit their personal style. Here are their choices:

- The scene painter wore painted painter's pants that she created herself by wearing them to the scene shop; they got covered with paint splashes that looked amazing. This is a field-specific element. In addition, she always had a clean shirt and a black blazer in her bag. The rest of her "interview attire survival kit" included an exfoliant cream to remove paint from her hands, hand cream to moisturize her hands, a hair brush, and lip gloss. She always looked neat and artistic.

- The makeup/hair artist would remove the black nail polish and finger rings whenever he was on location. His "interview attire survival kit" included odorless nail polish remover. He decided that his black leather pants, black shirt, and always sleek hair were enough of a statement for his field. He learned early on to have flawless hands if he was going to put makeup on the face of the star of a show.

- The technical director who looked like a supermodel was something fierce. Very much aware that her looks could be distracting, she always made sure to bring her motorcycle helmet, long Doc Martin boots, and her steel metal portfolio to the work sites where she interviewed. She also kept her long red hair tucked in a ponytail, and she made sure that her leather motorcycle jacket wasn't bulky but instead very stylish. When I asked her about her choices, she said: "Nobody messes with me; I can wear hard hats and manage a crew, and I can handle power tools like the best of them."

The point I am trying to make is that as designers and technicians we can add a personal style to conventional professional attire. We don't have to wear a Brooks Brothers suit; we can create our own "interview attire survival kit." A basic kit would include clean hands, hair, and clothes; a blazer or dress jacket, a clean shirt, and accessories such as a tie or necklace; plus the proper portfolio case for your specific field. The black suit jacket and the wrench in the back pocket of the TD are as effective as the vintage Chanel dress and faux brooch the costume designer wears (see Figure 9.1).

Foundations of Presenting

The *Merriam-Webster Dictionary* online defines the word *present* as an adjective, a verb, and a noun. The adjective function refers to the definition of something now existing or in progress; the verb function refers to the definition of introducing or bringing before someone; and the noun function refers to something presented—a gift or an impression. These definitions are the three keys to presenting a portfolio in a successful manner. First, the designer/technician needs to be present (now existing, involved); second, the designer/technician needs to present (bring work before) to an audience; and third, the designer/technician needs to leave a present (a lasting impression).

Being Present, Presenting, and Leaving a Present

Being present refers to affect and personal appearance (see Figure 9.2a). The designer/technician wants to make sure that his or her voice can be heard and pronunciation understood. The designer/technician must be alert and listen to the panelists' questions carefully; voice projection and listening can create instant rapport. Another factor to consider is grooming; dressing professionally and appropriately to the occasion will give confidence to the individual presenting a portfolio. It will also signal care and commitment to future possibilities.

FIGURE 9.1

From left to right: Costume designer and hair/makeup artist Courtney Irizarry wears a black blazer with vintage accessories and flawless hair and makeup to a senior portfolio review. Technical director Bill Hawkins wears a black dress jacket with a silver-gray shirt. He also wears his trademark red hair stripe. The specific color red is part of his brand; he uses it in his company logo. Scenic and costume designer Tyler Kinney dresses for success in a vintage jacket and tie. He is a great vintage shopper and has a classic Hollywood style. Photos courtesy of Kirk Miller, from the Design-Tech Senior Portfolio Reviews, Emerson College, 2009.

Presenting refers to the ability to communicate the important aspects of a project with good organization and clarity (see Figure 9.2b). A well-organized project should have a beginning, a middle, and an end. The layouts should show process and final product. Pages should be properly labeled and research sources clearly acknowledged. A designer/technician needs to make sure that he or she has all needed information, including historical period, artistic styles, source names, and technical jargon, so that the interviewers can put the information in context. Content knowledge will build trust between the parties involved.

Leaving a present refers to how the designer/technician wants to be remembered after an interview; it refers to the impression he or she wants to make on the panelists (see Figure 9.2c). Has the designer/technician included plenty of materials illustrating technique, artistic sense, versatility, and capabilities? Visual content, layout, and personal style can set a designer/technician apart from the rest or signal that he or she is right for a specific project.

FIGURE 9.2A

Being present. Illustration by former student Arika Cohen.

FIGURE 9.2B

Presenting. Illustration by former student Arika Cohen.

Doyle says: "One of the big concerns with presenting a sound design portfolio is your format. You are usually going to be presenting to very visual people, and it can be hard to show off your sound in a visual way. Try to take aural moments that were important to the production and then find an image from the production that shows the moment. Finding a picture that exemplifies the same moment that your sound exemplifies really helps to put a cue in context and will allow your audience to appreciate what you did there.

"Having a medium for your sounds to be heard is also very important. Do not assume that whomever you are meeting with will have a means to play back your audio. You want high enough quality that the people listening can appreciate all the nuances of your work, but you need to make it portable and simple; if you have ten minutes to show off your work, you simply cannot afford to spend five of those minutes setting up your speakers. High-quality headphones can be a solution if you are setting up an exhibit for people to interact with, but in an interview setting, you don't want to make your interviewer shift from listening to your work to listening to you explain it by taking the headphones on and off repeatedly, nor do you want to have only one of your interviewers able to hear at a time. Using a laptop to run a presentation program such as PowerPoint, Keynote, or PDF file that allows you to show images and play sounds is a good solution, provided you augment your laptop speakers with a lightweight and easily portable subwoofer, since very few laptops have any real frequency response below 500 Hz, which can make your work sound hollow and unfinished." (See Figures 9.3a through 9.3c.)

Show Case
Presenting a Sound Design Portfolio

Brendan F. Doyle is a sound designer, engineer, and artist currently pursuing his Master's in sound design at the University of Edinburgh. His previous work has been heard at the Lyric Stage Company of Boston, Boston Children's Theatre, Company One, Axe to Ice Productions, 11:11 Theatre Company, the University of Massachusetts at Lowell, Boston University, Wellesley College, Emerson Stage, Russell Sage College, and the New York State Theatre Institute as well as other venues in the Northeast.

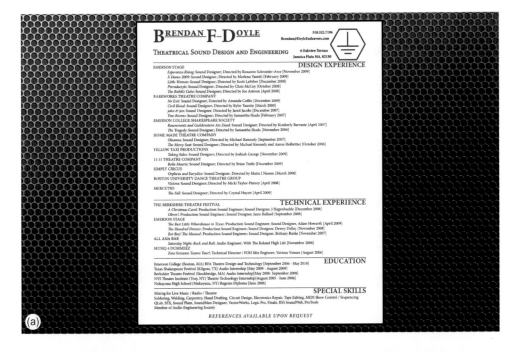

(a)

Doyle says: "I actually have three portfolios. The first is a set of storyboards for each project that has images, paperwork examples, speaker plots, and background research (shown here), with audio files to show what each show sounded like, either a montage of the whole show or a particularly interesting sequence as a whole. The second is a PDF of the storyboards with embedded audio files. The third is an audio CD with liner notes about each track and each production. Shifting between those three allows me to show off something tactile in person, show them my website where they can download the PDF, and leave behind a CD for them to refer to later."

Esperanza Rising

Produced by Emerson Stage
November 2009: At Emerson College's Cutler Majestic Theatre

Concept Statement:

Esperanza Rising is a play about homes: having one, losing one, and finding a new one. Esperanza starts off in her comfortable home in Mexico, and is torn away from that familiar place, and has to find a new space to exist in. Therefore, the sound of the show reflects that idea of home. In the beginning of the play, the sound originates from upstage center, Esperanza's Aural Home. As her home burns, and she is forced to leave her home, her Aural Home is destroyed, pulling the sound away from the hill that represents her center, and goes offstage, and further into the house. The sound continues to roam, just as Esperanza does, until she eventually becomes comfortable and establishes her new home, and the sound settles down with her.

Act II, Scene 6: Esperanza Listens in Vain for the Earth to Speak to Her

Earth Sounds:

In creating the sound of the earth, the velocity of the Earth, both in its orbit around the sun and rotation around its axis, as well as the orbit of the moon around the Earth. Those speeds were then converted to cycles per second and modulated up thirty-one octaves to bring it into the audible frequency ranges. Then using additive synthesis a timbre was developed to represent the shape and mass of the Earth, with slight variations for Esperanza's home of Aguascalientes and her new home in California.

Preshow Look: Burlap Drop

(b)

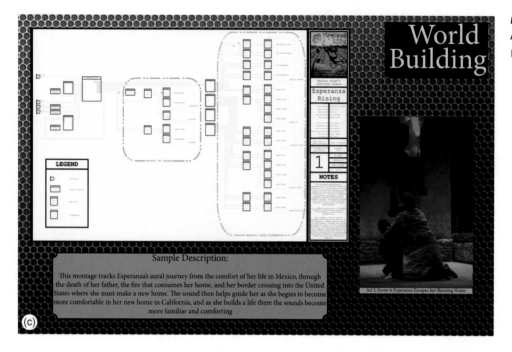

World Building

Esperanza Rising

1

NOTES

Sample Description:

This montage tracks Esperanza's aural journey from the comfort of her life in Mexico, through the death of her father, the fire that consumes her home, and her border crossing into the United States where she must make a new home. The sound then helps guide her as she begins to become more comfortable in her new home in California, and as she builds a life there the sounds become more familiar and comforting

Act I, Scene 4: Esperanza Escapes her Burning Home

(c)

Post-Interview Maintenance

Here are some guidelines that can be helpful to both the beginner and the seasoned designer/technician in maintaining presentation skills:

- Remember to introduce yourself right away and take a few moments to meet the interviewers, make eye contact, share general information, and the like.

- Make sure that you have plenty of current résumés and business cards to give to reviewers and prospective employers.

- Designer/technicians must review and update their portfolios regularly and make it a habit that allows them to be in touch with their work.

- Plan a summary for each project (basic concept, key techniques, and short anecdotes); make sure they have a beginning, middle, and end.

- Make sure the portfolio layout is clearly organized (by project) so it shows skill, versatility, and progress. Plan transitions between projects.

- Start strong and end strong; get the reviewers' attention and leave them wanting more.

Self-Evaluation

After the interview, it is important to integrate received feedback, to prepare for future opportunities. Since designer/technicians can be their own worst critics, it is important to do a self-assessment in a self-supporting, honest, and caring way. A neutral evaluation should include the panelists' feedback and future goals or next steps. A self-assessment questionnaire would include questions about style, voice, rapport, and content. These are some examples:

- *Style.* Were personal grooming and appearance favorable, average, or unfavorable, and why? What are the next steps?

- *Voice.* Were volume and articulation favorable, average, or unfavorable, and why? What are the next steps?

- *Rapport.* Were conversations empathic, with accurate listening and comprehensive answers? Was this aspect favorable, average, or unfavorable, and why? What are the next steps?

- *Content.* Was there enough preparation, research, work samples, and subject knowledge? Was this aspect favorable, average, or unfavorable, and why? What are the next steps?

Networking: What's Next?

Networking refers to the creation of an ever-expanding list of future opportunities, resources, and business relations. Since most industry people in each region refer to the design-tech field as small community, six degrees of separation almost always applies. Designers and technicians should always keep this in mind. They should keep business affiliates' names, resources, and places on their radar, even if they don't get a job. This network knowledge may help with future connections and projects. At the end of a meeting they can plant seeds to follow up. For example: "I look forward to hearing from you soon," "I would really like to work with you," "Let's talk about possible future collaborations," and so on. Sending a letter (before or after an interview) expressing interest in a company can open doors. Sending a thank-you note after an interview is a very good thing; it demonstrates good interpersonal manners and appreciation for someone else's time. Asking for feedback is also helpful. For example, if after an interview students think that they are not going to get into their first choice for a grad program, they should ask the reviewers for feedback and what next steps they would recommend. The most powerful networking tool, in my opinion, is a résumé. It can leave a lasting impression, it can be submitted prior to an interview to create interest, or it can be left afterward as a present.

If the résumé is one of the "presents" we leave after our interview, how do we make it unique? What is an effective résumé?

WORKBOOK

What presentation techniques would I want to focus on for my next portfolio review?

_____

_____

_____

_____

_____

_____

_____

PRACTICE YOUR PRESENTATION . . . IF YOU HAVE A GOOD IDEA OF WHAT YOU
WANT TO SAY, YOU WILL COME ACROSS AS BEING CONFIDENT.

DAVID C. ("KIP") SHAWGER, JR.

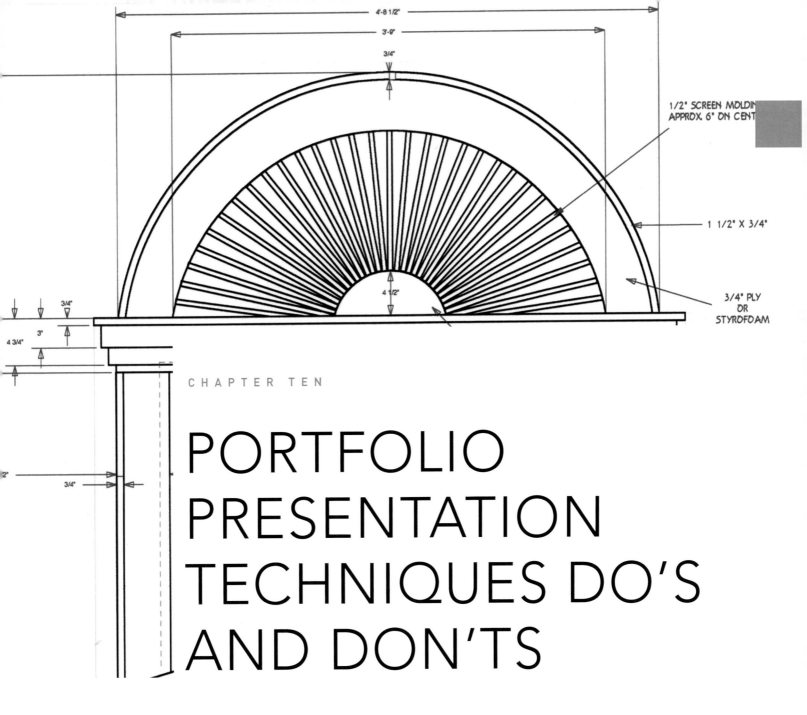

1/2" SCREEN MOLDIN
APPROX. 6" ON CENT

1 1/2" X 3/4"

3/4" PLY
OR
STYROFOAM

4'-8 1/2"

3'-9"

3/4"

4 1/2"

3/4"

3"

4 3/4"

2"

3/4"

CHAPTER TEN

PORTFOLIO PRESENTATION TECHNIQUES DO'S AND DON'TS

The following are the teaching points I usually share with students and colleagues.

Do's

Do the following:

- Plan a beginning, a middle, and an end for your portfolio presentation.

- Take time to meet the interviewers and establish eye contact.

- Project your voice and speak clearly.

- Remember good grooming and professional manners and appearance.

- Review your portfolio materials often and always prior to your interview.

- Plan a short summary to describe each project.

- Make sure the portfolio layout is clear.

- Make sure that project sequences don't compete with each other.

- Make sure projects are labeled and keyed properly.

- Make sure to have source lists for research, materials, and the like.

- Have support materials in the back pocket of your portfolio.

- Have updated résumés and business cards.

Show Case

David C. ("Kip") Shawger, Jr., is the former Kennedy Center/American College Theatre Festival national design vice chair. Currently he is associate chair and head of design in the Department of Theatre and Dance at Ball State University. He has been adjudicating students' work for many years. He adds the following do's to our list:

- Dress appropriately. A neat, clean appearance is a must. A tie isn't necessary, but take a moment to select clothing that makes you feel good about yourself.

- Personal hygiene is also noteworthy (clean hair, clean fingernails, etc.). You don't get a second chance at making a first impression.

- Practice your presentation . . . but don't memorize. If you memorize and get lost, you will not look good. However, if you have a good idea of what you want to say, you will come across as being confident. Present your portfolio to friends when practicing.

- Have your friends ask questions as you practice. This will make you more relaxed when the actual presentation takes place.

- Find out as much as you can about your prospective employer or school. It never hurts to know to whom you are talking.

- Put your best work in the front and in the rear of your portfolio. People more readily remember what they see first and last.

- Practice smiling and try to be pleasant. This will relax you.

Don'ts

Do not:

- Present a disorganized portfolio.
- Avoid looking at your interviewers.
- Look like you just finished pulling an all-nighter.
- Be badly groomed, including unkempt fingernails.
- Forget sketch labels or keys.
- Have different competing projects adjacent to each other.
- Use bad photographs or incomplete research or sketches.
- Use loose pages.
- End with a weak project.
- Forget to give credit to other artists' work featured with a project.
- Ignore questions or get defensive.
- Forget to pass around your résumé and/or business card.

Show Case

Kip Shawger adds the following don'ts to our list:

- Don't be cocky. Self-confidence is one thing, but coming across as a "know it all" is a very big turnoff.
- Don't rush. Take your time. While you may have a limited interview time, if you rush, you run the risk of getting flustered. If you take your time, you'll come across as composed. Know your time limit and plan on staying within your allotment. If you do this, you won't need to rush.
- Don't expect to be perfect. The more you expect of yourself, the more pressure you will feel. And feeling pressure can cause you to make any number of mistakes in your presentation.
- Don't spend too much time explaining why you did something or what your director wanted. The more time you spend talking about "why" leaves too little time spent on ideas.
- Above all, never apologize for any part of your design work. Be proud of it. If you have to make an apology for your work, it isn't worth putting in your portfolio.

EMPLOYERS LOOK AT RÉSUMÉS TO GAIN A SENSE OF YOUR

PROFESSIONALISM, RELEVANT EXPERIENCE, AND POTENTIAL TO FIT WELL WITHIN

THE EXISTING TEAM.

LESLIE CHIU

CHAPTER ELEVEN

DESIGN-TECH RÉSUMÉS, CVS, BUSINESS CARDS, AND STATIONERY

A résumé is a comprehensive document that contains a short account of a designer/technician's career. It is designed with a target audience in mind; it summarizes individual achievements and lists professional qualifications. It can be one or two pages long and, when well executed, can be a really powerful networking tool.

A curriculum vitae, or CV, is a longer, more detailed synopsis. Whereas the goal of résumé writing is to be concise, the CV is more detailed and includes a summary of educational and academic backgrounds and affiliations; teaching, research experience, and publications; and awards, honors, and grants. In the United States a CV is used in applying for academic, scientific, and research positions or when applying for fellowships or grants.

A Winning Résumé: Introductory Words of Wisdom

In the national bestselling book *The Pathfinder*, author Nicholas Lore describes a résumé as a "… tool with one specific purpose: to win an interview." This is the number-one purpose of a résumé; "if it doesn't (win), it isn't an effective résumé. It presents you in the best light. It convinces the employer that you have what it takes to be successful in this new position or career." Lore further adds that a résumé needs to be "so pleasing to the eye that the reader is enticed to pick it up and read it. It 'whets the appetite,' stimulates interest in meeting you and learning more about you. It inspires the prospective employer to pick up the phone and ask you to come in for an interview."

Intent and Purpose of a Résumé

The Rockport Institute website (www.rockportinstitute .com/résumés.html) contains an award-winning guide for résumé writing by author Nicholas Lore. He describes the following possible reasons to have a résumé:

- To pass the employer's screening process
- To provide up-to-date contact information

- To establish you as a professional person with high standards and excellent writing skills, based on the fact that the résumé is so well done
- To have something to give to potential employers, your job-hunting contacts, and professional references
- To use as a covering piece or addendum to another form of job application, as part of a grant or contract proposal, or as an accompaniment to graduate school or other application
- To put in an employer's personnel files
- To help you clarify your direction, qualifications, and strengths, boost your confidence, or start the process of committing to a job or career change

How to Present Your Work History and Education

"Most résumés are not much more than a collection of 'evidence' and various facts about your past," writes Lore. "By evidence, we mean all the mandatory information you must include on your résumé: work history with descriptions, dates, education, affiliations, list of software mastered, etc. All this evidence is best placed in the second half of the résumé. Put the hot stuff in the beginning and all this less exciting information afterward." The evidence includes some or all of the following:

- Experience (also Professional History or Professional Experience)
  - List jobs in reverse chronological order; focus on the most recent and/or relevant jobs
- Education (also Education and Training)
  - List educational entries in reverse chronological order, degrees or licenses first, followed by certificates and advanced training, college major and distinctions or awards

- If you are working on an uncompleted degree, include the degree and afterward, in parentheses, the expected date of completion: BS (expected 200*X*).

- If you didn't finish college, start with a phrase describing the field you studied, then the school and the dates (the fact that there was no degree may be missed)

- Awards
  - If the only awards received were in school, put these under the Education section
  - Mention what the award was for, if you can (or simply "for outstanding accomplishment" or "outstanding performance"); this section is almost a must if you have received awards

- Professional Affiliations
  - Include only those that are current, relevant, and impressive; include leadership roles if appropriate

- Publications
  - Include only if you have published; summarize if there are many, and include juried articles and chapter contributions to books or specialty magazines

- Personal Interests
  - Personal interests can indicate a skill or area of knowledge that is related to the goal, such as photography for someone in public relations or carpentry and woodworking for someone in construction management

- References
  - You may put "References available upon request" at the end of your résumé, or you can list three names with titles and email addresses; you can also bring a separate sheet of references to the interview, to be given to the employer upon request

---

The Design-Tech Résumé: Specific Expectations

Design-tech résumés have formatting guidelines that may differ from most traditional business résumés. To expand the information provided by the Rockport Institute, I've reached out to Leslie Chiu from the company Building Better Job-Seeking Skills (www .buildingbetterjobseekingskills.com). Leslie presents workshops and provides professional consultations on résumés, interviewing, and building careers in the entertainment industry. She has also worked as a production and stage manager for 15 years. She is currently the production manager and a lecturer in theatre arts at Brandeis University in Massachusetts.

Leslie describes the expectations for résumés in the design-tech field as follows: "Employers look at résumés to gain a sense of your professionalism, relevant experience, and potential to fit well within the existing team. Finding the right fit is important in any industry, but let's face it, there are a lot of strong personalities in theatre, and all of our work is dependent on collaboration, so finding the right fit is important for everyone. This allows you to use your style and personality to show how you are the unique combination of skill and fit for which the employer is looking. However, remember the goal of your résumé is to show your professionalism, skills, and, ultimately, to get you the interview where you can best represent yourself."

Leslie continues: "Remember to consider the perspective of the person who will be reviewing your résumé in the hiring process. Most employers go through a screening process, especially when they have several positions available. Résumés are often skimmed in less than thirty seconds, to be sorted into 'yes,' 'maybe,' and 'no' piles. You can avoid the 'no' pile by leading the reader's focus to specific areas. Your area of specialty should be clear. Write the résumé for the ultimate job you want, not what you would settle for in the meantime. If you are interested in several areas, you should have a separate résumé focused on each area."

Résumé Formatting

When it comes to general formatting, I have noticed that design-tech résumés tend to be organized in "chunks" via paragraphs or columns. Leslie Chiu observes that the formatting can be divided in two categories, namely a list format, which is more favored, and a paragraph format. She explains, "For the list format, consider how you subdivide your listing of positions. For instance, a scenic designer with equal amounts of design and assistant design experience should consider a scenic design section at the top, followed by an assistant scenic design section. This way, even if the most recent job was as an assistant designer, it is the most recent scenic design position the reviewer will see first. And the supporting sections shouldn't be larger or appear to carry more weight than the top section, which is presumably your desired position.

"For the paragraph format favored by administrators and some production positions," Leslie continues, "consider the order in which you list your responsibilities. Make sure that the tasks that illustrate the most significant responsibilities and skills are listed first. Include only the most relevant highlights of the position, not a job description. To round out the focus of your résumé, make the most of your Special Skills or Related Skills section by including specifics on all skills that could be relevant to the position for which

you are applying. Consider including things such as specific software programs and equipment you have been trained to use, such as specific light boards, types of welding methods, and so on.

"Potential employers often request references or recommendation letters," Leslie adds. "There are a few key rules to follow. Most important, always remember to ask if someone will be a reference for you before listing them as a reference. Getting an unexpected call for a reference means that the reference will not be well prepared to discuss your work. It is also a good idea to find out in advance what the reference would say about you, especially about what you need to work on professionally. You should try to match the references you provide to the specific job so that the reference will be able to discuss your qualifications relevant to the job requirements. The same applies for letters of recommendation. Last, provide your reference with information, including the job description, required qualifications, and why you are interested in the job. When asking for a letter of recommendation, you should also provide any specific instructions and requests from the employer, the name, title, and address of the recipient, and the deadline. The person acting as a reference or writing the letter of recommendation is doing you a favor, so be respectful of his or her time and make it easy for that person to give you a good reference."

Finally, both Leslie and I agree that a résumé needs to be maintained and updated regularly. "Keep an all-inclusive list of positions and skills as you gain them, and be prepared to edit each résumé that you send. Use the most relevant positions and information dependent on the position for which you are applying. In the entertainment industry you never know how your previous work may factor into your future work."

A Blueprint for an Effective Résumé Presentation

Once the formatting and the list of credits have been sorted out, you must plan the layout or organization of the résumé. This, of course, will depend on the number of credits to be included. There are many books, software programs, and websites dedicated to résumé design that you can use as a reference, but perhaps the most important aspects to consider in developing your résumé are that it complements your portfolio and that it represents your personality and professional approach. Sometimes it is necessary to have multiple résumés (that is, one for design and one for technical work) that can be used to apply for jobs where a specific talent is needed. Other times we need to include multiple credits when the job requires multiple skills (for example, a technical director's position that includes teaching stagecraft and designing a show for the organization's season).

Remember that just like your portfolio, your résumé will have a beginning (your name, expertise, and contact information), a middle (work credits), and an end (related experience, education, and so on). For students and established professionals, a one-page résumé is appropriate. In academic settings, the CV is the norm; it has four or more pages. In all cases, the formatting needs to be clear and consistent, and it needs to be updated regularly.

When enumerating your work credits, keep in mind that you need to include the following:

- Job title

- Production name: show, special event, etc.

- Date of production

- Production company, production agent, producer, etc.

- Artistic director, director, choreographer, supervisor, etc.

- Venue: theatre, TV studio, museum, etc.

Show Case

Design-Tech Résumé Formatting Samples

The information in your résumé can be arranged in different ways, but the line entries, paragraphs, or columns must be consistent within the whole document's body. This way the reader can make sense of the information at a glance (see Figure 11.1).

Sometimes there are a lot of credits to be included. When more information needs to be included in a résumé, the format could be organized into various columns and presented as a double-sided document, still keeping the information in consistent order (see Figures 11.2a through 11.3b).

When you're choosing paper, fonts, and effects, make sure that they represent your personality while looking professional. Make sure that the paper color and the fonts will photocopy well in black and white; often a producer will make copies of your résumé, so you have to plan for it to be readable and look good in black and white (Figures 11.4a and 11.4b).

When you're choosing a logotype, make sure it represents you as an artist. Color, shape, and font should be part of the whole design. The same formatting principles apply but with added personality (see Figures 11.5a and 11.5b.)

CORY RODRIGUEZ
Scenic Designer

1929 Porters Point Rd
Colchester VT, 05446
e-mail: csrodriguez29@gmail.com
phone: (203) 232-5346

2007-2010 PROFESSIONAL PRODUCTIONS
Scenic Designer, The Full Monty
Stowe Theatre Guild, Stowe VT, Director Carole Vasta Folley
Assistant Scenic Designer, Treasure Island
Roundhouse Theatre, Bethesda MD, Designer Jeff Modereger
Assistant Scenic Designer, 42nd Street
North Shore Music Theatre, Beverly MA, Designer Jeff Modereger
Assistant Scenic Designer, Souvenir
Vermont Stage Company, Burlington VT, Designer Jeff Modereger
Scenic Painter, Inspecting Carol
Vermont Stage Company, Burlington VT, Designer Jeff Modereger
Scenic Painter, On The Verge
Town Hall Theatre, Middlebury VT, Designer Melissa Lourie
Scenic Painter, Opus
Vermont Stage Company, Burlington VT, Designer Jeff Modereger

2005-2009 ACADEMIC PRODUCTIONS
SCENIC DESIGNER (ROYALL TYLER THEATRE, UNIVERSITY OF VERMONT)
Festival of One Acts 2006-2009
The Last Five Years Director, Catherine Durickas
The Seagull Director, Peter Jack Tkatch
ASSISTANT SCENIC DESIGNER, DESIGNER JEFF MODEREGER
Ring Round the Moon
MacBeth
The Compleat Female Stage Beauty
SCENIC ARTIST
Beyond Therapy   The Underpants
Hair   Miss Firecracker Contest
La Ronde   Arms of the Man
Found A Peanut

AWARDS
2010 KCACTF National Barbizon Award for Excellence in Scenic Design Region 1

RELATED SKILLS
Scenery Construction and Scenic Painting
Hand Drafting and Model Building
Furniture Upholstery and Refurbishing
Props Construction
Basic Lighting, Sound, and Costume Knowledge
Adobe Photoshop, Illustrator, InDesign and Flash knowledge

EDUCATION & INTERNSHIPS
2004-2007 Theatre/Scenic Design, University of Vermont
2007-2009 BS, Graphic Design, Champlain College
2010 O'Neill Center Internship in Scenic Design

REFERENCES
Jeff Modereger, Chair, UVM Dept. of Theatre   Peter Jack Tkatch, Director
jeffrey.modereger@uvm.edu   ptkatch@zoo.uvm.edu

FIGURE 11.1

The information in Cory Rodriguez's scenic design résumé includes professional experience, academic experience, and related skills. Notice that the name and title at the top of the page are clearly legible; contact information is included and important memberships are highlighted. The information is organized in various paragraphs, with key points in the same order for each one of the projects mentioned. Adding color to the heading is a simple way to create a stationery page.

FIGURES 11.2A AND 11.2B

Michele Macadaeg's costume technician résumé lists the information organized into columns. It includes professional design experience, related experience, education, and references. Notice that contact information is included.

MICHELE MACADAEG

57 Grove Street
Dover, NH 05820
941.447.4484
macadaeg@mac.com

PRODUCTION EXPERIENCE

Stitcher	Erin Jean Designs; Ballroom Dance Costumes, Newburyport, MA	2006
Draper/Stitcher	Wanda's World, Off-Broadway, New York City	2008
Draper/Stitcher	The Great American Trailer Park Musical; National Tour.	2007
Swatcher	Romeo and Juliet Minnesota Opera, Minneapolis	2007
Costume Design Assistant	Weston Playhouse Theatre, Weston VT.	2007
Stitcher	Sarasota Opera, Sarasota	2007
First Hand/Stitcher	Asolo Repertory Theatre, Sarasota	2003-2007
Ast. Costume Shop Supervisor	Chautauqua Opera, Chautauqua	2004-2005
Costume Design Assistant	Starlight Productions, Pittsburgh	2003
Women's Head	Carnegie Mellon University, Pittsburgh	2002
Resident Costume Design Assistant	Huntington Theatre Company, Boston	2001 - 2002
Costume Shop Manager	Walnut Hill School, Natick, MA.	2001
Shop Assistant	American Repertory Theatre, Cambridge	2000 - 2001
First Hand	Emerson Stage, Boston	2000 - 2001
First Hand	Commonwealth Shakespeare Company, Boston	2000
First Hand	Massachusetts General Hospital Mural Project, Boston	1999
Costume Shop Co- Manager/Cutter	Emerson Summer Stage, Boston	1999
Stitcher	Michael Menger's Really Big Dance Company, Portland, OR.	1997
Stitcher	Portland Stage, Portland, OR.	1997

EDUCATION

B.F.A. Theatrical Design Tech.	Emerson College, Boston	May, 2000

AWARDS

Evvy Award for Excellence in Theater Design, Emerson College, Boston		May, 2000

REFERENCES

Jennifer Caprio	Adrienne Webber	Anita Canzian
Costume Designer	Costume Shop Manager	Head Draper
25th Annual Putnam County Spelling Bee	Barter Theatre	Huntington Theatre Co.
17 W. 20th St. 6E	133 W. Main St.	264 Huntington Ave.
New York, NY. 10011	Abingdon, VA. 24210	Boston, MA. 02115
917.575.0225	276.619.3306	617.629.7085

(a)

RELATED EXPERIENCE

Draper/Stitcher	Wanda's World, Off-Broadway, New York City	2008
Draper/Stitcher	The Great American Trailer Park Musical; National Tour.	2007
Swatching (in NYC)	Romeo and Juliet Minnesota Opera, Minneapolis	2007
Costume Design Assistant	Weston Playhouse Theatre, Weston VT.	2007
Stitcher	Sarasota Opera, Sarasota	2007
First Hand/Stitcher	Asolo Repertory Theatre, Sarasota	2003-2007
Ast. Costume Shop Supervisor	Chautauqua Opera, Chautauqua	2004-2005
Costume Design Assistant	Starlight Productions, Pittsburgh	2003
Women's Head	Carnegie Mellon University, Pittsburgh	2002
Resident Costume Design Assistant	Huntington Theatre, Boston	2001 - 2002
Costume Shop Manager	Walnut Hill School, Natick, MA.	2001
Shop Assistant	American Repertory Theatre, Cambridge	2000 - 2001
Cutter	Emerson Stage, Boston	2000 - 2001
First Hand	Commonwealth Shakespeare Company, Boston	2000
First Hand	Massachusetts General Hospital Mural Project, Boston	1999
Costume Shop Co- Manager/Cutter	Emerson Summer Stage, Boston	1999
Stitcher	Michael Menger's Really Big Dance Company, Portland, OR.	1997
Stitcher	Portland Stage, Portland, OR.	1997

EDUCATION

B.F.A. Theatrical Design Tech.	Emerson College, Boston	May, 2000

AWARDS

Evvy Award for Excellence in Theater Design, Emerson College, Boston		May, 2000

REFERENCES

Jennifer Caprio	Adrienne Webber	Cathleen Crocker-Perry
Costume Designer	Costume Shop Manager	Costume Designer/Draper
25th Annual Putnam County Spelling Bee	Barter Theatre	7728 Abbott St. #1
17 W. 20th St. 6E	133 W. Main St.	Pittsburgh, PA. 15221
New York, NY. 10011	Abingdon, VA. 24210	941.775.5228
917.575.0225	276.619.3306	

(b)

Tracy Wertheimer's lighting résumé has a lot of credits; she has organized it into various columns using effective margins and a clear organization of information.

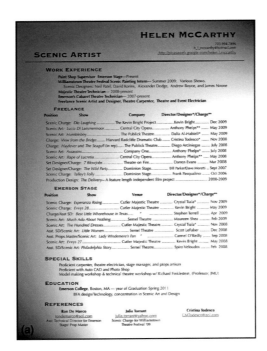

(a)

(b)

Your résumé's paper color, letter fonts, and graphics need to photocopy well in black and white in case copies are made. Notice the contrasts in the two versions of Helen McCarthy's résumé for scenic painting. The grading in the two-tone résumé may not copy well, though it will email well as a PDF file.

(a)

FIGURE 11.5A

Jenny Lind Bryant's wardrobe-styling résumé has a dynamic heading and uses original artwork as a page logo. This heading could easily be used for stationery page or a brochure.

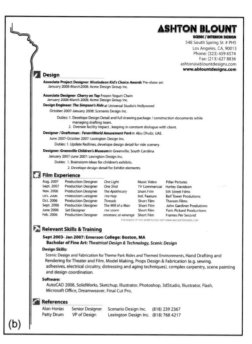

(b)

FIGURE 11.5B

Ashton Blount's scenic/interior design résumé is contemporary and confident. It represents an individual working on the West and East Coasts in theatre, film, TV, and advertising.

The Bio and the Curriculum Vitae

Your bio is a very brief synopsis of accomplishments pertaining to your profession. You use your bio to create a summary of your life's activities that relate to your work in your field of concentration. Your bio should not read like an online CV; it should not be too detailed. Bios usually run with a word count of 75 to 150 words, depending on the organization's catalogue space or the Web page space. They may also be longer, depending on the individual's status and accomplishments.

The box contains an example of a bio with a word count of 147 words.

Rafael Jaen has been designing costumes for over 25 years. He is a member of the prestigious United Scenic Artists (USA) Chapter 829. Recent theatre works include the Lyric Stage's *Kiss Me, Kate* and Beau Jeste's *Madame LeMonde* (Tennessee Williams Provincetown Festival, 2009), both recipients of the Hubie Award and nominated for IRNE Awards for Best Costume Design 2009. Recent film credits include costumes for the PBS/American Experience series *God in America*. Jaen is the design, technology, and management co-chair for the Kennedy Center American Theater College (KCACTF) Region 1. His work has been featured in full-page articles in the

Boston Globe, Boston Herald, Theatre Design & Technology (*TD &T*), *LIVE DESIGN*, and USITT's *Sightlines*. Jaen is the recipient of the USITT 2008 Grant, *Modern Tailoring Techniques*. The second edition of his book *Developing and Maintaining a Design-Tech Portfolio* (Focal Press, 2006) is scheduled for publication in Fall 2011.

A CV or curriculum vitae is an account of a person's education, qualifications, and experience. It is formatted as a document with multiple pages. It is used mostly in academic settings. It's important to know that the term *curriculum vitae* means résumé, and the word *résumé* means CV, in some countries across Latin America and in Europe. The information in a CV would include a detailed, expanded account of someone's career. Someone with 20 years of experience in the business would have a CV that includes detailed credits from all those 20 years. The website http://jobsearch.about.com/cs/curriculumvitae/a/curriculumvitae.htm features good CV samples and helpful information.

These are some elements that should be included in a CV:

- Name, title, and contact information
- Detailed educational degrees and certificates
- Professional appointments (commissioner, chair, vetted chairing panels, etc.)
- Committee service (at a school or organization)
- Publications (including journal articles, feature articles, book chapters, books, etc.)
- Professional experience (credits in the fields of expertise)
- Teaching experience
- Invited presentations at regional and national conferences
- Professional memberships
- Awards and honors
- Research grants

Other Marketing Tools: Business Cards and Brochures

Business cards and brochures are personal networking tools that can highlight an individual's personality, artistry, and area of expertise. There are many options for business card design and brochures; many digital programs offer images and templates. Some designers also use postcards to promote a particular aspect of their businesses.

Tips on Successful Use of Business Cards and Brochures as a Marketing Tool (or as a "Present")

Here are some helpful tips in creating and using business cards and brochures in your marketing efforts:

- The design of a business card or brochure should be professional and attractive. Logos and color schemes become part of the designer's "brand."
- Cards should minimally list the designer/technician's name, field of expertise, phone number, and email address. A card could also list key affiliations and a business address. If logos are included, they should match the logos in the professional's stationery, brochures, and websites.
- Brochures should show a sampler of the work of the designer/technician. They work as a mini-portfolio with a beginning, a middle, and an end. The opening page is the bio, the middle section highlights skills (using images), and the end offers quotes and other points of interest. Colors need to be coordinated with the résumé and the business card.
- When handed out, marketing items should be in good shape and always clean. Designers and

technicians should always carry some business cards with them so they can be distributed when the occasion arises.

- Designer/technicians should always be prepared to hand out and exchange business cards in informal meetings and settings.

- In addition, they should always add prospective employers to their contact list upon receiving a business card.

Show Case

Stephanie Deitzer is the founder of *Style at Work*. With her 20-plus years of corporate experience, she empowers clients to dress stylishly, yet appropriately, for business and other life roles where confidence and capability matter—to feel good from the inside out. With her help, clients develop a look that makes them stand out in a crowd, bridges from work to play, and promotes self-confidence. Marketing materials help her in that endeavor (see Figures 11.6a through 11.6c).

Joe Rossi has designed makeup for film, theatre, television, and opera. Joe has worked as head of the makeup department for companies such as Disney, Showtime, Warner Brothers, Miramax, Samuel Goldwyn Films, Twentieth Century Fox, and many popular shows at NBC and ABC. He has provided makeup services for many national political figures, including President Bill Clinton, Hillary Rodham Clinton, and Vice President Al Gore. He was makeup designer for the Ronald Reagan and George Bush Inaugural Concerts at the Kennedy Center in Washington, D.C.

When I asked Rossi about the design behind his résumé, business cards, and website, he said: "The main idea behind the advertising and marketing use of my brochure and website is to show the diversity of my business. Although one function is to draw in new

(a)

FIGURES 11.6A, 11.6B, AND 11.6C
Stephanie Deitzer uses note cards that contain her logo (brand) and evoke her website design. Her cards reflect her serene personality and field of expertise. Notice the design choices used for both shown here; they create a brand by using specific color palette and logotype.

(b)

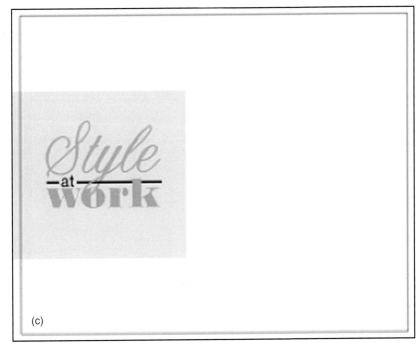

(c)

clients, the secondary function has been to market myself to existing clients in a new way. Many of the companies and designers using my services would normally hire different artists to design beauty makeup, prosthetics, and handmade hairpieces. My advertising shows that I provide full-service design and creation." (See Figures 11.7a through 11.7c.)

We now have our portfolio case, portfolio materials, and our résumé. What's the next step?

(a)

(b)

(c)

WORKBOOK

What information would I like to include
in my résumé, and how will I format it?

_____

_____

_____

_____

_____

_____

_____

IF YOU REALIZE THAT A GREAT RÉSUMÉ CAN BE YOUR TICKET TO GETTING EXACTLY THE JOB YOU WANT, YOU MAY BE ABLE TO MUSTER SOME GENUINE ENTHUSIASM FOR CREATING A REAL MASTERPIECE.

NICHOLAS LORE

CHAPTER TWELVE

DESIGN-TECH RÉSUMÉS, CVS, BUSINESS CARDS, AND STATIONERY DO'S AND DON'TS

A résumé is in many ways a work of art; it requires skill acquired by practice, learning, and observation. It also requires a conscious use of creative imagination, especially in the production of its aesthetic. The following excerpt from *The Pathfinder: How to Choose or Change Your Career for a Lifetime of Satisfaction and Success* (www.rockportinstitute.com/résumés.html) helps illustrate my theory.

The Pathfinder: How to Choose or Change Your Career for a Lifetime of Satisfaction and Success
by Nicholas Lore

It is a mistake to think of your résumé as a history of your past, as a personal statement, or as some sort of self-expression. Sure, most of the content of any résumé is focused on your job history. But write from the intention to create interest, to persuade the employer to call you. If you write with that goal, your final product will be very different than if you write to inform or catalog your job history. Most people write a résumé because everyone knows that you have to have one to get a job. They write their résumé grudgingly, to fulfill this obligation. Writing the résumé is only slightly above filling out income tax forms in the hierarchy of worldly delights. If you realize that a great résumé can be your ticket to getting exactly the job you want, you may be able to muster some genuine enthusiasm for creating a real masterpiece rather than the feeble products most people turn out.

Questions a Résumé Must Answer

- What key qualifications will the employer be looking for?

- What qualifications will be most important to them?

- Which of these are your greatest strengths?

- What are the highlights of your career to date that should be emphasized?

- What should be deemphasized?

- What things about you and your background make you stand out?

- What are your strongest areas of skill and expertise? Knowledge? Experience?

- What are some other skills you possess—perhaps more auxiliary skills?

- What are characteristics you possess that make you a strong candidate (things like innovative, hard-working, strong interpersonal skills, ability to handle multiple projects simultaneously under tight deadlines)?

- What are the three or four things you feel have been your greatest accomplishments?

- What was produced as a result of your greatest accomplishments?

- Can you quantify the results you produced in numerical or other specific terms?

- What were the two or three accomplishments of that particular job?

- What were the key skills you used in that job? What did you do in each of those skill areas?

- What sorts of results are particularly impressive to people in your field?

- What results have you produced in these areas?

- What are the "buzzwords" that people in your field expect you to use in lieu of a secret club handshake? These should be included in your résumé.

Design-Tech Résumés, CVs, Business Cards, and Stationery Do's

After many years of reviewing résumés at USITT (and other venues), plus researching effective ways to use it, I have observed that there are some simple guidelines that have proven very helpful. Let's take a look at those guidelines now.

- Always include your contact information, especially your email address and business phone number, at the top of your résumé.

- Remember to include your expertise (for example, costume technician) as part of the title so your résumé can be archived properly. It is okay to have different résumés with different titles for different skills.

- The identification, title, and contact info on the top of your résumé should match the information on your business card. It is best if the font and style match as well so that you create a brand for yourself.

- It is recommended to use the same banner design at the top of your résumé for the top of your stationery.

- Clear presentation, good grammar, and correct spelling will always help make a good impression. Make sure to proofread your documents before making many copies.

- In preparing a digital résumé, make sure it is in Microsoft Word format so it can be edited and updated easily, then save it to a folder in your computer where you can easily find it.

- When planning to email or upload a résumé to a website, save it first as a PDF file. When you send a résumé as an email attachment, PDF files can be opened easily by any prospective employer. Make sure to label the file with your name—for example, RafaelJaenrésumé.pdf.

- Most employers prefer to read your career history in reverse-chronological order (starting with the most recent credits). It is also important to include your title on the job, the venue, show, director, direct supervisor, and so on. Include what's relevant for each project you've completed.

- The number of résumé pages should correspond with your years of experience. The consensus seems to be to keep the résumé between one single-sided page to one double-sided page.

- Save more detailed information, such as community service, courses taught, juried articles, and the like, for your CV.

Design-Tech Résumés, CVs, Business Cards, and Stationery Don'ts

Here's what *not* to do:

- Never describe your experience inaccurately or alter the show credits. Such oversights may be interpreted as lies.

- Avoid typos and misspelling of names of contributors, directors, and others.

- Avoid artsy layouts or overwhelming designs that won't photocopy well. Always make a test run to see how your résumé looks when photocopied or how easy it is to email and open the file.

- Avoid storytelling. Be careful not to fill it with unnecessary information regarding hobbies, personal philosophies, and the like. The résumé should really be a well-organized summary of your credits, a tool that will help you find a job match to your skills.

WHEN LOOKING AT A PORTFOLIO, THE REVIEWER WILL NOT ONLY BE LOOKING AT THE QUALITY OF THE ART, BUT DOES IT COMMUNICATE A PROCESS? IS THERE EVIDENCE OF COLLABORATION?

DONNA MEESTER

CHAPTER THIRTEEN

ESTABLISHING GOALS AND REVIEWING, CHOOSING, AND UPDATING WORK

When I started to collect materials for this book, I wanted to be able to offer different options to readers who are planning to develop and maintain their portfolio. We can establish goals and review our objectives, but we still have to choose the work that best represents us and update our portfolio often. Since rules aren't set in stone, I wanted to suggest some common guidelines or points that design-tech professionals need to think about.

In this chapter I use the comments of three of my colleagues to motivate a dialogue and then add my own "teaching points" to help explain the portfolio planning and development process.

Putting it Together: The Large Case
by Anthony R. Phelps

Anthony R. Phelps has chaired portfolio reviews for the USITT Lighting Commission for various years. I asked him if he would share some points regarding his portfolio setup. He says: "My portfolio is a heavy, large case. I chose this for two reasons: first, I was tired of having my wimpy vinyl portfolio cases, as well as their contents, destroyed at the airport on the conveyer belt; second, I wanted a larger format to display my work. I have approximately 14 portfolio plates that are 20 × 30 inches and the photos are mounted on matte board. I chose this because the matte board can withstand abuse and is easy to come by. Each 20 × 30-inch portfolio plate contains pictures, drafting, drawings, and research materials for a particular show. Sometimes I use two plates to present a show. I never present all 14 plates during an interview. I choose the plates and productions that I feel show me in the best light to the employer. The other plates I hold in reserve for another interview or if the interviewer wants to see more."

Phelps adds: "The materials on the plates vary from show to show. All plates have at least one 8 × 10-inch photo of the production and several smaller photos,

showing both full stage and detail shots of the production. I include on several plates some research materials that influenced the design—a painting that I used the colors from or a piece of furniture that we replicated. I also like to show bits of my drafting so you can have a better understanding of the stage and objects on it while looking at the production photos. The drafting mounted to the portfolio plate is either shrunk down to a smaller scale or just part of the original drafting, such as a detail of a wall. I have full drafting plates for several shows with me in the portfolio in their original format on 24 × 36-inch paper, so if someone wants to see what the light plot or ground plan really looked like and what their shop could expect from me, I could show them. I do not carry the drafting for every show in my portfolio, most people are not that interested in your drafting to see pages and pages of it. I feel it only necessary to show a couple of shows with all the drafting to prove that I can produce the necessary drawings for my job."

When asked about drawbacks, Phelps says: "The major drawback of my portfolio is its size and weight, which is also why I like my portfolio. This portfolio is great for larger interview settings with several people. I can present it a plate at a time, or set it up as a display and let people ask questions if the interview is less formal. When I need to do a smaller one on one interview, I use a smaller portfolio that I can fit easily on someone's desk."

When suggesting next steps to students and colleagues who are in the process of developing their portfolio, I share teaching points. I divide them into five categories:

- The carrying case
- Featured works
- Portfolio size
- Communicating process
- Organization

FIGURES 13.1A AND 13.1B

The author assembling his portfolio case and making decisions. Take notice of the materials that you need for a basic layout (double-sided tape, rubber cement, matte board, portfolio pages, etc.) and always have plenty on hand. Photos by Ariel Heller.

FIGURES 13.1C AND 13.1D

The author trying different configurations. He recommends: "Include good quality sketches and photographs in different sizes." Photos by Ariel Heller.

Rafael Jaen Teaching Points 1: The Carrying Case

Here are my guidelines regarding the carrying case for your portfolio (see Figures 13.1a and 13.1b):

- Choose a case that will hold and protect your work.
- If you travel a lot, choose a sturdy case that is easy to carry.
- Choose the display technique that best suits your style.
- Take notice of the materials that you need for a basic layout (double-sided tape, rubber cement, matte board, portfolio pages, etc.).
- Make sure you always have plenty of layout materials.
- Plan all pages starting with your base display technique and layout.

Rafael Jaen's Teaching Points 2: Featured Works

Regarding your portfolio's featured works, I suggest that you (see Figures 13.1c and 13.1d):

- Include research materials to inform the process and choices made.
- Include written paragraphs or a concept narrative to explain the project (when needed).
- Include good-quality photographs in different sizes. Make sure that there are a few 8.5 × 11-inch photos.
- Shrink drafting and CAD drawings or include partials of the original size plans next to the fully realized project.
- Make sure to have materials that showcase your various talents.

Rafael Jaen's Teaching Points 3: Portfolio Size

Regarding portfolio size:

- Plan the portfolio sizes based on the interview setting; larger portfolios work best with large groups.

- Plan to have more than one portfolio if you will interview in different settings, taking into consideration the case portability and efficiency.

- Make color copies and reduce your samples to be used in multiple portfolios.

- Plan to have a digital portfolio (or CD) with samples of your work that can be mailed or included in promotional materials.

- Professional Web pages can be used as an alternate portfolio that any interested party can preview.

Putting It Together: Words of Wisdom
by Donna Meester

Donna Meester is an assistant professor in the Department of Theatre and Dance at the University of Alabama. There she is head of the MFA and undergraduate Costume Design and Production Program. She writes: "Process and collaboration are two terms that are incredibly important when talking about the relationships between directors and designers. When looking at a portfolio, the reviewer will not only be looking at the quality of the art, but does it communicate a process? Is there evidence of collaboration? In addition to displaying the final sketch and production photographs, research, notes, thumbnails, and any other additional pieces of information are welcome to see in a portfolio."

She adds: "Paper and choice of media are important. A heavy, dark show probably is not best represented with a light, soft media on clean white paper. For example, Shakespeare's *Titus Andronicus* is a dark show, best presented with dark, gritty medium on dark gritty paper. Always include photographs of the final product. While backstage costume shots are nice, particularly because they are often closer and clearer than an onstage shot, people looking at a portfolio want to see onstage shots. These tell many things: the quality of the overall production, how things work together on stage, if they look on stage as well as they do in the sketches or backstage, along with any number of other stories!"

Meester continues: "Sometimes work is included because the style and genre of the show are quite different from other shows featured in the portfolio. For large shows, particularly those with identifiable groups, one way to organize the presentation is by groupings of such groups. These pages, when found in a portfolio, can be presented with the research and photo pages with the painted sketches next to the group they belong with. Another presentation would be to have all of the research/photo pages together followed with the complete set of sketches. Don't feel compelled to include one sketch per page. If more than one fits, use the space! While research is important for the designer to base designs on and to help communicate ideas to the director, it is also often necessary to share this information with the shop. Research can be attached to sketches, drafting, etc., or stand on its own. Sometimes a designer wants to keep the Show Production Bible (binder) intact. Regardless of the method of presentation, everything should be organized. Don't be afraid to show where ideas began. Include everything that helped you get to the final product!"

Rafael Jaen's Teaching Points 4: Communicating Process

Here are some ways to communicate process in your portfolio:

- Include research materials and other pertinent materials that show evidence of collaboration, such as the color palette of the other designers in a show.

- Make sure your layout materials are congruent with the style of the play and that they evoke the emotions, qualities, and actions of the show—dark, gritty paper for a dark and gory show.

- Include backstage shots when they inform the process, but remember that what the reviewers are looking for is the final product.

- Let the page layout tell the story; let your visuals speak for themselves.

Putting It Together: Featuring Models in Your Portfolio
by Crystal Tiala

Crystal Tiala is an associate professor at Boston College and a United Scenic Artists Local 829 freelance scenic designer. Her other design experiences include interior design, event design, charge scenic artist, and lead construction on films. She says: "When presenting your models in a portfolio, take the time to clean up all the details and the surrounding model box. Photographing it well will take some skill with a camera. It is also helpful to light it in a way that shows its best form and color and to help the viewer envision it as a full-scale design" (see Figure 13.1e).

FIGURE 13.1E
Zanna Don't! SpeakEasy Stage Company, Boston 2007; model in ¼-inch scale. Set design: Crystal Tiala; director: Paul Daigneault; lighting accomplished with fiberoptic model lights from Thematics Lightbox.

Tiala continues: "Lighting a model can be as simple as a few small flashlights or clip-lights or more complex solutions of incorporating miniature model lights to simulate practical lamps. Have a few basic lighting gels on hand and some tape and plan to spend some time creating a great look for the model. More complex and expensive products, such as Thematic Lightbox systems, are superb at simulating lighting effects in model scale and a good investment if you want to invest in really showing off your model work. If you have taken the time to build an impressive model, don't shortchange your work with a poor photographic representation."

Rafael Jaen's Teaching Points 5: Organization

Finally, a few points about your portfolio's organization (see Figures 13.1f and 13.1g):

- The work in the portfolio can be organized to show variety and range of artistry.

- Group sketches in different sizes to fit the portfolio page when doing the layout of a large show.

- The order of your portfolio items is important; the standard order is research, sketches, and final product.

- Save production books if they demonstrate added expertise and inform the process.

- Keep production workbooks neatly organized for easy reading during a review.

I understand the portfolio teaching points and I am ready to start my planning. What steps can I take to apply these teaching points to actually create my portfolio?

FIGURES 13.1F AND 13.1G
The layout order is important; research, sketches, and final product constitute the standard order. In a more relaxed setting, the author chooses a vertical layout to present a well-polished portfolio. Photos by Ariel Heller.

What teaching points can I apply in
developing and maintaining my portfolio?

_____

_____

_____

_____

_____

_____

_____

SINCE DESIGNERS AND TECHNICIANS CAN BE THEIR OWN WORST CRITICS, IT IS IMPORTANT TO DO A SELF-ASSESSMENT IN A SELF-SUPPORTING, HONEST, AND CARING WAY.

RAFAEL JAEN

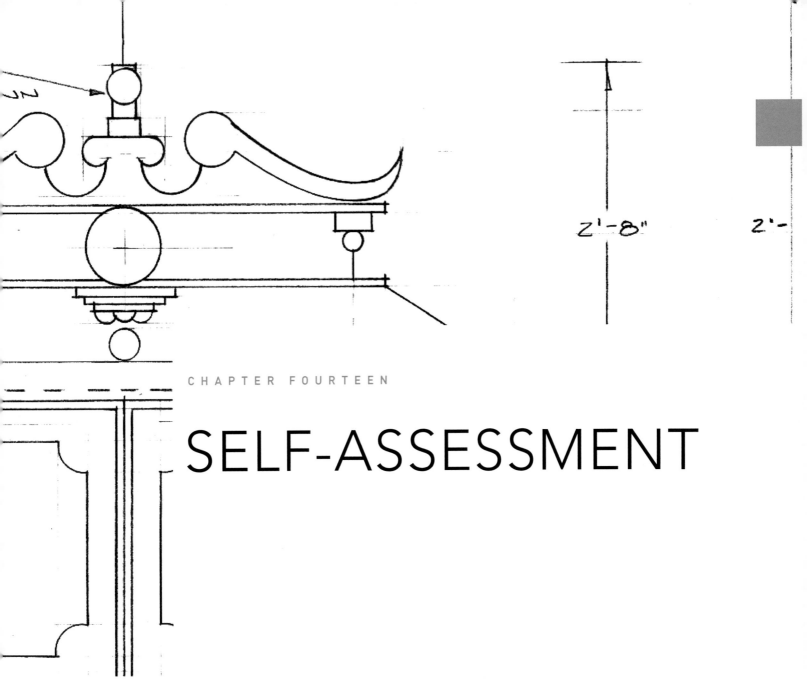

CHAPTER FOURTEEN

SELF-ASSESSMENT

Developing and maintaining a design-tech portfolio can be a structured and well-organized job; however, we have to remember that it is, in its very nature, more of an organic process than a scientific one. This is why it is important to assess where we are in the developing of our showcase on an ongoing basis; we need to integrate feedback and keep perspective as we move forward. As we archive our work, we should ask what to put aside for the portfolio and do some loose planning in anticipation of the time for updating. Sometimes we are prompted by our own internal clock and time off; at other times a job interview comes along or we are invited to present at a conference; at still other times there are timelines and requirements that organizations will impose.

The Basics of a Self-Evaluation

After an interview, it is important to integrate received feedback to prepare for future opportunities. Since designer/technicians can be their own worst critics, it is important to do a self-assessment in a self-supporting, honest, and caring way. A neutral evaluation should include the panelists' feedback and future goals or next steps. A self-assessment includes questions about style, voice, rapport, and content.

There are various self-evaluation areas to consider, such as these:

- *Style.* Were personal grooming and appearance favorable, average, or unfavorable, and why?

- *Voice and rapport.* Were volume and articulation favorable, average, or unfavorable, and why? What are the next steps? Were conversations empathic, with accurate listening and comprehensive answers? Was this aspect favorable, average, or unfavorable, and why?

- *Content.* Was my portfolio complete? Was there enough research, good layout, work samples, and subject knowledge? Was this aspect favorable, average, or unfavorable, and why?

We can all agree that it is important to self-evaluate after an interview in order to integrate feedback, but we have to be discriminating and clear about what we choose to integrate and what we choose to dismiss. Maybe the feedback we get is good for applying to a school program, but it may not work to apply for a position in a professional organization or a teaching job. It is important that we self-assess what our next steps are based on our career concept and our blueprint for short-term goals.

The Comprehensive Self-Evaluation

The following is a Workbook that I have developed for this purpose; it contains basic questions or prompts that will help clarify our process. I suggest referring to these questions as you go through your archives and take notice of what needs attention, then take care of your portfolio and go back to your career master plan!

Workbook: The Self-Assessment Questionnaire
Rate yourself as you go through this list. Then choose a strategy for each item that needs attention.

- My portfolio case:

  - Is it a clean, appropriate, and professional-looking portfolio case? Is it easily handled?

    Rating: 1 ( )   2 ( )   3 ( )   4 ( )   5 ( )
    Note: (1) = Needs improvement, (5) = It is
        excellent!
    Strategy: Does this item need attention?
        What steps will I take to take care
        of this?

- My portfolio inside supplies:

  - Are my sheets holders in good shape, clean and smudge free? Do I have enough extra sheets?

    Rating: 1 ( ) 2( ) 3( ) 4( ) 5( )
    Note: (1) = Needs improvement, (5) = It is excellent!
    Strategy: Does this item need attention? What steps will I take to take care of this?

- My portfolio content:

  - Is my first page well designed? Do I have an updated résumé and business cards, with multiple copies available?

    Rating: 1 ( ) 2( ) 3( ) 4( ) 5( )
    Note: (1) = Needs improvement, (5) = It is excellent!
    Strategy: Does this item need attention? What steps will I take to take care of this?

  - Do I have clear transitions between projects, with continuous layout, either horizontal or vertical?

    Rating: 1 ( ) 2( ) 3( ) 4( ) 5( )
    Note: (1) = Needs improvement, (5) = It is excellent!
    Strategy: Does this item need attention? What steps will I take to take care of this?

  - Do I have careful project organization with comprehensive display of the process, including research, plans, and rough and final sketches?

    Rating: 1 ( ) 2( ) 3( ) 4( ) 5( )
    Note: (1) = Needs improvement, (5) = It is excellent!
    Strategy: Does this item need attention? What steps will I take to take care of this?

- Do I have clear concept translation to design choices and palette? How is my attention to detail?

  Rating: 1 ( ) 2( ) 3( ) 4( ) 5( )
  Note: (1) = Needs improvement, (5) = It is excellent!
  Strategy: Does this item need attention? What steps will I take to take care of this?

- How is my sketch quality? Are things clearly labeled, is the color media fixed properly, do my sketches need to be bordered and/or matted?

  Rating: 1 ( ) 2( ) 3( ) 4( ) 5( )
  Note: (1) = Needs improvement, (5) = It is excellent!
  Strategy: Does this item need attention? What steps will I take to take care of this?

- Do I have final renderings next to production photos? How is the quality of my photos? Are my photos true to the production?

  Rating: 1 ( ) 2( ) 3( ) 4( ) 5( )
  Note: (1) = Needs improvement, (5) = It is excellent!
  Strategy: Does this item need attention? What steps will I take to take care of this?

- My portfolio back pocket:

  - Do I have (or need) available production books and some paperwork?

    Rating: 1 ( ) 2( ) 3( ) 4( ) 5( )
    Note: (1) = Needs improvement, (5) = It is excellent!
    Strategy: Does this item need attention? What steps will I take to take care of this?

- Me, the presenter:

  - How are my grooming, presence, and appearance? Am I dressed properly for my interview? Do I need a haircut? Do I have the proper wardrobe?

    Rating: 1 ( )   2( )   3( )   4( )   5( )
    Note: (1) = Needs improvement, (5) = It is
        excellent!
    Strategy: Does this item need attention? What
        steps will I take to take care of this?

  - How about my voice projection, listening skills, and idea articulation? Do I need to rehearse prior to my interview? Am I missing something on paper (such as properly labeled projects) that could facilitate my verbal presentation?

    Rating: 1 ( )   2( )   3( )   4( )   5( )
    Note: (1) = Needs improvement, (5) = It is
        excellent!
    Strategy: Does this item need attention? What
        steps will I take to take care of this?

- Is my verbal presentation clear and to the point? Does it match my organization (beginning, middle, end, charts and forms)?

  Rating: 1 ( )   2( )   3( )   4( )   5( )
  Note: (1) = Needs improvement, (5) = It is
      excellent!
  Strategy: Does this item need attention? What
      steps will I take to take care of this?

BUT DO NOT COMMIT YOURSELF SOLELY TO . . . TECHNOLOGY; ALWAYS HAVE A REAL, HONEST-TO-GOODNESS, HOLD-IT-IN-YOUR-HAND-AND-TURN-THE-PAGES PORTFOLIO.

DAVE TOSTI-LANE

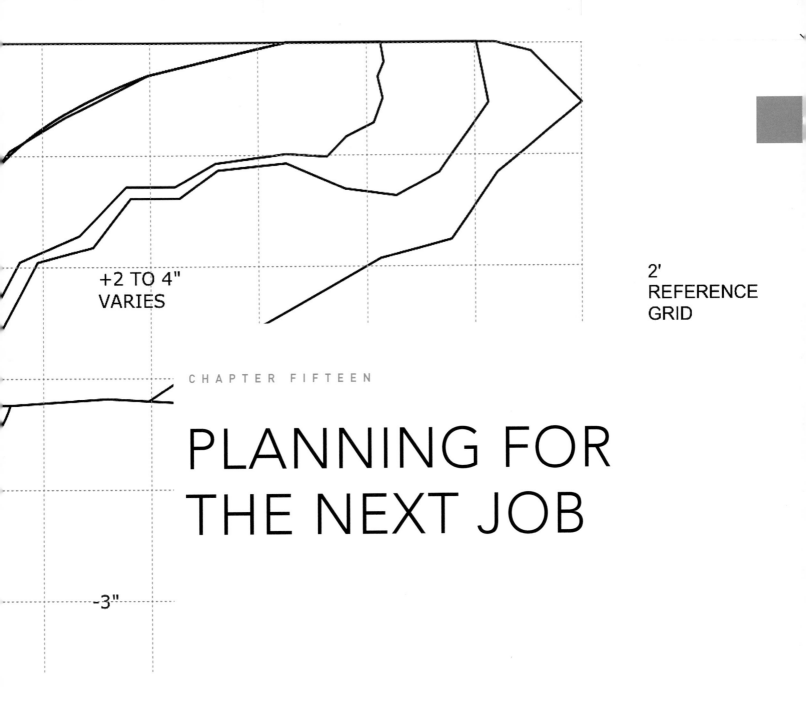

+2 TO 4"
VARIES

2'
REFERENCE
GRID

-3"

CHAPTER FIFTEEN

PLANNING FOR THE NEXT JOB

Why Planning? What Planning?

There are two sayings in theatre that have stayed with me through the years (I'll paraphrase): "Even if you are good, you still have to audition" and "You are only as good as your last project." We are no different from professionals in other fields; we share the same concerns regarding advancement, opportunity, better pay, recognition, getting a new job, growing in the job, making changes, leaving a legacy, and planning for retirement. How many times did you find yourself competing for a job when you knew you were the person best qualified for it, but you didn't get it? How many times have you had a fantastic process working on a show and yet have gotten a critic's bad review? (Producers say that it is okay, but we wonder if they'll call us again.) Or you had an interview at a college and the reviewers didn't think you had an impressive enough body of work? Or you expected a raise or bonus that never came?

Our field is very competitive and sometimes it is challenging to break into new territory due to demanding schedules, constant deadlines, and closed networks of people. Sometimes resources are limited, creating a scarcity mentality. How do we keep ourselves prepared for the next "audition," and how do we overcome a bad "last project"? The answer is to remain inspired, marching forward with clear vision and a plan.

In a profession that is highly creative, it is important that we take time to map out our future, to come up with a "career concept" (or vision) and to create a "blueprint" (or next steps) for what we want to do next. We need to produce, market, and take our own show on the road! (See Figures 15.1a through 15.1c.)

Putting It Together

The process of preparing, developing, and maintaining a portfolio can help us set goals in planning for the next step in our career development. We are creatures of habit, so it is important to plan for downtime in our schedules; incorporating portfolio maintenance days in our calendars is of the utmost importance. The portfolio will inform how we are doing. What information can we get from reviewing our projects? It could be as simple as realizing that we need to get more pages or as challenging as adding new state-of-the-art production work.

There are some basic considerations to include in our planning. There is a vision of the big picture—what I call the *career concept*—and next steps or short-term goals, which I call the *blueprint*. In my experience, this process works best when it is fluid; we need to balance it with other life demands. Keep an eye on the goals, but don't obsess too much about them.

The Big Picture: The Design-Tech Career Concept

Back in the mid- to late 1980s I had the opportunity to take various business courses at Boston University. Since then there is one thing that has remained with me, even today; Business planning mirrors (in many ways) the process of designing and producing a show. First, we need to have a vision that addresses what we ultimately want; this vision becomes the *concept*. This concept includes all sorts of things, from practical to philosophical. We start with the question: Where do we want to be in five years? Once we have one or more answers, we can work our way back to decide the steps to take starting right now.

Your Concept: Identifying Practical Considerations

First we have to come up with a list of accomplishments that we would like to achieve in five years. I call this the *wish list*—a list of 5 to 10 items is always helpful. Next, just as in a production, we have to consider the interpersonal factors: budget, timelines, venue, specific script needs, and the like. It is important to take time to brainstorm, take notes, and make lists; the one advantage in our career planning is that we are producer and director, therefore the final choices are ours!

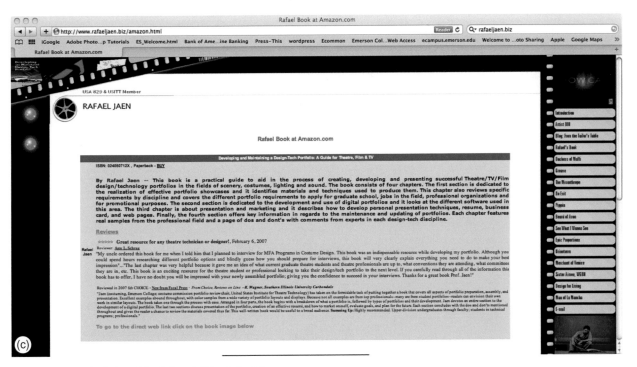

FIGURES 15.1A, 15.1B, AND 15.1C

The author's website is part of the main business plan; the menu includes tabs for various design projects and tabs for his published books and blogs.

The following points show how these aspects would translate into our plan and what to put on our list:

- *The wish list.* This list includes anything from better income to awards; from getting a color marker collection of 150 colors to buying a larger drafting table; from owning a scenic company to having a staff of 20 workers; from having a retirement account to getting comprehensive health insurance. This step is perhaps the hardest part of this plan.

We are used to supporting the vision of others, so coming up with our own may feel alien to us. I say write your list anyway and include big and small items in it.

- *Interpersonal relations.* This refers to our network and people resources. Our field survives on teamwork; therefore it is important that we realize who is on our team as we plan. This list includes key people that could become a resource when and if the need arises. It includes friends, colleagues, newspaper critics, independent press reviewers, specialty magazine editors, organizations (regional and national), unions and guilds, group insurance, vendors, computer technicians. We do not have to anticipate every need here, but write what is key in the first year. If I want to be designing at a League of Resident Theatres (LORT) theatre in five years, it would help to get in the United Scenic Artists Union in three years.

- *The budget matter.* This refers to the obvious, such as income, but it could also include scholarship opportunities, grants, renting a studio with other design-tech folks, or recycling materials. It is important to be creative and daring when you're thinking money. We need to assess what kind of income we need to take care of our living expenses and financial goals. Do we need to get new skills in order to get better pay? Do we need to change companies? Do we need to branch out into an allied field? Remember that we can be very resourceful in putting a show together, and this is a five-year plan, so every day will take you closer to realizing your career design.

- *The venues.* This refers to geography, environment, space, and location. Do you need to work in warm weather, or does your family need to be in a certain region? Do you aspire to work in a shop that is Occupational Safety and Health Administration

(OSHA) compliant? Would you like to have a larger studio with better equipment? Would you like to be closer to the store that sells the supplies you need for your work? Do you want to be the TD for a drama department in an elementary school in Vermont?

- *Your script, your needs.* Since this plan is self-scripted, you will find that as you put your big ideas and vision on paper, some other considerations will arise. I call these the script needs. The design-tech career concept will need to be revised and updated, just like a show. For example, say you want to be on Broadway in five years but you just started your undergraduate degree; maybe your goal should be to get in the proper union and work as an assistant first. Or you want to get a big award that can be mentioned in a promotion and tenure file; in this case it's best to be general with the idea, making your goal "Professional Recognition" instead of "Winning an Oscar." Maybe you won't get a Tony, Emmy, or Oscar next year, but you could enter a juried event (writing a design-tech paper or sharing some new technology). Sometimes we need to change some of the big specific goals into more general ideas; what's important is to be going in the general direction of your plan.

The Small Steps: Your Blueprint for Short-Term Goals

Once we have come up with the design-tech career concept, we need to look at our portfolios and résumés in order to assess what short-term goals to put into place. This is the idea I call the design-tech blueprint, or the "nuts and bolts" of the process; it will help us tighten the loose ends and set short-term goals. I keep a list of short-term goals in a visible place that I can refer to as a reminder. In our field we tend to create what we focus on. In the same manner as the design-tech concept part of the plan, it is important to let the process be fluid and balance it with other life demands.

The blueprint list includes five to 10 short-term goals. The objective is to cross out as many of these goals as possible in a chosen time frame. Some people work well with quarterly goals; others need to structure them in a year span. The list includes items such as portfolio materials, new works development, promotion and marketing, and education and training.

___

These are some of the questions that can assist in creating the blueprint list:

- Is my portfolio case in good shape; does it look professional?

- Is the portfolio up to date? Do I need to add my last few shows?

- Which works do I keep or incorporate in the portfolio, and what works go into the archives?

- Do I have all production sketches, swatches, photos, programs, and so on to add to new portfolio pages?

- Will I need a digital portfolio to apply for grad school or as part of my promotional package?

- Are my résumé and business card up to date? Do I have at least two dozen copies available with my portfolio?

- Do I need to mail my résumé to companies in another state?

- Should I create a Web page for my business? If I have one, is it up to date?

- Do I have press reviews and promotional materials? Do I need to mention an award I won in my portfolio?

- Do I need new or different projects to expand my portfolio?

___

Remember that "Even if you are good, you still have to audition" and "The art of making art (in this case, developing and maintaining a design-tech portfolio) is putting it together." The goal of the blueprint is to help develop, maintain, and even reassess a portfolio that can assist you in achieving the larger concept or vision you hold for yourself as a professional in your field. Every bit and every piece counts!

START WITH YOUR STRONGEST PRODUCED WORK. DO ONLY SHOW
WORK THAT YOU FEEL CONFIDENT ABOUT.

KITTY LEECH

CHAPTER SIXTEEN

WORDS OF WISDOM: DO'S AND DON'TS HIGHLIGHT SUMMARY

In previous chapters we learned the guidelines that many experienced professionals and seasoned academicians recommend in developing a portfolio. Although there are no hard-set rules, some standards do apply. This chapter looks at some commonly accepted practices and things to avoid. These are the golden keys, or the do's and don'ts, of portfolio development, presentation techniques, and marketing.

Portfolio Development Do's: Good Practices

- Most reviewers will say that a portfolio must be put together in such a way that it answers questions specific to its goals. Include the materials needed to apply for a specific job. A portfolio prepared for graduate school will meet different expectations than one used to, for example, apply for a job as designer or technician in regional theatre.

- Students should begin the portfolio with the strongest class projects, including art classes, photography, and the like. At the professional level the same rule applies: Always start with your strongest produced work. Do only show work that you feel confident about.

- If the portfolio is full of produced work and design-tech class projects, don't be afraid to have art projects at the end of the portfolio or in a separate binder.

- Review the portfolio materials often so you are able to talk about your work from a number of different points of view: concepts, process, budget.

- Include a piece of promotional material (a program or flyer, not reviews) as well as a minimum of one or two sketches and production photographs for each production being shown. Students should include class projects, but at the end, not at the beginning of the presentation.

- The sketch lettering should be neat, edges should not be ragged, pastels need to be fixed, and so on.

Sketches, swatches, research, and the like should be affixed to the page neatly when put in the portfolio.

- Although many people like to present their portfolios in chronological order, the reverse may be more effective. There is no rule saying that a portfolio needs to be in any type of chronological order.

- Drafting, blueprints, and CAD drawings need to be a readable size. Photographs (digital and otherwise) need to be true to stage color and must contain detail.

- Research and reference materials should include their sources and titles.

- News and media articles should include dates and title pages. The goal is to give reviewers as many contexts as possible so that at a glance they can understand the scale and venue of the work that you are presenting.

- Layout and design of the portfolio pages is as important as the work on the page. Keep the principles of design in mind in planning your page layout and your rendering plates.

Portfolio Development Don'ts

- Stay clear of badly organized materials, incomplete projects, and pages that must be turned a different way for each picture.

- Avoid too much information spread over too many pages. Do not include the kitchen sink!

- Don't apologize for anything in your portfolio. If it requires an apology, it probably doesn't belong there.

- If your pictures don't look good, it doesn't matter how good the work looked in real life. Become your own photographer.

Digital Portfolio Do's and Don'ts

There are some basic things to remember in planning and executing a digital portfolio for a CD or website. Always remember that, above all, the work should represent you and your skills.

CD and Web do's:

- Ask for help from your computer wizard friends.

- Save your work (on CD) using at least two programs so anyone can read it.

- Attach a written statement with your CD that explains the contents of the portfolio.

- Choose the best images of completed projects as well as media clips.

- Look for website domains that offer templates so you can design a professional-looking site.

- Start your website with a few pages, keeping things simple and short.

- Plan for easy and inexpensive maintenance.

- Label things clearly; add notes as needed for instant gratification!

CD and Web don'ts:

- Use low-quality photos in your website or CD.

- Rely on scanning photos; it's best to start with digital "film."

- Retouch pictures (color correction) so they don't look like the staged production.

- Make the site all about flash and splash.

- Make your website complicated so it takes a long time to load.

- Make the focus the layout above content.

Theatre, TV, and Film Portfolio Presentation Techniques Do's and Don'ts

Do:

- Plan a beginning, a middle, and an end for the portfolio presentation.

- Take time to meet the interviewers and establish eye contact.

- Project your voice and speak clearly.

- Remember good grooming, professional manners, and appearance.

- Review your portfolio materials often and always prior to your interview.

- Plan a short summary to describe each project.

- Make sure the portfolio layout is clear.

- Make sure that project sequences don't compete with each other.

- Make sure projects are labeled and keyed properly.

- Make sure to have source lists for research, materials, and the like.

- Have support materials in the back pocket.

- Have updated résumés and business cards ready.

Don't:

- Present a disorganized portfolio.

- Avoid looking at your interviewers.

- Look like you just finished pulling an all-nighter.

- Exhibit bad grooming, including unkempt fingernails.

- Forget sketch labels or keys.

- Have different competing projects adjacent to each other.

- Use bad photographs or incomplete research or sketches.

- Use loose pages.

- End with a weak project.

- Forget to give credit to other artists' work featured with a project.

- Ignore questions or get defensive.

- Forget to pass your résumé and business card.

Résumé, CVs, and Business Cards Do's and Don'ts

After many years of reviewing résumés at USITT and other venues, I have observed some guidelines that have proven very helpful.

Do:

- Always include your contact information, especially your email address and business phone number, at the top of your résumé.

- Remember to include your expertise as part of the title so that your résumé can be archived properly. It is okay to have different résumés with different titles for different skills.

- The identification, title, and contact information at the top of your résumé should match the information on your business card. It is best if the font and style match as well.

- Clear presentation, good grammar, and correct spelling will always help make a good impression. Make sure to proofread your documents before making many copies.

- In preparing a digital résumé file, make sure it is in Microsoft Word format so that it can be pasted easily (in an email message) and opened easily (as an attachment) by any prospective employer. Make sure to label the file with your name.

- Most employers prefer to read information in reverse chronological order. It is also important to include your title on the job, the venue, show, director, and so on. Include what's relevant.

- The number of résumé pages should correspond with your years of experience. The consensus seems to be to keep the résumé to one page (less experience) to three pages (more experience).

- Save more detailed information such as community service, courses taught, juried articles, and the like for your CV.

Don't:

- Never describe your experience inaccurately or alter a show's credits. Such actions may be interpreted as intentional lies.

- Make typos and misspell of names of contributors, directors, and so on.

- Create artsy layouts or overwhelming designs that won't photocopy well. Always make a test run to see how your résumé looks when photocopied or how easy it is to email and open the file.

- Engage in storytelling. Your résumé is really an organized summary, a tool to match you to a job. Be careful not to fill it with unnecessary information regarding hobbies, personal philosophies, and the like.

A theatrical design-tech portfolio is a showcase of a designer/ technician's process, resourcefulness, and artistry. This showcase is key in opening new doors and getting into recognized colleges, obtaining scholarships, and getting new jobs in the field. Putting a portfolio together for presentation can seem like an impossible undertaking, and it can become a time-consuming and challenging process. The tips provided in this book should help ease you through that process. I hope you keep finding this process useful, inspiring, and helpful!

3"

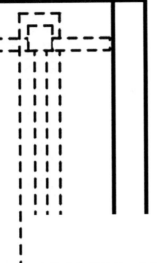

NOTE:
PAINT LIKE WOOD.

CHAPTER SEVENTEEN, PART 1

CONTRIBUTOR BIOS, FIRST EDITION (2006)

Many people contributed to the first edition of this book, including many mentors, colleagues, students, academicians, freelancers, and professionals in allied fields. Their feedback was always helpful and encouraging. Each one of them shares my passion and love for design technology, and each one believes in the importance of design-tech portfolio development. In this chapter I feature their bios with some credits, some quotes, and some samples.

April Bartlett says: "Make your portfolio tell a story. You're not always there to talk about every page. You may only have a fifteen-minute interview slot; having your portfolio able to speak for itself allows you to focus on answering the interviewer's questions. You've mapped out a book for yourself to read when showing your portfolio; instead of thinking about what you're going to say next, all you have to do is turn the page."

April Bartlett, scenic designer. MFA Carnegie Mellon University, 2007. BFA Emerson College, 2004. Meritorious Achievement in Scenic Design; American College Theatre Festival, 2004. *Who's Who Among American Students*; Emerson College, 2004. Evvy Award for Achievement in Scenic Design, 2004.

Jessica Champagne is currently a first-year graduate costume design student at the University of California, Irvine, and graduated from Emerson College with a BFA in design/technology with a concentration in costume design in 2005. She won the 2004 KCACTF Barbizon Award for Excellence in Costume Design Region I and also attended U/RTA Auditions in 2005, where she got a full-paid scholarship to attend UCI Irvine.

Arika Cohen graduated from Emerson College with a BFA in design technology (scenic and costumes) and a minor in theatre education. During 2005, while in the Boston area, Cohen managed to combine her teaching and design into her daily schedule. Her last works could be seen in the productions at the Boston's Children Theatre.

Eric Cornell owns and operates Cornell Consulting, an arts management consulting business focused on aiding and establishing emerging companies and artists in New York, Boston, and Washington, D.C. Additionally, Cornell has worked extensively throughout the country: On Broadway: *The Producers, Hairspray*; Off-Broadway: *Perfect Crime, In the Air*; New York: *People Like Us* (NYMF); regionally: The Barn Theatre, Peterborough Players, American Repertory Theatre, Broadway in Boston/Clear Channel Entertainment. Originally from Oklahoma, Eric Cornell received his BA in theatre from Emerson College in Boston and now resides in New York City. www.ericcornell.com.

Ann Cudworth has worked professionally in the four realms of set design: theatre, film, television, and virtual reality. In 1977, she started by designing a production of *The Nutcracker* for the Lexington Ballet Company in Lexington, Kentucky. Shortly afterward, she designed shows for the MIT Shakespeare Ensemble with director, Murray Biggs, and at the Nucleo Ecclectico in Boston. Moving to New York City in 1983 for graduate school, she worked on many student films and stage presentations for New York University and Columbia University. After graduation from NYU in 1986, she continued to work in the Art Department on feature films and commercials. By 1987 she was an art director for feature films shooting in New York. Soon to come was television, starting with soap operas. Ann holds the unusual distinction of designing four soap opera disasters for three different soap operas in one season. Eventually, this work led to a permanent freelance position with CBS in 1994. For the last 13 years Cudworth has been a production designer for shows such as *60 Minutes*, *48 Hours*, *CBS News Productions*, and *CBS Evening News* special events. The creation of virtual scenic pieces for the 1994 election coverage started Ann's virtual set design career. Her current work can be seen on projects for *Market Watch* and *CBS News Promotions*. She has won two Emmys, one for a real set and one for a virtual set.

Ariel Heller, photographer, is a 2006 graduate of Emerson College with a BFA in musical theatre. He has also studied acting as an apprentice at Brown University's Trinity Repertory. A New Hampshire native, he has performed in regional theatre as well as at Boston's Majestic Theatre and the Boston Lyric Stage. His credits include *Guys and Dolls* (Harry the Horse), *Pippin* (Lewis), and *Urinetown, The Musical* (Ensemble). Mr. Heller is also an avid photographer and a world champion target archer.

William Gordon Henshaw, MFA in drama from San Diego State University, 1996, is the resident costume designer at Henderson State University in Arkadelphia, Arkansas. Henshaw's awards include the Kennedy Center American College Theater Festival Regional Costume Design Nominee, the Bernice Prisk Award for Excellence in Theatrical Costuming, and the Wendell Johnson Award for Excellence in Design. Henshaw is a member of USITT, both national and regional chapters.

Janie E. Howland, scenic designer, holds an MFA from Brandeis University (1993) and a BA in art history, University of Pennsylvania (1987), and is a member of United Scenic Artists Local 829. She is also an Elliot Norton Award winner, 1997, and founding member of the CYCO SCENIC production company.

John Iacovelli has done theatrical set designs for Broadway and regional theatre productions; art direction and production design for TV and film; and art direction and production design for video and industrials. Some of his impressive career credits include set design for many Broadway productions such as *Peter Pan*, art direction for TV shows such as *The Cosby Show*, production design for *Resurrection Boulevard* and *Babylon 5*, art direction for the film *Honey I Shrunk the Kids!*, and industrial installations for the Summer 1996 Olympics and Disney.

Andrew Kirsch, BFA in technical theatre from Emerson College, 2006. Kirsch pictures for this book arrived just as he completed technical direction for the Emerson Stage production of *Undiscovered Country*. He spent Summer 2005 as the scenic construction intern for the Westport Country Playhouse's 75th season. At the Playhouse, Kirsch worked on *Dear Brutus* and *Journey's End,* directed by Gregory Boyd, and *Member of the Wedding,* directed by Joanne Woodward. His interest in theatre tech began at Camp Dudley in Westport, New York, when he was eight years old. Kirsch is from Westport, Connecticut, and supplemented theatric construction with building EuroClosets for three years.

Kitty Leech says: "Don't ever say anything negative or derogatory about another designer, director, or actor while you are discussing the work in your portfolio. Everyone in this business knows everyone else. If you found someone difficult to work with, just say that it was a 'challenge.' Everyone will know what you mean. We've all been there!"

Kitty Leech, BA Pennsylvania, MFA New York University Tisch School of Design. Costume design credits include seven companies of *Gross Indecency; The Three Trials of Oscar Wilde*, including the original New York productions as well as productions in San Francisco, Los Angeles, Toronto, and London's West End. Other notable Off-Broadway credits include *The Novelist, A Romantic Portrait of Jane Austen,* by Howard Fast, and *Goblin Market,* for which she received a Maharam Award nomination. Currently she is chair of the Costume Design Exam Committee for USA Local 829, a committee she has served on since 1987, and chair of the Young Master's Award Committee for the Theater

Development Fund's Irene Sharaff Awards. She is on the faculty at New York University's Tisch School of the Arts Drama Department and the Playwright's Horizon's Theatre School. Leech has been a guest artist at the American International School in Salzburg, Austria, and a guest lecturer at the Parsons School of Design, Pratt Institute, and Lincoln Center Theatre. She has reviewed hundreds of portfolios.

Andy Leviss, sound designer and nationally touring sound engineer, BFA Theatre Design/Technology, Emerson College. Winner 2003 EVVY Award for Outstanding Achievement in Sound Design. Author/owner of OneFromTheRoad.com: Tools, Toys and Tales for the Theatrical Technician.

This is an excerpt from *The Pathfinder: How to Choose or Change Your Career for a Lifetime of Satisfaction and Success*, written by Nicholas Lore and published by Simon & Schuster: "If you plan to have a deeply satisfying career, one that goes beyond the ordinary level of satisfaction and success most people accept, then it may be worth noticing that there seems to be a mechanism at work that tends to keep people stuck to the same spot on the flypaper of life. The better you are at unsticking the stuck, the more power you have to say how your life will be."

Nicholas Lore is the founder of the Rockport Institute, an international career consulting firm that has coached many thousands of clients through midcareer change or first-time career decisions. He and his staff have worked with business executives, government officials, technical people, support staff, artists, musicians, and professionals in all fields. He has been commended for excellence by two U.S. presidents. As the director of the Rockport Institute he is a mentor to many of the most gifted career, personal, and business coaches around the world. Lore also serves as a personal consultant to chief executive officers (CEOs) who want their organizations filled with happy, committed, productive people. He has been a corporate CEO, manufacturing plant manager, entrepreneur, researcher in the field of psychology, market gardener, blues singer and guitar player, well driller, and newspaper boy. He lives by a lake under ancient oaks with his wife and best friend Mitra.

Donna Meester is an assistant professor in the Department of Theatre and Dance at the University of Alabama. There she is head of the MFA and undergraduate Costume Design and Production Program. She has served as the design chair for the Kennedy Center American College Theatre Festival Region VI and is currently the design vice chair for Region IV. Meester is also an active member of USITT and Southeastern Theatre Conference (SETC).

Mark Newman is an award-winning journalist who was most recently the managing editor of *Entertainment Design* and *Lighting Dimensions* magazines. His career has spanned television talk shows to an off-Broadway theatre's box office to numerous editorial jobs in New York City. A native of Alabama, he currently resides in Chillicothe, Ohio.

Amanda Monteiro. The privilege of working with Rafael opened doors I had never even contemplated. After beginning his first design class, a passion awoke that was never there before. Before I knew it I had taken every one of his classes. In 2003, I graduated from Emerson College with a bachelor's degree in theatre studies with emphasis in both acting and costume design. After I was told I was too young to begin my graduate degree, I began working in a shop, sewing as well as doing some freelance design projects in Boston and working retail to make ends meet. Before I knew it I was asked to move to New York and take a position in the buying office of French Connection. While at French Connection I began taking draping classes at the Fashion Institute of Technology (FIT). Today I find myself not designing but working with designers as part of the buying team at Giorgio Armani. I owe much of my success to Rafael Jaen and his teachings.

Karen Perlow. Freelance lighting designer, 1986 to present; instructor, Massachusetts Institute of Technology; Stage Source board member, 2002 to present; IRNE winner, 2003, for best lighting design. Somerville Arts Council Grant Reviewer, 2002.

Here is an excerpt from *Avoiding a Portfolio Imbroglio*, by Mark Newman: "Who am I anyway? Am I my résumé?" So goes the lyric from the opening number of *A Chorus Line*, sung by an aspiring triple threat. For aspiring theatre designers, the answer to the lyric is yes . . . and no. Design faculty at top colleges can easily see through the gloss of a slick portfolio. An attractive presentation is nice, but if the talent and the ability are not there, the presentation is moot."

Anthony R. Phelps has worked as an associate technical director at Harvard University. He holds an MFA in design from Minnesota State University, Mankato. Teaching credits include the University of Kentucky and Bradley University. Design credits include Theatre L'Homme Dieu, the Publick Theatre, and the Old Log Theatre. Professional memberships include USA, IATSE, and USITT. Phelps is the founder and executive editor of *The Painter's Journal*.

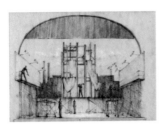

Brian Prather most recently designed the premiere production of *Fuente* for Barrington Stage Company. Recent work includes the premiere of *My Heart and My Flesh* for Coyote Theater at Boston Playwright's Theater, *Working* for Emerson Stage at the Cutler Majestic Theatre, *First Love* for StageWorks Hudson, and *Thief River* for Barrington Stage Co. Prather is a recent MFA graduate of Brandeis University.

Carrie Robbins has designed costumes for more than 30 Broadway shows, including 2001's *A Class Act*, *Grease* (Tony nomination, Best Costumes), *Over Here* (Tony nomination, Best Costumes), *Agnes of God*, *Yentl*, *Octette Bridgeclub*, *Sweet Bird of Youth*, *The First*, *Frankenstein*, *Happy End*, *Boys of Winter*, *Cyrano*, *Shadow Box*, *The Iceman Cometh*, and *Secret Affairs of Mildred Wilde*. Among awards she has won are five Drama Desk Awards, a Maharam, and several international design awards. She created designs for the Lincoln Center Rep, Chelsea Theatre Center, Acting Co., and the New York Shakespeare Festival. Regionally she has designed at Mark Taper Forum (*The Tempest*, FIT Surface

Design Award) and *Flea in Her Ear* (LA Dramalogue Award), Guthrie Theatre, and Williamstown Theater Festival. Her film and television work includes *In The Spirit*, *SNL*, PBS's *Arts in America* series, and several unseen pilots. Her opera designs include San Francisco Opera (*Samson et Dalila*), Houston Grand Opera, Sarah Caldwell's Opera Co. of Boston, Hamburg Statsoper, and Washington Opera. She was profiled in *Costume Design, Techniques of Modern Masters and Contemporary Designers*, among others. She has been a master teacher of costume design at NYU for more than 25 years. Her recent work includes *Exact Center of the Universe* for the Women's Project, *Tallulah Hallelujah*, *Toys in the Attic*, *Rags* at Paper Mill Playhouse, *The Wedding Banquet*, and *Belle* (directed by Tazewell Thompson), and currently *White Christmas*, a new musical based on the film, directed by Walter Bobbie and opening at the Curran Theatre in San Francisco in November. She also designed uniforms for *The Rainbow Room* and *Windows on the World* (Image of the Year Award).

Kristina Tollefson has her MFA in costume design and technology from Purdue University and is currently an assistant professor and resident costume and makeup designer at the University of Central Florida in Orlando. She serves as the vice commissioner for communication for the Costume Design & Technology Commission of USITT.

Nicholas D. Vargelis, lighting designer, graduated
from Emerson College in May 2003, Magna Cum
Laude with a BFA in theatre design technology.
At Emerson he received an EVVY Award for
outstanding work in lighting design. He worked
as a freelance lighting designer in Boston and
New York and then went to Europe. He is currently
living in Berlin and has two upcoming photography
exhibitions, the first a solo exhibit with a mix of
work from the United States and Paris and the
second a group showing in Spring 2006 focusing
on his current work in Berlin. Vargelis designed
lighting in Fall 2005 for an outdoor dance
performance sponsored by the city of Berlin—
a "night of arts" in NeuKolln.

3"

NOTE:
PAINT LIKE WOOD.

CONTRIBUTOR BIOS, SECOND EDITION (2012)

This, the second edition of this book, features many teachers, colleagues, students, academicians, freelancers, and professionals in the design-technology and allied fields. I am very proud to add their names to the list of contributors; each one of them shared their wisdom generously and wholeheartedly. I am especially thankful to my students Joshua Stewart and Allison Hill, who helped me edit the text in most chapters.

Allison Hill (Show Case text editing; www.allison-hill .com) says: "As a costume designer, I can apply my visual art skills with my love of fashion and my fascination with analyzing and understanding people, their motivations, and the way that they work, and applying that in how they would select their clothes. Through sound, I can exercise the nerdier side of my brain, building systems and seeing designers' auditory visions coming to life. My goals as a costume designer are to get into large stage productions, perhaps even touring, so as many people can see my work as possible. With sound, I would like to get into system design and see where that takes me."

As an English major at Bates College in Maine, *Amy Whitten* (www.amywhitten.com) volunteered to help start the campus TV station—and soon forgot all about *Beowulf*. Her fascination with "the biz" led her to Emerson College, where she got her master's in mass communication and broadcasting in 1992. She's been a freelancer in production ever since. By 1997 she was busy as a coordinator/associate producer. But the joy of arranging caterers and location permits couldn't match the toil of making pictures happen—so she made a sharp turn into the art department. It was a risky move, but it paid off with lots of interesting gigs, challenges, people, and travel to faraway places. Amy also started working more seriously in photography. Her work has appeared in several group shows, including the National Boston "Box" gallery and, most recently, Boston's 375th anniversary exhibit.

The career of art director *Ashton Blount* (www .ablountdesigns.com) has taken him from Los Angeles to Dubai to New York. He's created trees from scratch and even flooded an entire set. We caught up with him in his Brooklyn office to learn more about his career and pick his brain. His advice and experience are useful to anybody who wants to become an art director as well as anybody who works or plans to work with one.

Brendan F. Doyle is a sound designer, engineer, and artisan working primarily on live performance applications. He is currently a master's candidate in sound design at the University of Edinburgh after receiving his BFA from Emerson College in theatre design and technology. His previous work has been heard at the Lyric Stage Company of Boston, Boston Children's Theatre, Company One, Axe to Ice Productions, the University of Massachusetts at Lowell, Boston University, Wellesley College, Russell Sage College, and the New York State Theatre Institute, as well as other venues in the northeastern United States and the United Kingdom.

Stage manager *Colin Dieck*, originally from Gloucester, Massachusetts, has worked in technical theatre since his days at Bowdoin College, including working as a technician during the Edinburgh Fringe Festival and as lighting designer and production manager for Cho-In Theatre of Seoul, South Korea. He now resides in Washington, D.C., and recently served as a venue manager for the Capital Fringe Festival. He has worked with Beau Jest, stage-managing *Samurai 7.0* and both managing stage and designing lights for *The Remarkable Rooming House of Madame Lemonde,* for the Provincetown Tennessee Williams Theatre Festival.

Brian White is currently a freelance scene designer in Houston, Texas. He received an associate of arts degree from San Jacinto College Central and a BFA in scene design from Texas State University. Recent awards for scene design include the 2007 KCACTF Scene Design Fellowship to the Eugene O'Neill Theatre Center in Waterford, Connecticut, and the 2007 KCACTF Region VI Barbizon Scene Design Award.

Cory Rodriguez (www.coryrodriguezdesigns.com/scenic-design.html) worked as a scenic designer for four years in Vermont and decided it was time to go to New York City. His past set design credits include designing *The Seagull* at the University of Vermont and, most recently, *Closer* at the Flamboyant Theatre in New York. He has assistant-designed at the Roundhouse Theatre in Bethesda, Maryland, and the North Shore Music Theatre in Beverly,

Massachusetts. Rodriguez also worked as a scenic artist on many shows over the past five years in Vermont, which include productions at UVM and the Flynn Theatre and in Middlebury. He studied scenic design at the University of Vermont under Jeff Modereger's mentorship. He has a BS in graphic design from Champlain College and has done a few graphic designs for UVM.

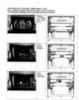

Crystal Tiala (https://www2.bc.edu/crystal-tiala) is an associate professor at Boston College and a USA Local 829 freelance scenic designer. Her other design experiences include interior design, event design, charge scenic artist, and lead construction on films. Tiala has served as the chair of the USITT New England Section, chair of design and technology for Region 1 of the Kennedy Center American College Theatre Festival, and advisor for the Ballard Institute and Museum of Puppetry. She received her MFA from the University of Connecticut.

Don Childs began his theatrical career at the San Francisco Actors Workshop during the theatrically active 1960s. During his tenure with the Workshop he spent five summers at the Colorado Shakespeare Festival working as a technician, lighting designer, and, finally, as technical director. When the Workshop founders went to New York to take over the Lincoln Center Theatres, Don returned to college, where he obtained a BA from the University of Iowa, an MA from San Jose State University, and an MFA from Indiana University. A teaching career has taken Don from San Diego to Montreal and many places in between.

Don has designed over 200 plays, musicals, dance concerts, and exhibitions. His work has been displayed at the Prague Quadrennial, where the production that he lit for set designer Ladislav Vychodil won the Gold Medal for Scenography. Among Child's favorite designs is the production of *Not About Nightingales,* produced at Sam Houston State. *Nightingales* brought him a number of awards, including an invitation to exhibit in the inaugural World Stage Design exhibition in Toronto in 2005. The Texas Educational Theatre Association named Don Childs Artist of the Year in 2007.

Don left the world of academia to concentrate on the consulting and designing areas of his career but has returned as a visiting professor at Oklahoma State University. He founded the Stagecraft Institute of Las Vegas in 2005 to train designers and technicians for the high-tech world of entertainment technology at its center in Las Vegas. Don is a member of USITT, IATSE-USA 829, and IAAM.

Glen Anderson (www.andersonportfolio.com) is pursuing an MFA in scenic design at the University of Florida, Gainesville. He holds a degree in scenic design and technology from Ball State University. At the 2007 KCACTF Anderson was awarded the Barbizon Excellence in Scenic Design Award. He is a member of USITT and participated in World Stage Design 2005 in Toronto.

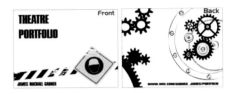

James Garner (www.wix.com/garner_james/portfolio) is a technical director and freelance technician currently based in the greater Boston and Washington, D.C., areas but is also looking to broaden his horizons to include other locales. Garner has over seven years of experience in the fields of theatre and broadcasting, and he holds a BFA from Emerson College's Theatrical Design and Technologies Department with an emphasis in technical direction.

Joanna (Joa) Stenning (joastenning.carbonmade.com) is a recent graduate of Emerson College with a BA in theatre studies (emphases on design technology and performance). She currently lives and works as a freelance properties designer in Boston, though she considers Western Massachusetts her home. Stenning plans to continue her work in theatrical design and to grow as an artist whenever and wherever possible.

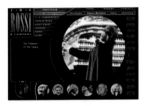

Jenny Lind Bryant is a wardrobe stylist whose experience includes film and theatre. Her credits cover on-set costumer, fashion stylist, makeup and hair design, fashion design, costume design, and wardrobe supervision. Her special skills include draping, pattern making, Lectra Modaris, U4ia, Adobe Photoshop, Microsoft Word, Microsoft Power-Point, Microsoft Excel, and digital photography. She received an MFA in theatrical design from the University of Georgia in 2009 and her BS in textiles and consumer sciences from Florida State University.

Joe Rossi (www.rossimakeup.com) has designed makeup for film, theatre, television, and opera. Joe was head of the makeup department on the Disney feature film *Underdog*; the Showtime series *Brotherhood*; the Warner Brothers feature *Osmosis Jones*; the Miramax feature *Outside Providence*; and the Samuel Goldwyn Films feature *Passionada*. He was key makeup artist on David Mamet's *State and Main*. Other film work includes the Twentieth Century Fox features *Stuck On You*; *Fever Pitch*; *Shallow Hal*; and *Me, Myself and Irene* and the features *Meet Joe Black*, *The Last Shot*, *Little Black Book*, *Thirteen Days*, *Mona Lisa Smile*, *The*

Human Stain, Moonlight Mile, Session 9, Prozac Nation,
and *Lift* as well as the German feature *Private Lies.*
His network credits include NBC's *Saturday Night
Live, Providence, Dateline, Unsolved Mysteries,* and
The Today Show as well as ABC's *The Century.* Joe
has provided makeup services for many national
political figures, including President Bill Clinton,
Hillary Rodham Clinton, and Vice President Al Gore.
He designed special makeup for Christopher Reeve
in *Death Takes a Holiday,* Robert Foxworth in *Cyrano
de Bergerac,* and Cameron Mitchell in *Battle for the
Lost Planet II.* He was makeup designer for the Ronald
Reagan and George Bush Inaugural Concerts at the
Kennedy Center in Washington, D.C.

John Paul Devlin (www.smcvt.edu/academics/theatre/
johnpauldevlin.asp) earned an MFA in drama
and an MA in history from Syracuse University as
well as a BA in history and communication arts/
theatre from Allegheny College. He is an assistant
professor of fine arts at Saint Michael's College in
Vermont, where he specializes in scenic and lighting
design and serves as technical director during the
academic year and resident designer and production
manager for the Saint Michael's Playhouse during
the summer. Devlin has 70 professional scenic,
light, and properties design credits among his 170
designs. He is the vice chair for design, technology,
and management for KCACTF Region One and a
member of the National and New England section of
USITT, active in the Education Commission.

Joshua Stewart (Show Case text editing and software
research; http://biography.jrank.org/pages/2450/
Chase-Debra-Martin.html) holds an MA in visual
media arts from Emerson College in Boston. He
earned a BA in communication from Virginia Tech
in 2006 and, in his senior year, received the Donald
F. Morris Memorial Award for excellence in student
broadcasting. He is also a member of the National
Society of Collegiate Scholars. Stewart is currently
an executive assistant at Martin Chase Productions
in Burbank, California.

David C. ("Kip") Shawger, Jr. (trailer: How Do I Paint?:
www.youtube.com/watch?v=422t4dodQSM), is
the Kennedy Center/American College Theatre
Festival national design vice chair. A native of New
Jersey who received a BS degree in Drama from
Nebraska Wesleyan University and an MFA degree
in design from Bradley University, he is an award-
winning designer with over 300 design credits and
30 years' experience in education, community,
professional theatre, television, and film. Currently
he is associate chair and head of design in the
Department of Theatre and Dance at Ball State
University.

Kirk J. Miller (www.kirkjmiller.com) is a graduate of Emerson College in Boston, where he received a BFA in Theatrical Design. He is a Lighting Designer, Director, and Programmer working in theatre, dance, live event, television, and film. Based in New England, he is also a freelance theatre and event photographer. In his free time he enjoys drumming and traveling. Born in Connecticut, he now splits his time between Boston and Los Angeles. He is grateful for the opportunity to follow his dreams of pursuing a career in the world of art and entertainment.

KJ Kim is a makeup and hair designer. She is a senior undergraduate student from the University of Evansville who graduated in May 2011. She is majoring in theatre design with a minor in fine art. In January 2011, Kim received the USITT Young Designers & Technicians Award in the makeup design area, sponsored by Kryolan Corporation. Simultaneously, she also won first place in the Alcone Company Makeup Design Award of Region III, KCACTF. She received an all-expense-paid trip to the Kennedy Center in Washington, D.C. in April 2011 as one of only eight national finalists in her field. This was the second year in a row for KJ Kim to advance to national competition.

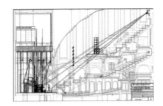

Kristin M. Hayes (www.kristinhayes.com) earned her BFA in theatre design and technology from Emerson College in May 2007. During her senior year, she was honored with the Barbizon Award for Excellence in Lighting Design at the Region 1 Kennedy Center American College Theatre Festival for her work on Emerson Stage's production of *The Witch of Blackbird Pond* in the Cutler Majestic Theatre. She then went on to win a fellowship at the National Festival held in Washington, D.C. Her work on the 25th Annual EVVY Awards was featured in the August 2006 issue of Lighting and Sound America. She currently works as a freelance lighting designer in the New England area. She has plans to attend graduate school in the future.

Leslie Chiu (www.buildingbetterjobseekingskills.com) has worked as a stage manager and production manager for 15 years. She is currently the production manager and a lecturer in theatre arts at Brandeis University. Her most recent credits include production manager for Commonwealth Shakespeare Company's *Othello* and production stage manager for the long-running hit Off-Broadway show *Blue Man Group* (Boston). Leslie received her MFA in stage management from the

University of Cincinnati College Conservatory of Music and her BFA in theatrical design and technology from Florida State University. Chiu also presents workshops and provides professional consultations on résumés, interviewing, and building careers in the entertainment industry.

Mallory Frers (www.malloryfrers.com/costume-design) is a freelance costume designer working in the New England area. Based in Boston, Mallory is currently employed by Emerson College, where she is the wardrobe supervisor for Emerson Stage. Frers's design work has been seen throughout the area in multiple theatre companies, including ART and Lyric Stage. Other proficiencies include makeup and hair design. Her specialties include period styles for theatre and film, makeup and hair styling for special occasions, and even special-effects requests for blood and guts.

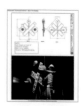

Bill Hawkins is a freelance technical director. He holds a BFA in theatre design and technology from Emerson College (2011). Hawkins markets his freelance project management and theatrical construction business as Mohawk Theatrical Associates.

Nicole Wilson began her career in costumes at the Pacific Conservatory of the Performing Arts, where she worked four consecutive summers as a costume technician. At PCPA she was able to stitch on such shows as *Brigadoon, A Little Night Music,* and *Beauty and the Beast* and to work as a costume crafts artisan on *Ragtime* and *The Imaginary Invalid.* In Fall 2008 Nicole transferred to Emerson College, where she completed her BFA in theatre design and technology in December 2010. While at Emerson she was fortunate to work as the draper on *Esperanza Rising, Into the Woods,* and *Light Up the Sky.* Since leaving Emerson Wilson has worked as the draper and wardrobe supervisor on ArtsEmerson's *The Color of Rose,* the draper on *Dollhouse* at the New Repertory Theatre, and as the costume coordinator for Boston Children's Theatre's production of *A Year in the Life of Frog and Toad.* Nicole has been honored to work with some of theatre's leading professionals and looks forward to continuing her work in costume technology.

Rosalind Robinson (www.rosalind-robinson.co.uk) trained as a scenic artist with the BBC after studying for a fine art degree in London, acquiring the skills of *trompe l'oeil* painting, marbling, gilding, and graining. She has worked as a professional artist and specialist decorator for more than 30 years, producing fine decorations on walls and furniture in the United Kingdom and abroad. She has studied botanical painting in courses at Kew Gardens and the Chelsea Physic Garden and teaches occasional botanical painting classes. She is a member of the Traditional Paint Forum, the Bath Society of Botanical Artists, and the Calne Artists Group. Murals commissioned in public buildings include:

- Normansfield Theatre, Teddington, Middlesex. Recreation of the Victorian stage scenery. Langdon Down Centre Trust.

- Grosvenor House Hotel, Park Lane, London W1. Fourteen large mural panels for the Grosvenor Suite Ballroom.

- Harrods, Knightsbridge, London SW1. Redecoration of the Food Halls with painted and gilded plasterwork, tiled medallions and marbling, and mural panels in the Safety Deposit Vaults.

- Clermont Club, Berkeley Square, London SW1. *Trompe l'oeil* grisaille work to the restaurant ceiling.

- The Inn on the Park, Hyde Park Corner, London SW1. Painted and gilded decoration to the banqueting room ceiling.

- Kansas City Hotel, Kansas City, USA. Paintings to the Ballroom reception area.

- Wiltshire Heritage Museum, Devizes. Murals for the Mediaeval Galleries.

Other works, involving more than 30 years' experience painting for discerning clients, are in private residences throughout Britain and in Gøteborg, Rome, Paris, and the United States. Her paintings and drawings have been exhibited at the Royal Academy of Art London, the Royal Watercolour Society London, the Mall Galleries London, Devizes Museum, Chichester Festival Exhibition, and The Podium, Bath.

Ryan Fischer is a theatrical lighting designer and new MFA Architectural Lighting Design student at Parsons The New School for Design in New York City.

To view examples of his work, visit www.fischerlighting.com, or visit his Facebook page at www.facebook.com/fischerlighting.

Scott Clyve (http://sclightingdesigns.com), lighting, set, and Web designer, has designed on Broadway, Off-Broadway, regionally, and internationally. Clyve's wide range of design experience has included such areas as theatre, dance, opera, industrials, and television. Clyve is a member of USA Local 829 and holds a BFA from Purchase College at SUNY.

Seághan McKay (www.seaghanmckay.com) is a Boston-based projection designer whose work has been seen at the SpeakEasy Stage Company, the Boston Conservatory, the Brandeis Theatre Company, and others. As a designer, technician, and educator for 17 years, McKay has been affiliated with the American Repertory Theatre, the Huntington Theatre Company, Blue Man Group, the Commonwealth Shakespeare Company, Brandeis University, Boston College, and others. McKay also performs as a live visualist, creating real-time interactive motion graphics for the popular Thunderdome series of club events in Boston. McKay is Lighting Supervisor at Brandeis University, where he also holds a position as lecturer in theatre arts.

Shanna Parks (www.wix.com/shannaparks/portfolio) started sewing at age eight with the help of her mother and grandmother. She found her way into a costume shop by age 13. Soon after, she decided to pursue a career in theatrical costuming, first choosing design but soon discovering her real interest lay in construction. Parks completed her BFA at Emerson College and her MFA at the University of North Carolina at Chapel Hill. Her work experience includes the Utah Shakespearean Festival; PlayMakers Repertory Company, North Carolina; the Oregon Shakespeare Festival; PCPA Theatrefest, California; and the Huntington Theatre, Boston.

Stephanie Deitzer, founder of Style at Work (www.styleatwork.biz/about/), has always endeavored to be stylish, creative, and memorable in what have typically been conservative work environments. With her 20+ years of corporate experience, Deitzer now empowers clients to dress stylishly yet appropriately for business and other life roles where confidence and capability matter—to feel good from the inside out. With her help, clients develop a look that makes them stand out in a crowd, bridges from work to play, and promotes self-confidence. Deitzer's love affair with fashion began at the age of four when she learned how to sew from her grandfather, an Italian tailor. Wearing custom-tailored clothing and helping friends and family with their wardrobe choices during her formative years, Deitzer observed fabric, style, silhouette, and fit first-hand, and she began to understand that everyone is born with his or her own look. Her talents for styling and fashion were further applied through her college years and studies at Vanderbilt University, where, as a drama major, her experience broadened to include costuming, hair, and makeup techniques. These skills proved useful upon graduation, when she helped launch the Prescriptives skin care and cosmetics line in New York. During her years of corporate life, she represented prestigious firms, including the Boston Consulting Group and IBM, where she successfully assisted colleagues and managers who enlisted her aid with their business, business casual, and personal looks. After many loyal years in big business, it was time for her to explore the next chapter of her life and determine how to best follow her passion. Recognizing that helping others through style was the common thread throughout her entire life, the direction was clear, and Style at Work was born. Deitzer is currently VP of education and acting VP of membership for the Association of Image Consultants International (AICI) New England Chapter.

Production designer *Thomas A. Walsh* (www
.thomasawalsh.net) was born in Los Angeles
into a show-business family. His father, Arthur
Walsh, who was a jitterbug champion, appeared
in many musicals, comedies, dramas, and short
films while under contract to MGM Studios. Later
his father was a successful nightclub comedian
on the Las Vegas/Lake Tahoe/Reno circuit.
Walsh's interest in narrative design developed
at Hollywood High School, where he designed
and staged plays and musicals. He received his
BFA in theatre design from California Institute
of the Arts. He has designed for feature films,
Imax/Omnimax, television movies and series,
documentaries, Broadway dramas and musicals,
and regional theatre. Walsh is the winner of a
Primetime Emmy for art direction and an ADG
Award nomination for *Buddy Faro* (1998). He is also
winner of the 2004 ADG Excellence in Production
Design Award for a Single Camera Series for the
hit ABC-TV show *Desperate Housewives*. His work
on *In Search of Dr. Seuss* (1993) garnered another
Emmy nomination as well as a Cable Ace Award.
Walsh also did production design work on *MGM:
When the Lion Roars* (1992), which won an Emmy
for Best Informational Special. Walsh is a leader
in designing for IMAX and one of his projects, *The
Living Sea* (1995), received a Documentary Academy
Award nomination. He designed the Tony Award–
winning Best Production of 1980 (*Children of a
Lesser God*) and was associated with three other
Tony Award wins for best production from his work
as an associate designer with famed production

designer Tony Walton (*I'm Not Rappaport*, 1986;
The Real Thing, 1984; *My One and Only*, 1984). In
addition, Walsh was nominated for a second
Cable Ace Award for *Kingfish, A Story of Huey
P. Long* (1994). He most recently was the originating
production designer on ABC-TV's hit series
Desperate Housewives for four seasons. Walsh
is co-chairman of the Art Directors Guild Film
Society and is also a member of USA Local 829 in
New York. He is also a member of the Academy
of Motion Picture Arts and Sciences, the Academy
of Television Arts and Sciences, and the Board of
Directors of the Center for Film and TV Design and
is a founding member of the 5D: The Future
of Immersive Design Conference. He has been
serving as president of the Art Directors Guild
since January 1, 2003, IATSE Local 800. It
represents scenic, title, graphic artists, digital
artists, set designers, model makers, illustrators,
and matte artists. The total ADG membership now
numbers 2,000.

Tracy Lynn Wertheimer (www.tracesoflightdesigns.
com) is a freelance lighting designer based in New
York City. After growing up in the Washington,
D.C., area, Wertheimer moved to Boston, where
she received a BFA in theatrical design and
technology from Emerson College. She now
resides in New York City and is thrilled to be
working with companies up and down the East
Coast. Wertheimer was awarded first place for the
Barbizon Award for Excellence in Lighting for her
design of *Esperanza Rising*. She was also awarded

the American College Theatre Festival (ACTF) Region 1 Merit Award for Excellence in Lighting Design. She was chosen by Emerson College to be a part of *Who's Who Among Students in American Colleges and Universities* and was awarded the 2010 Emerson College Theatre Design/Technology Award.

Tyler DeMotte Kinney (www.tylerkinney.com) is a costume and scenic designer from Boston. His credits include costume designing *Striking 12* (Speakeasy Stage Company), *Tonya & Nancy the Rock Opera* (Club Oberon), and *BARE: A Pop Opera* (Suffolk University PAO) and assistant costume designing *The Life and Adventures of Nicholas Nickleby* (Lyric Stage Company). Kinney is a recent BFA Theatre Design/Technology graduate from Emerson College. He was also the recipient of a National Barbizon Award for Excellence in Scenic Design at the 2011 Kennedy Center American College Theatre Festival Region 1.

A

A Chorus Line, 66
Adding Machine, 41f, 42f, 43f, 44f
Adobe Acrobat family
  InDesign, 130
  PDF, 127–129
  Photoshop Creative Suite, 130–139
Adobe Flash Professional, 122
A Little Night Music, 17
AllArtSupply.com, 34
aluminum portfolio binders, 24f, 26
American Experience series
  God in America, 88
American National Standards Institute (ANSI), 31
American Tragedy: The Case of Clyde Griffiths, 7–11, 10f
Anderson, Glen
  vertical layout of portfolio, 49f
The Angel and the Woodcutter, 159f
ANSI. *see* American National Standards Institute (ANSI)
Antigone, scanned slide from, 125f
appearance, professional/ appropriate
  for portfolio presentation, 164–165
appropriate/professional appearance
  for portfolio presentation, 164–165
Assassins, 7, 9f
A Year in the Life of Frog and Toad, 17

B

Babylon, *5*, 56
back pocket, 55–56, 55f
Bamboo laminate, 30, 30f
Barlett, April, 106–108
Beauty and the Beast, 17
beginning part, portfolio, 40, 40f
being present, defined, 165, 167f
Beudert, Peter, 67, 69
binders, 24–30, 26f, 27f
  aluminum portfolio binders, 24f, 26
  easel binders, 25
  multiring binders, 25, 26f
  slide-in pocket page portfolio binders, 26, 27f
  standard three-ring binders, 26, 27f
bio, 184–185
Blount, Ashton
  résumé, 184f
blueprint, 210
  for short-term goals, 212–213
Boston Marriage, 129f
branding, 122–123
Brigadoon, 17
brochures, 185–189
  points to avoid, 193
  points to remember, 193
Brother MFC-6490CW, 35–36
Bryant, Jenny Lind
  résumé, 184f
Buddy Faro, 143
budget, 210–212
Building Better Job-Seeking Skills, 179
business cards, 185–189
  steps to avoid, 218
  steps to consider, 218
business planning, 210, 211f. *see also* career

C

career
  planning and, 210, 211f
  portfolio and, 210
career concept, 210–212
  identifying practical considerations, 210–212
carrying case, for portfolios, 197, 197f
cases, portfolio, 204–205. *see also* carrying case, for portfolios
Bamboo laminate, 30, 30f
binders, 24–30, 26f, 27f. *see also* binders
categories, 24–25
folios, 24–25, 29–30. *see also* folios
presentation cases, 24–32, 28f
supplies and materials, 31–32. *see also* supplies and materials
Tera-Cover, 30, 30f
Vista, 30f, 31
CD showcases
  e-portfolios, 125
  points to avoid, 161
  points to remember, 158–160
Champagne-Hansen, Jessica, 7, 7f, 8f
Charrette, 34
Chiu, Leslie, 179–180
clear polyester archival, 31
Clyve, Scott, 160, 160f
college applications, 60
color scheme, for digital portfolio, 122
Colours Artist Supplies, 34
communicating process, in portfolios, 198, 199–200, 199f

computers
  in design studio, 112
  new capabilities and new uses, 115
  relearning and learning for the first time, 113–115
  working with collaborators and, 112–113
costume and makeup designer
  Tollefson, Kristina, 133, 134f
costume designer
  Champagne-Hansen, Jessica, 7, 7f, 8, 8f
  Deitzer, Stephanie, 164, 186, 186f
  Henshaw, William, 7–11, 10f
  Irizarry, Courtney, 166f
  Jaen, Rafael, 129f, 184–185
  Kinney, Tyler, 130, 131f, 132f, 166f
  Macadaeg, Michele, 182f
  Parks, Shanna, 135, 136f
  résumé, 182f
costume design portfolio, 71–73, 73f, 74f
costume technician, 80
  Wilson, Nicole, 17, 18f, 20, 80, 81f, 82f
Cudworth, Ann, 145–146, 147f
curriculum vitae (CV), 178–179, 184–185
  points to avoid, 193
  points to remember, 193
  steps to avoid, 218
  steps to consider, 218
CV. *see* curriculum vitae (CV)
CYCO SCENIC, 7

D

Deitzer, Stephanie, 164, 186, 186f
designer's archives, 56
design-tech blueprint, 212–213
design-tech portfolio
  avoiding confusion, 66–70
  back pocket, 55–56, 55f
  basics, 70–80
  beginning part, 40, 40f
  cases. see cases, portfolio
  creation of, 4
  defined, 4
  end part, 41–43, 44f
  function served by, 4
  general considerations, 40
  inserts, 50f, 51f
  marketing and networking, 56–62
  middle part, 41, 41f, 42f, 43f. see also middle part, portfolio
  page layout options, 43–50. see also page layout options
  photographs in, 11, 52, 91–98
  planning and creation of, 24–30
  steps to avoid in development of, 105–108, 107f
  steps to consider in development of, 102–105, 104f, 105f
  type of case, 24
  types, 64
  visual content, presentation, 43–50
  winning design portfolio, 4–11
  winning technical portfolio, 15–20

design-tech résumés, 179–181
  effective presentation, blueprint for, 181
  formatting, 180
  formatting samples, 181, 182f, 183f, 184f
  points to avoid, 193
  points to remember, 193
Devlin, John Paul, 103–108, 104f, 105f, 107f
Dick Blick (formerly Art-Store), 34
Dieck, Colin, 158, 159f
Digital Art Supplies, 34
digital portfolio, 68–69, 110
  defined, 112, 116–118
  developing techniques, developing techniques, digital portfolio
  points to remember/avoid, 156
  steps to avoid, 217
  steps to consider, 217
digital portfolio, developing techniques
  graphic design principles and branding, 122–123
  interactive portfolios, 152–154
  multimedia sharing and social media, 139–152
  photo editing software, 130
  PowerPoint and Adobe PDF, 127–129
  software applications and CD showcases, 125
  websites and web archives, 130–139
domain name
  purpose of, 154
  registration, 154
Doyle, Brendan F., 161, 161f, 168, 169f

durability
  supplies and materials, 32–33

E

easel binders, 25
easel folios, 29, 29f, 30f
education, in résumés, 178–179
Elliot Norton Award, 125
end part, portfolio, 41–43, 44f
Entertainment Design, 66–70
Esperanza Rising, 17

F

Facebook, 122, 142–152, 142f
featured works, of portfolios, 197–198, 197f
film, portfolio presentation for
  steps to avoid, 217–218
  steps to consider, 217
first impressions, importance of, 164
First Love, 70–71
Fischer, Ryan, 152–154, 153f
Flash sites, 137–139
Flickr, 140, 140f
folios, 24–25, 29–30
  easel folios, 29, 29f, 30f
  oversized expandable portfolios, 29, 29f, 30f
Fornes, Maria Irene, 11, 13f
Frers, Mallory, 124f
Fuente, 70–71

G

Garner, James Michael, 30, 137–139, 139f
Google Analytics, 137–139

graphic design, principles, 122–123

H

Hall, Eric, 118f
Hallelujah, Tallulah, research cut sheet for, 117f
hard portfolio, 7
Hawkins, Bill, 15, 16f, 17f, 124f, 166f
Hayes, Kristin, 4, 5f, 6f
  page layout of portfolio, 45f, 47f
Henshaw, William Gordon, 7–11, 10f, 105–106
Honey, I Shrunk the Kids, 56
horizontal layout, 46, 46f, 47f, 48f
Howland, Janie E., 7, 9f, 125, 125f

I

IATSE. see International Alliance of Theatrical Stage (IATSE)
ICANN. see Internet Corporation for Assigned Names and Numbers (ICANN)
identification page, 40
InDesign, Adobe, 130
inkjet-printed fabrics, 117f
inserts, 50, 50f, 51f
interactive portfolios, 152–154
International Alliance of Theatrical Stage (IATSE), 62
Internet Corporation for Assigned Names and Numbers (ICANN), 154
interpersonal relations, 210–212

Into the Woods, 17
Irizarry, Courtney, 166f
Isackes, Richard, 66

J

Jaen, Rafael, 129f, 184–185
 teaching points, for
  portfolios, 196–201
Jaworski, Ellen, 123f

K

KCACTF Barbizon Award,
 130
Kim, KJ, 20, 20f, 73, 75f, 76f
Kinney, Tyler, 130, 131f,
 132f, 166f
Kintish, Will, 164
Kirsch, Andrew, 83, 85f,
 86f, 87f

L

Lacovelli, John, 56
large case, portfolio, 196
laser archival, 31
"lazy Susan effect", 45–46
leaving a present, defined,
 166–168, 168f
Leech, Kitty, 102
legibility
 supplies and materials, 33
Leviss, Andy, 11, 15f
Lewis, Andy, 77–80, 79f, 80f
Lighting Design Award, 61
lighting designer
 Clyve, Scott, 160, 160f
 Dieck, Colin, 158, 159f
 Hayes, Kristin, 4, 5f, 6f,
  45f, 47f
 Perlow, Karen, 52–55, 53f,
  54f, 55f
 résumé, 183f
 Wertheimer, Tracy, 183f

lighting design portfolio,
 73–77, 77f, 78f
Light Up the Sky, 17
LinkedIn, 122
Lore, Nicholas, 178, 192–193

M

Macadaeg, Michele
 résumé, 182f
Macromedia Dreamweaver,
 130–139
Madison Art Shopping, 34
Maiden's Prayer, scanned
  slide from, 126f
makeup and hair designer
 Kim, KJ, 20, 20f, 73, 75f,
  76f
makeup and hair design
  portfolio, 73, 75f, 76f
makeup designer
 Rossi, Joe, 186–188, 188f
Marine, Alexandre, 11
marketing, 56–62
marketing tools
 bio, 184–185
 brochures, 185–189
 business cards, 185–189
 CV, 178–179, 184–185
 résumés, 178–179
McCarthy, Helen
 résumé, 183f
McKay, Seághan, 146–148,
 148f
Meester, Donna, 66, 74f,
 102, 198
Microsoft Office
 PowerPoint, 127–129
middle part, portfolio, 41,
 41f, 42f, 43f
 production, 41
 type of work, 41
 venue, 41
Miller, Kirk J., 91–98
 interview with, 94–98

Monteiro, Amanda, 71, 73f
Mud, 11, 13f
multimedia portfolio, 83–88
multimedia sharing, 122,
 139–152
multiring binders, 25, 26f
multiring refill pages, 31
 clear polyester archival,
  31
 laser archival, 31
 polypropylene archival, 31
musical *Rags*, 115, 116f
My Heart and My Flesh,
 70–71

N

NETC. *see* New England
 Theatre Conference
 (NETC)
networking, 56–62, 171
New England Theatre
 Conference (NETC), 61
Newman, Mark, 66–70
Nicholas Nickleby, 140, 141f
 horizontal layouts for, 48f

O

Office Depot, 34
organization, of portfolio,
 200–201, 200f
organizations offering
  portfolio reviews, 60–62
oversized expandable
  portfolios, 29, 29f, 30f

P

Paar, Jennifer, 114f
page layout options, 43–50
 horizontal layout, 46, 46f,
  47f, 48f
 opening page, 45–46
 vertical layout, 49, 49f

Parks, Shanna, 135, 135f,
 136f
Participatory Media
 Guidebook, 139–140
PAT. *see* Photographic
 Activity Test (PAT)
The Pathfinder, 178
 *How to Choose or Change
  Your Career for a
  Lifetime of Satisfaction
  and Success*, 192–193
patterned room color &
  texture study, 114f
PDF. *see* Portable
 Document Format (PDF)
Pearl Fine Art Supplies, 34
Perlow, Karen, 52–55, 53f,
 54f, 55f
Phelps, Anthony, 11, 14f,
 77f, 77, 78f, 83, 83f, 196
photo editing software, 130
Photographic Activity Test
 (PAT), 31
photographs, 52–56, 91–98,
 95f, 96f, 97f
Photoshop, 115, 115f, 118f
Photoshop Creative Suite,
 Adobe, 130–139
Pina Zangaroo, 30
Pippin
 vertical layout of costume
  designs, 49f
polypropylene archival, 31
Portable Document Format
 (PDF), 127–129
portfolio(s)
 back pocket, 205–206
 carrying case for, 197,
  197f
 case, 204–205
 communicating process
  in, 198, 199–200, 199f
 content, 204, 205
 featured works of, 197–198,
  197f

featuring models in, 199–200, 199f
guidelines for, 196–197
large case, 196
organization, 200–201, 200f
presenter, 206
size, cf, 198
portfolio development
steps to avoid, 216–217
steps to consider, 216
portfolio presentation, techniques, 162
appearance for, professional/ appropriate, 164–165
first impressions, 164
foundations, 165–170
networking in, 171
points to avoid, 174–175
points to remember, 174
post-interview maintenance in, 170
self-evaluation, 170–171
Portfolios-and-Art-Cases, 34
post-interview maintenance, 170
PowerPoint, 127–129
Preparing Narrative Artists and Practitioners for a New Century, 145
presentation cases, 24–32, 28f
presenting, 165–170
defined, 166, 167f
printers, 35–36
production designer
Cudworth, Ann, 145–146, 147f
production design portfolio, 88–91, 92f, 93f
professional/appropriate appearance
for portfolio presentation, 164–165

projection designer
McKay, Seághan, 146–148, 148f
properties design portfolio, 88

R

Rags, 115, 115f, 116f
Ragtime, 17
Rapidweaver, 146
Realmac Software, 146
real registrars, 154
registrars
domain name, 154
real, 154
The Remarkable Rooming House of Madame LeMonde, 158, 159f
research cut sheet, 117f
résumés, 178–179, 192–193
design-tech, 179–181
effective presentation, blueprint for, 181
formatting, 180
intent and purpose, 178
steps to avoid, 218
steps to consider, 218
work history and education in, 178–179
Resurrection Boulevard, 56
review
news/media, 52–56
steps to avoid in, 69
Rex Art, 34
Rigoletto, 73f
Robbins, Carrie, 112–113, 115f, 116f, 117f
Robinson, Rosalind, 148–152, 150f
Rockport Institute website, 178
Rodriguez, Cory
résumé, 182f

room composite, using Photoshop, 118f
Rossi, Joe, 186–188, 188f

S

safety
supplies and materials, 33
scenic artist
McCarthy, Helen, 183f
résumé, 183f
scenic designer
Howland, Janie E., 7, 9f
Kinney, Tyler, 166f
Prather, Brian, 70–71, 71f, 72f
résumé, 182f
Rodriguez, Cory, 182f
scenic design portfolio, 70–71
script needs, 212
self-assessment. see self-evaluation
self-evaluation, 170–171
basics, 204
comprehensive, 204–206
questionnaire, workbook, 204–206
SETC. see Southeastern Theatre Conference (SETC)
set designer
Beudert, Peter, 67, 69
Howland, Janie E., 125, 125f
Kinney, Tyler, 130, 131f, 132f
White, Brian, 45f, 47f
Shawger, David C. (Kip), Jr., 40, 40f, 41f, 42f, 43f, 44f, 174, 175
sheet protectors, 31, 32f
size, portfolio, 198
slide-in pocket page
portfolio binders, 26, 27f

slide presentation
points to avoid, 161
points to remember, 158–160
social media, 122, 139–152
social networking sites, 122
software applications, for digital portfolio, 125
sound designer, 69
Doyle, Brendan F., 161, 161f, 168, 169f
Lewis, Andy, 77–80, 79f, 80f
sound design portfolio, 77–80, 79f, 80f, 168
Leviss, Andy, 11, 15f
Southeastern Theatre Conference (SETC), 61
stage managers, 70
standard three-ring binders, 26, 27f
Staples, 34
stationery, 185. see also brochures
Stenning, Joanna (Joa), 88, 89f
storage pages, 31
style, 204
supplies and materials
durability, 32–33
legibility, 33
multiring refill pages, 31. see also multiring refill pages
safety, 33
strategies for obtaining, 34–36
three-ring binder sheet protectors, 31–32, 32f. see also three-ring binder sheet protectors
versatility, 33
websites, 34
Sweeney Todd, scanned slide from, 126f

T

tab dividers, 31–32, 33f
Teague, Bill, 66, 67, 73
technical director, portfolio
    of, 83–88, 83f, 85f, 86f,
    87f
technical directors, 69–70
    Garner, James Michael,
        137–139, 139f
    Hawkins, Bill, 15, 16f, 17f,
        166f
technician's archives, 56
technician's portfolio, 80
television, portfolio
    presentation for
    steps to avoid, 217–218
    steps to consider, 217
Tera-Cover, 30, 30f
theatre, portfolio
    presentation for
    steps to avoid, 217–218
    steps to consider, 217
Theatre Designers and
    Computers, 112–113
theatrical design-tech
    portfolio, 218
The Color of Rose, 17
The Cosby Show, 56
The Duchess of Malfi
    horizontal layouts for, 48f
The Idiot, 11, 12f

The Imaginary Invalid, 17
The Painter's Journal, 83
The Shakespeare Stealer, 7,
    7f, 8f
Thief River, 70–71
three-ring binder sheet
    protectors, 31–32, 32f
    sheet protectors, 31, 32f
    storage pages, 31
    tab dividers, 31–32, 33f
Tiala, Crystal, 199–200
Tollefson, Kristina, 102–105,
    133, 134f
Tosti-Lane, Dave, 66–67, 68
Trainer, Molly, 123f
Twelfth Night, 74f
Twitter, 122, 142–152, 142f

U

United Scenic Artists (USA),
    62
University/Resident Theatre
    Association (URTA), 60–61
URTA. *see* University/
    Resident Theatre
    Association (URTA)
The U.S. Institute for
    Theatre Technology, Inc.
    (USITT), 61–62
USA. *see* United Scenic
    Artists (USA)

USITT. *see* The U.S. Institute
    for Theatre Technology,
    Inc. (USITT)
Utrecht Art, 34

V

Vargelis, Nicholas, 11, 13f
venue, 210–212
versatility
    supplies and materials, 33
vertical layout, 49, 49f
Vista, 30f, 31
    mist variety, 31
    onyx variety, 31
    snow variety, 31
voice and rapport, 204

W

Waiting for Godot, 134f
Walsh, Thomas, 143–145,
    144f
websites
    beginners and
        experienced users,
        sites for, 155
    designing, 154–155
    points to avoid, 161
    points to remember,
        158–160
    Rockport Institute, 178

supplies and materials, 34
and web archives,
    130–139
*We Don't Get a Second
    Chance to Make a First
    Impression*, 164
Wertheimer, Tracy
    résumé, 183f
White, Brian
    page layout of portfolio,
        45f, 47f
Whitten, Amy, 88–91, 92f,
    93f
Wikipedia, 154
Wilson, Nicole, 80, 81f, 82f
Winlarski, Jo, 114f
winning design portfolio,
    4–11
winning technical portfolio,
    15–20
wish list, 210–212
work history, in résumés,
    178–179
Working the Musical, 72f
World Wide Web, 122

Y

YouTube, 142–152, 142f